NEOCONSERVATIVE POLITICS AND THE SUPREME COURT

Neoconservative Politics and the Supreme Court

Law, Power, and Democracy

Stephen M. Feldman

NEW YORK UNIVERSITY PRESS
New York and London

NEW YORK UNIVERSITY PRESS
New York and London
www.nyupress.org

LIBRARY OF CONGRESS CATALOGING-IN-PUBLICATION DATA
Feldman, Stephen M., 1955-
Neoconservative politics and the Supreme Court : law, power, and democracy / Stephen M. Feldman.
p. cm.
Includes bibliographical references and index.
ISBN 978-0-8147-6466-4 (cl : alk. paper) — ISBN 978-0-8147-8589-8 (ebook) — ISBN 978-0-8147-7076-4 (ebook)
1. Political questions and judicial power—United States. 2. United States. Supreme Court. 3. Conservatism—United States. I. Title.
KF8748.F45 2012
320.520973—dc23 2012024882

New York University Press books are printed on acid-free paper, and their binding materials are chosen for strength and durability. We strive to use environmentally responsible suppliers and materials to the greatest extent possible in publishing our books.

Manufactured in the United States of America
10 9 8 7 6 5 4 3 2 1

As always, to my family: Laura, Mollie, and Samuel

CONTENTS

ACKNOWLEDGMENTS

This book evolved from a planned article focusing on two questions. First, what is neoconservatism? The term *neoconservativism* has been used so loosely that its meaning has become obscure, yet its frequent use suggests an underlying importance. Thus, I wanted to go to its origins and understand why so many have thought neoconservatism so important. Second, given the apparent importance of neoconservatism, how has it influenced the Supreme Court? I started work on the article—in a sense, a sequel to my previous book, on free expression and democracy—and before I knew it, I was at work on a new book. A number of people helped along the way. I especially thank those individuals who commented on the entire manuscript or its parts (including article manuscripts that I later developed into chapters or sections of the book): Mark Tushnet, Noah Feldman, Richard Delgado, and Tom Grey. Debbie Gershenowitz, senior editor for history and law at NYU Press, showed great faith in this project and was instrumental in bringing it to print. I also appreciate the feedback that I received from the fall 2008 participants in the Georgetown/Maryland Discussion Group on Constitutionalism, held at the University of Oregon. Likewise, I appreciate the comments from my colleagues at the University of Wyoming who participated in faculty colloquies related to this project. The Housel/Arnold endowment provided financial assistance for the work. The librarians at the College of Law, including Tim Kearley, Susan Wozny, and Tawnya Plumb, constantly aided my research, often tracking down obscure out-of-print texts. Finally, I thank Deans Steve Easton and Jerry Parkinson for their support of my scholarship.

Articles that, to different degrees, served as the bases for various parts of the book were published in the *William and Mary Bill of Rights Journal*, the *Cardozo Law Review*, and the *Denver University Law Review*.

1

Reagan, Cross-Pollination, and Neoconservatism: An Introduction

For more than twenty-five years, starting in 1980, neoconservatives stood at the intellectual forefront of a conservative coalition that reigned over the national government. Neocons earned this prominent position by leading an assault on the hegemonic pluralist democratic regime that had taken hold of the nation in the 1930s. Pluralist democracy accepts ethical relativism: No preexisting or higher principles limit the interests, values, and goals that can be urged in the democratic arena. Thus, individuals and interest groups legitimately seek to satisfy their own interests and values, whatever their content. From the diverse asserted interests and values, the government pursues those goals that emerge through certain established procedures. Process rather than substance determines legitimacy.[1]

While neoconservatives began to assail pluralist democracy in the 1960s and '70s, they simultaneously advocated for a resurrection of republican democracy, which had predominated before the 1930s. Republican democratic theory declares that virtuous citizens and officials pursue the common good rather than their private interests. Thus, neocons rejected the ethical relativism that supports the pluralist democratic regime and instead championed "traditional American values" or virtues that were to direct society toward the common good. In a sense, neocons wanted the United States to return to Pleasantville: They believed that the nation would be renewed by returning to republican democracy, just as the protagonist in the movie *Pleasantville* believed his life would improve if he were to live in the eponymous small town of an old black-and-white television sitcom.[2]

Well, things didn't go as expected in *Pleasantville*—or for the neocons. Most important, they never succeeded in undermining the pluralist democratic framework. To the contrary, the necons themselves operated as just one more interest group competing within the (pluralist) democratic arena, albeit a highly successful one. And then the political winds shifted in 2008: The neoconservatives found themselves out of power in Congress and the executive branch. Even so, at that point, they were not totally bereft of vigor. Neoconservative justices still controlled the Supreme Court and will continue to do so for years to come. Of course, with congressional elections every two years and presidential ones every four, the precise ratio of conservative Republicans and progressive Democrats in official positions will vary depending on the most recent electoral results. When Democrats control the coordinate branches, conflict with the Court in partisan-charged cases will be intense and frequent. Decisions such as *Citizens United v. Federal Election Commission* could become the norm. To describe *Citizens United* in stark terms, the five conservative justices outvoted the four progressive justices to reach the conservative outcome, holding that congressionally imposed limits on corporate and union spending for political campaign advertisements violate the First Amendment. Undoubtedly, when Republicans control the coordinate branches, such vivid conflict will be less likely. Yet, even during times of Republican sway, the aggressive and confident neoconservative justices will push ahead, seeking to implement their distinct interpretation of the Constitution, which will inevitably clash with congressional and executive actions. In fact, Congress enacted the campaign finance restriction invalidated in *Citizens United* in 2002, when Republicans controlled the House of Representatives and the presidency.[3]

Hence the question: What consequences will follow from having neocons steering the Court for the foreseeable future?

* * *

At the outset, neoconservativism should be distinguished from other political outlooks. Start with a distinction between progressivism (or liberalism) and conservatism. In general, progressives resist governmental efforts to impose moral values but favor governmental intervention in the economic marketplace when necessary to promote equity. Conservatives often favor both governmental and nongovernmental promotion of traditional moral and religious values yet prefer an unregulated economic marketplace because it ostensibly rewards individual merit. To understand neoconservatism per se, though, it must be distinguished from other forms of conservatism. After World War II, traditionalist conservatives such as Russell Kirk expressed a Burkean reverence for tradition and religion as sources of values. They preferred minimal or restrained government, but they brooded that individuals might abuse liberty and become licentious. Libertarian conservatives, inspired by Friedrich Hayek's *Road to Serfdom*, emphasized the protection of individual liberties, especially economic liberties. They worried little about license, and for that reason, they stressed minimal government above all else. In contrast, neoconservatives were more willing to accept an assertive government, but one that pursues (conservative) goals embodied in the concept of the common good. Confident and aggressive, neocons believed that they could rationally discern universal truths and the best policies for achieving desired goals consistent with those truths. Because supposedly not all individuals could decipher the universal truths, some neocons advocated for the use of tradition and religion to inculcate what they deemed to be suitable values.[4]

After the neoconservatives rose to political prominence in the 1980s, a new or altered form of traditionalism emerged: paleoconservatism. Some commentators viewed paleoconservatism as no more than traditionalism under another name, some viewed it as traditionalism on steroids, and some viewed it as a whole new (or very old) form of conservatism. Like traditionalists, paleos such as Patrick Buchanan emphasized traditional and religious values, but paleos were far less optimistic. Traditionalist conservatives generally believed that traditional American values continued to be vital, though they needed to be vigorously defended. Paleos tended to be bitter and angry: They "can fairly be said to despise much of contemporary American life." They feared that Americans were "irrevocably cut off from a living, sustainable tradition," so they would insistently "hark back to that which is lost." With their echoes of the pre–Cold War "Old Right," paleos vehemently criticized the neocons as "interlopers," as not being truly "conservative at all." Especially wary of neoconservative foreign policy, paleos denounced neocons as "an alien cabal intent on promoting a utopian, Bolshevik revolution around the globe." Neocons, in turn, worried that the paleos displayed "a neoisolationist nativism tinged in a few cases with antisemitism."[5]

To be sure, these definitions of conservatism and liberalism as well as the competing forms of conservatism are roughly hewn, and such generalizations can be misleading. For instance, as is often noted, conservatives tend to protect and celebrate the status quo, while progressives question it. Yet, over recent decades, neoconservatives have led the charge against the pluralist democratic regime—that is, against the status quo. Besides, in the 1980s, President Ronald Reagan managed to consolidate the various forms of conservatism under a big tent. Undercurrents of disagreement always remained, but the competing conservative movements, in a sense, cross-pollinated. Traditionalists, libertarians, and the general public adopted many neoconservative views, which became well publicized in the mainstream media, while neoconservatives shifted to adopt positions more closely aligned with those of their conservative competitors. This cross-pollination arose partly because of Reagan's charisma; somehow, all conservatives could accept him as their leader. Then the reality of Reagan's political success contributed to further conservative intermixing. When conservatives first tasted political power with Reagan, they naturally hungered for more. "The task," explained neocon Irving Kristol, "was to create . . . a Republican majority—so political effectiveness was the priority." Conservatives of diverse stripes realized they could garner more power only by working with other conservatives. Francis Fukuyama, a neoconservative intellectual leader during the 1980s and '90s, admitted that, after a while, "it became increasingly hard to disentangle neoconservatism from other, more traditional varieties of American conservatism." During this time, the categorization of particular conservatives as one type or another became problematic. Regardless, with Republicans occupying the White

House for so many years since 1980, numerous Supreme Court as well as other federal judicial appointees were unequivocally conservative, if not neoconservative. Currently, four justices can be reasonably classified as neocons: Antonin Scalia, Clarence Thomas, John Roberts, and Samuel Alito.[6]

* * *

New York Times columnist David Brooks has written, "If you ever read a sentence that starts with 'Neocons believe,' there is a 99.44 per cent chance everything else in that sentence will be untrue." If Brooks is correct, if most descriptions of neoconservatism get it wrong, whether intentionally or unintentionally, then what, precisely, is neoconservatism? Hence, the first goal of this book: to explain neoconservatism, its purposes and policies. This goal necessitated my method: to present a narrative history of neoconservatism. To understand neoconservatism, one must go to its origins and follow its development, especially if one seeks to avoid the typical mischaracterizations that arise because of media caricatures as well as its cross-pollination with other conservative movements. Indeed, critics often use the label of neoconservatism as an epithet (like "liberal" in the 1980s). Consequently, I describe why early leaders, such as Irving Kristol and Norman Podhoretz, transformed from being liberals into neocons. Most important, I explain how neoconservatism fits within our (pluralist) democratic system; such an understanding is crucial to a full appreciation of neoconservatism, given that the neocons sharply attack pluralist democracy. This focus on pluralist democracy raises several questions that need to be addressed: Why did pluralist democracy supplant the republican democratic regime in the 1930s? Why did Leo Strauss and other European émigrés criticize the emerging American pluralist democratic regime in the 1940s and 1950s? Why did incipient neoconservatives then draw specifically on Straussian themes in forming their own critiques of pluralist democracy? How, meanwhile, did the pluralist democratic regime evolve during the period running from World War II to the turn of the twenty-first century? My position, in part, is that the entrenchment and evolution of pluralist democracy combined to thwart neoconservative efforts to achieve their overarching purpose: to undermine the pluralist democratic regime and return us to republican democracy.[7]

This neoconservative failure nonetheless leads to my second major goal: to explain how neoconservatism succeeded in numerous significant ways, even though it did not (and could not) fulfill its ultimate end. In particular, I focus on how neoconservatism influenced Supreme Court adjudication in several realms of constitutional law. My position, here, is that neoconservative justices have cut and pasted: cutting elements of pluralist democracy and pasting in swatches of republican democracy, when possible, while largely leaving the pluralist democratic fabric intact. The Court, for example, decided Establishment Clause cases and modified First Amendment doctrine to promote "moral clarity," a favorite neoconservative theme, even though the justices otherwise reinforced the pluralist democratic regime (for instance, by continuing to use techniques, such as balancing tests, characteristic of pluralist democracy).

What, then, does the future hold? This is the subject of the final chapter, which has two specific goals. First, it explores how the neoconservative justices might shape constitutional law over the next several years. In which subject areas might or might not neocons stamp their imprint? Second, it suggests how progressives might confront the challenge of a Court infused with neocons. What strategies might effectively diminish neoconservative influence? My position is that the neoconservative justices, always needing to hold the cautiously conservative Justice Anthony Kennedy's vote, will likely continue to cut and paste with moderate success. Given this reality, progressives who must bring their cases before the Court (and they should avoid doing so whenever possible) should aim their arguments at a single target: Justice Kennedy. In most politically controversial cases, progressives will win only if they can persuade Kennedy to cast his vote with the liberal rather than the neoconservative bloc. And even if they cannot win, progressives will benefit if they can nudge Kennedy enough to the left that he impels the neocon justices to temper their positions, to diminish the forcefulness of their neoconservative pronouncements.

Three caveats clarify my interrelated goals. First, even though the final chapter recommends progressive strategies, I wrote the book with a sympathetic ear: I aim to make sense of neoconservatism within the historical context in which it arose. To reach a full understanding of any intellectual or political movement, one must approach it from the inside. One must appreciate why those within the movement believed in their various efforts and strategies, why such efforts and strategies seemed to insiders at the time to be reasonable or even compelling. Given this, one should remember that the early neoconservatives were disenchanted liberals. From their perspective, then, they sought to appreciate the prominence of the individual without descending into narcissism or solipsism. They sought to appreciate that self-interest inevitably motivates but must be tempered with values traditionally associated with virtue, like independence, self-reliance, and altruism. They sought to appreciate the importance of diversity without tolerating decadence. They sought to appreciate the beneficence of reason without allowing it to push society into an abyss of relativism. Whether these are worthwhile objectives and whether the neoconservative efforts were justified, I leave to the reader to decide.

Second, I describe the Court—or more precisely, four of the justices—as being neoconservative rather than merely conservative. The crux of my argument is that the corpus of the Court's work over approximately the past twenty years more closely matches the themes of neoconservatism, as I define it, than those of the leading alternative forms of conservatism: traditionalism and libertarianism. Certainly, some readers will object to this characterization and maintain that, for instance, Scalia is instead a traditionalist.[8] And, in fact, I do not insist that neoconservatism is the only accurate description of the Court (or of the four neocon justices) in all cases. In some cases, one might reasonably conclude that such-and-such a justice sounds more like a libertarian, or that another justice sounds like a traditionalist. Nonetheless, I still argue that *neoconservatism* best categorizes the Court's decisions and opinions over the preceding two decades. Two predominant factors, though, are likely to generate categorization disputes. First, as already discussed, the various forms of conservatism have cross-pollinated in recent years to the point where their boundaries sometimes blur. Second, neoconservatism, traditionalism, and libertarianism, even when properly defined, overlap. More specifically, neoconservatism shares important themes with both traditionalism and libertarianism, but, significantly, traditionalism and libertarianism diverge in many instances. Thus, numerous cases might fairly be characterized as both neoconservative and traditionalist, or both neoconservative and libertarian, but far fewer cases could be called both traditionalist and libertarian (and those few cases would also be neoconservative).

Third, and finally, I do not critically analyze either neoconservatism or the neoconservative reliance on Straussian themes. I do not attempt to demonstrate that certain neoconservative policy prescriptions might fail in any of the following ways: to follow from broader neoconservative principles, to tie logically together in a coherent whole, or to reflect Strauss's writings accurately. All of which is *not* to say that I am uncritical. Rather, my critique arises from within the historical narrative of neoconservatism: thus, my argument that neoconservatives did not and could not achieve their overarching purpose of resurrecting republican democracy. Whether one agrees or disagrees with neoconservative tenets, one should recognize that in the venue of the Supreme Court or elsewhere neoconservatism bears inherent limits because of its social and cultural context. A return to Pleasantville, in the end, is no more than a fantasy.

2

From Republican to Pluralist Democracy

Republican Democracy

From the framing through the 1920s, the United States operated as a republican democracy. Citizens and elected officials were supposed to be virtuous: In the political realm, they were to pursue the common good or public welfare rather than their own private interests. The 1776 Virginia Bill of Rights, for instance, stated: "[G]overnment is, or ought to be[,] instituted for the common benefit, protection, and security of the people, nation, or community." The pursuit of "partial or private interests" amounted to the corruption of republican government. Therefore, the promotion of civic virtue was paramount. "[N]o free government, or the blessings of liberty, can be preserved to any people," the Virginia Bill of Rights pronounced, "but by a firm adherence to justice, moderation, temperance, frugality and virtue and by frequent recurrence to fundamental principles." Within a republican democratic system, individual rights and liberties were important, but the common good always bounded their scope. The government, that is, could restrict individual rights and liberties if it did so in pursuit of the common good.[1]

Political leaders of the framing generation claimed that the American people were especially well suited for republican democratic government. An agrarian economy where "almost every man is a freeholder" engendered a material equality unknown elsewhere, particularly in Europe. This widespread land ownership imbued individuals, moreover, with an independence that intertwined with the community and promoted a virtuous commitment to the common good. "I think our governments will remain virtuous for many centuries," wrote Thomas Jefferson, "as long as they are chiefly agricultural; and this will be as long as there shall be vacant lands in any part of America." And with an overwhelming number of Americans being committed to Protestantism and tracing their ancestral roots to western or northern Europe, the people seemed sufficiently homogeneous to join in the pursuit of the common good. As John Jay wrote, "Providence has been pleased to give this one connected country to one united people—a people descended from the same ancestors, speaking the same language, professing the same religion, attached to the same principles of government, very similar in their manners and customs, and who, by their joint counsels, arms, and efforts, fighting side by side throughout a long and bloody war, have nobly established general liberty and independence."[2]

Of course, some Americans did not fit the mold. Not all were white Protestant Anglo-Saxons. Exclusion from the polity, however, preserved at least a surface homogeneity. According to republican democratic theory, nonvirtuous individuals (or a nonvirtuous societal group) would not willingly forgo the pursuit of self-interest. Instead, they would form factions bent on corrupting republican democratic government. Thus, an alleged lack of civic virtue could justify the forced exclusion of a group from participation in democratic processes. On this pretext, African Americans, Irish Catholic immigrants, women, and other peripheral groups were precluded from participating in republican democracy for much of American history. Typically, then, the concepts of virtue and the common good were interpreted to mirror mainstream white Protestant values and interests.[3]

Even so, during the nineteenth and early twentieth centuries, the specific meanings of *virtue* and *the common good* transformed in response to cultural, social, and economic pressures. For instance, in the 1790s,

Americans condemned political parties as factions seeking to satisfy their own interests. Political parties, it was believed, threatened the welfare of the republic. By the middle of the nineteenth century, though, the political party had become an accepted republican democratic institution. Parties, it seemed, promoted the common good by encouraging the average person to participate in the democratic process. In fact, with the acceptance of political parties, voter turnout increased dramatically during the first part of the nineteenth century. Voter turnout for the 1824 presidential election was only 16.2 percent, but with the help of political parties, turnout soared to an antebellum high of 77.5 percent in 1840. After the Civil War, turnout continued to climb, reaching a high of 82.4 percent for the 1876 election.[4]

Republican democracy thus proved flexible and resilient: Virtue and the common good remained the overarching principles of government even as their meanings periodically changed. Yet a variety of forces, including industrialization, urbanization, and immigration, placed the republican democratic regime under tremendous strain in the late nineteenth and early twentieth centuries. In 1859, the value added from manufacturing (equaling the value of shipments minus the cost of materials and the like) for the entire nation totaled less than $8.6 million. By 1899, that total had increased to approximately $4.6 billion. It leaped to more than $8 billion in 1909, then to nearly $24 billion in 1919. The leading industrial states of New York and Pennsylvania alone jumped from having approximately 73,000 manufacturing establishments in 1870 to 130,000 in 1900. During this same period, 1870 to 1900, even the Southern states of Virginia and North Carolina increased their manufacturing establishments to number more than 15,000, an increase of more than 50 percent. In 1870, agricultural workers far outnumbered industrial workers (in manufacturing, construction, transportation, and related jobs)—approximately 7 million to 4 million—but by 1900, the now nearly 14 million industrial workers outnumbered agricultural workers by more than 3 million.[5]

The growth of industry corresponded with a growth in urban populations, as a disproportionate number of factories were located in the burgeoning northeastern and midwestern cities. In 1870, more than 28 million Americans lived in rural settings, while only 9.9 million lived in urban areas. The ratio of rural to urban dwellers gradually decreased over the next decades. By the 1890s, the superintendent of the 1890 census could observe that the American frontier had finally been exhausted. The expanding population could no longer keep moving west in search of rural expanses. Unsurprisingly, then, the rural and urban populations were almost equal by 1910. By 1920, more Americans lived in cities than in rural areas—54.1 million compared with 51.5 million—and the trend toward urbanization would continue unabated over the following decades.[6]

Quite evidently, the American population not only became more urban, it also expanded rapidly, jumping from 39.9 million in 1870 to 63 million in 1890 to 92.4 million in 1910. By 1915, the population had soared to more than 100 million. Much of this increase arose because of immigration. Total annual immigration moved from 153,640 in 1860 to 387,203 in 1870 to 457,257 in 1880. The numbers remained high until the turn of the twentieth century, when they skyrocketed. In 1903, more than 857,000 immigrants came to the United States, and from 1905 to 1914, more than 1 million immigrants arrived annually six different years. Thus, even when many northeasterners were still heading westward—between 1870 and 1890, New York lost more than 313,000 and Pennsylvania more than 175,000 native whites—these states nonetheless grew in population, with New York gaining more than 750,000 and Pennsylvania 450,000 immigrants.[7]

The effects of industrialization, urbanization, and immigration rippled throughout society, intermingling with one another, influencing numerous components of American life. Partly because industrial leaders steadfastly encouraged immigration to maintain a large pool of surplus factory workers, immigrants continued streaming into the cities. Forty-six percent of the workers in the slaughterhouse and meatpacking industries were immigrants, while the textile industry had more than 75 percent immigrant workers. Given this, the cultural gulf between rural and urban America grew ever wider. Meanwhile, the desire for further industrialization, ever more progress, contributed to a change in education. After the Civil War, a new type of American university developed, "all but unrecognizable in comparison with the college of 1860." Antebellum colleges had focused on the liberal arts and the classics; education was to engender "mental discipline," as well as "piety and strength of character." The new universities instead emphasized culture, service, and research. The postbellum emphasis on culture signaled the strongest link to the antebellum college; educators did not totally repudiate the old concerns for the liberal arts, the classics, and the nurturing of mental discipline. But in the new universities, the dominance of this concern diminished vis-à-vis the growing and interrelated emphases on service and research, both fueled by industrialization. To a large degree, the universities were expected to be utilitarian: to serve the "emerging industrial technological society." And within the university setting, such service could be achieved through research. Consequently, much university research was oriented toward practical advances that might aid industry. Because of advancing secularism—a gulf between science and religion had opened and seemed to be spreading—many researchers sought to cloak themselves under the authoritativeness of objective science. This era thus saw the initial rise of modern social science: Many economists, psychologists, sociologists, and political scientists believed that their "job was to identify social problems and to formulate policies for solving them." The government, from this perspective, was to implement the recommended policies because they were "scientifically formulated." The economist Richard T. Ely, for instance, argued for "[c]onscious cooperation in industry": "Society sets before itself purposes, and attempts to achieve them through social action."[8]

To a great extent, higher education became professionalized, a predictable development given that industrialization sparked specialization and professionalization throughout the economy. Ely noted that while "[a] Boston directory for 1789 gives less than two hundred occupations; at the present time [in 1903] there are probably as many as ten thousand." Many of the new occupations were professional, as lay people hoped experts could guide them through this period of confounding technological and social change. While these new professionals served the developing industrial complex, their emergence also illustrates the growing segmentation of American society, which further strained republican democracy. Each profession tended to nurture its own outlooks, its own interests and values. Such parochialism was manifested in the flourishing of numerous professional organizations, such as the American Bar Association, founded in 1878. The rush to create professional organizations was nowhere more prevalent than in the new universities. The late nineteenth century saw the formation of the American Historical Association, the American Economic Association, the American Sociological Association, and the American Political Science Association—all topped off by the creation of the American Association of University Professors in 1915. Professional associations served their own members by helping them monopolize a lucrative share of the economic marketplace, and they did so partly by becoming more insular, wrapped in their own jargons and techniques, laying claim to their own respective specialized realms of knowledge. Yet, simultaneously, professional associations tended to invoke the common good, assuring lay people that their members satisfied certain standards of training and conduct, that members truly possessed the expertise to serve the public.[9]

During this time, the modern law school, with professional teachers and scholars, developed in the postbellum universities. From the framing until the Civil War, legal scholars and jurists had faithfully described a legal system grounded on natural law and natural rights, often explicitly linking natural law to Protestant Christianity. Indeed, republican democratic government had roots deeply implanted in natural law. Regardless, after the war, with secularism advancing, legal academics accentuated the importance of positive law as they sought to articulate a science of law: an academic discipline of "pure law" that deserved a place in the university alongside the natural and social sciences. Harvard law professor Joseph Beale, for instance, insisted that a principle could not be regarded as law "until it is established as a principle of some actually living and working system of positive law." Of course, despite this transition from natural law to positivism within the academic circles of jurisprudence, many politicians and judges continued to invoke natural rights. The preeminent constitutional law treatise writer of the postbellum period Thomas Cooley, who spent most of his professional career as a judge rather than as an academic, dealt ambivalently with natural rights. In his influential treatise *Constitutional Limitations*, first published in 1868 and by 1903 in a seventh edition, Cooley used language suggestive of natural rights. Yet he found such rights to be legally protected only if they had been adopted as positive law; and, as Cooley explained, positive law evolved largely as a matter of the historical and cultural development of a people and nation. Natural rights, therefore, remained significant only insofar as the people continued to support their positive enforcement and not because such rights existed in some hypothetical state of nature.[10]

In sum, the America that had engendered and supported republican democratic government no longer existed. The weakening of its natural law foundations was but one problem. More important, republican democracy had originally been based on a preindustrial agricultural economy and a relatively homogenous population. Yet by the early twentieth century, most workers were not farmers; they were wage laborers in factories. These new factory workers did not own their own land and had little hope of ever doing so. The economic and social equality that had emanated from widespread land ownership had previously generated a reasonable degree of political equality among white male Protestants. Now, deep inequalities and divisions cleaved the American populace. An increasing degree of wealth became concentrated in fewer hands. Laborers pushed to unionize and to garner higher wages, while capitalists beat back such demands with legal devices and, that failing, violence. Immigration changed the demographic makeup of the American population. Heterogeneity (or plurality) had gradually grown into preeminence: Even the thinnest veneer of homogeneity could not be maintained. Before the Civil War, most immigrants had come from Ireland, Germany, Scandinavia, and Britain, and as late as 1882, 87 percent of all immigrants arrived from western Europe. Within twenty years, however, that number had dwindled to only 22 percent of the total, with 78 percent instead coming from southern and eastern Europe. And from the perspective of white Anglo-Saxon Protestant Americans, these new arrivals were racially distinct—that is, inferior. The United States Immigration Commission issued in 1910 a report worrying that "Jewish immigration now exceeds in number annually that of any other race with the exception of the Italian." Italians, the report continued, were unlikely to become virtuous American citizens because of their alleged proclivity for criminal activity, illiteracy, and poverty. Of course, the English or Anglo-Saxons remained the ideal immigrants: "[T]here is no necessity [to discuss] the character, social institutions, and other qualities of the English as an immigrant people. It may be assumed that all Americans understand the race which has given us our language and laws and political institutions." Given such attitudes toward various immigrant groups, calls for limits on immigration, especially on that from southern and eastern Europe, became more common and aggressive.[11]

The Practice of Pluralist Democracy

Despite the pressures created by industrialization, urbanization, and immigration, republican democracy persisted through the 1920s. But in the late 1920s and early 1930s, the republican democratic regime finally collapsed, supplanted by a new one: pluralist democracy. Under pluralist democracy, one did not need to demonstrate civic virtue to qualify as a participant.

During the 1930s, many ethnic and immigrant urbanites who had previously been discouraged from partaking in national politics became voters and actively cast their support for Franklin Delano Roosevelt's New Deal. And with more widespread participation, the point of democratic politics changed: Politics became the pursuit of self-interest rather than of the common good. Interest group efforts to satisfy preexisting values and desires became normal and legitimate. Substantive governmental goals could no longer be condemned as contravening the common good; all goals were determined through interest group bargaining, coalition building, negotiation, and compromise. Ultimately, then, pluralist democracy was defined through a process that ensured full and fair participation and the assertion of one's interests and values, especially in the legislative arena.[12]

To be clear, pluralist democracy emerged first as a social and political reality. Only subsequently, in the late 1930s, would scholars begin to explicate and justify this new form of democratic practice in a coherent theory. But already by the early 1930s, the reality was that the American population was more heterogenous than ever before. The reality was that the majority of Americans lived in cities. The reality was that more Americans were working for wages in factories than working their own farmland. And the reality was that the American people were confronting a monumental economic depression. From 1929 to 1931, unemployment catapulted from 3.2 percent to a staggering 15.9 percent of the labor force. The ranks of the unemployed continued to swell, reaching nearly 25 percent in 1933. With factories closing at an alarming rate, unemployment stood even higher in large industrial cities; in Chicago, for instance, more than half the unskilled laborers were out of work at times. Those with jobs suffered, too; from 1929 to 1933, the average hourly earnings of factory workers fell by 22 percent. Meanwhile, during those years, the value of farm property sank by 36 percent, and overall, gross national product (GNP) dropped by 29 percent.[13]

With the arrival of the right leader, Franklin D. Roosevelt, the economic depression combined with already existing pressures to force the old republican democratic regime to succumb. Despite industrialization, urbanization, and immigration, the cultural distances between various groups of Americans had been narrowing over the prior decade partly because of legislative restrictions on immigration—fewer immigrants were stepping off the boats and alienating old-stock Americans—and partly because of the development of a mass-consumer culture that led many Americans to desire the same products, whether Coca-Cola, a Model T Ford, or a radio, and to exalt the same celebrities, whether Babe Ruth (from baseball), Rudy Vallee (from radio), or Rudolph Valentino (from movies). The widespread economic deprivations of the Great Depression further closed the gaps between Americans, at least temporarily. A second-generation Italian American Catholic man with a family and an Anglo-Saxon Protestant man with a family would, in all likelihood, be equally desperate if laid off and unable to find other jobs. The latter might previously have believed in virtue and the common good, understanding those concepts to correspond with the values and interests of white Protestant Americans in general. But after a few weeks of unemployment, he would have the same goals as the man from the immigrant family: a job with a decent wage, and if that was impossible, then some assistance in feeding and sheltering his family.[14]

President Roosevelt and the New Dealers facilitated the transformation of democracy by responding to these desires. Instead of dismissing the preferences and values of immigrants, indigents, religious minorities, and other peripheral groups as being nonvirtuous, instead of dismissing their desires and goals as contravening the common good, FDR sought to incorporate these groups into the polity and to satisfy their interests. Instead of preaching morality to immigrants and their children and trying to convert them to Protestant values—as the Progressives had tried to do earlier in the twentieth century—FDR focused on economic issues. As one of FDR's close advisors, Rexford G. Tugwell, said, "[T]he New Deal is attempting to do nothing to people, and does not seek at all to alter their way of life, their wants and desires." In Roosevelt's first inaugural address, he explained to the people that he sought "action, and action now" rather than "changes in ethics."[15]

Consequently, FDR purposively led the nation toward a more open and inclusive form of democracy. Mainstream and old-stock Protestant values, long the foundation for the ideals of virtue and the common good, were now to be balanced with the values of other Americans who constituted the demographically diverse population. No single set of cultural values was authoritative. Ethical relativism took hold as a political reality: All values, all interests—or at least a plurality of values and interests—mattered to Roosevelt and the New Dealers. Democracy now revolved around the assertion of interests and values by sundry individuals and groups. The pursuit of self-interest no longer amounted to corruption; rather, it defined the nature of (pluralist) democracy. Significantly, then, government could no longer be limited to pursuing some conception of a common good. Government responded to the pushes and pulls of interest groups as they pressed their claims through the democratic process. Labor became one of the most prominent and powerful societal groups to emerge in the 1930s, but it was not the only one. Diverse voluntary groups and associations openly sought to shape governmental decisions—they pushed open the doors to the polity. In cities, for instance, one might find a Polish Democratic Club or a Lithuanian Democratic League. Lobbying became open, aggressive, and institutionalized, as exemplified during the 1935 congressional debates and negotiations over the National Labor Relations Act (NLRA). A full list of the organizations lobbying Congress might seem endless; it would include a panoply of manufacturing and labor representatives such as the American Association of Creamery Butter Manufacturers, the National Electrical Manufacturers' Association, and the International Brotherhood of Boiler Makers, Iron Ship Builders, and Helpers of America. Two years later, the legal scholar Louis L. Jaffe observed that "all legislation . . . is an immediate response, in a greater or less degree, to some group pressure [so that] Congress and the state legislatures pass laws for the farmer, laws for labor, laws for business."[16]

When it came to the economy, Roosevelt subscribed fully to a modernist outlook. That is, he had a historicist attitude: History demonstrated that social, cultural, and political arrangements were contingent and changeable and that human inventiveness could produce endless (though not inevitable) progress. Thus, Roosevelt pushed for immediate action guided by lawyers and social scientists, experts grounded in empirical research. Before World War I, many Progressives and sociological jurisprudents had hailed the potential contributions of trained scientific and social scientific experts in politics and law. For many Americans, this faith in experts and empiricism grew even stronger after the war. The leader of the University of Chicago's political science department, Charles Merriam, devoted his first two books, published in 1924 and 1925, to the advocacy of empirical methods. He maintained that empiricism would enable political scientists to enhance human control over the future and make for a better social world. Legal scholars (the legal realists) also believed that expertise garnered through empirical studies could cure societal ills and produce progress. William O. Douglas, a future chair of the Securities and Exchange

Commission and a future Supreme Court justice, concluded his studies of the bankruptcy system: "[I]t is apparent that if a system were provided which took cognizance of the many economic and social problems antecedent to bankruptcy, it would be possible to integrate the bankruptcy power into programs of social planning in many fields and to effectuate different policies for different problems." Even the cynical political theorist Walter Lippmann equated statesmanship with expert knowledge grounded in empiricism: "[Statesmanship] requires the insight which comes only from an objective and discerning knowledge of the facts, and a high and imperturbable disinterestedness."[17]

FDR and his New Deal cohorts thus turned to legal and social science experts to help shape and administer legislation that responded to the economic needs of a multitude of American constituencies. Roosevelt repudiated the republican democratic assumption that the government could not infringe on individual rights and liberties unless acting for the common good. This assumption had minimized governmental regulations of the economy, particularly since laissez-faire ideology had infused republican democratic thinking in the late nineteenth century: Many potential restrictions on the marketplace had been deemed contrary to the common good, as manifested by the interests of big business. Freed of these republican democratic constraints on government, FDR and the New Dealers sprang into action. They passed fifteen pieces of legislation during the first one hundred days of Roosevelt's first term, and they continued enacting legislation in accordance with the needs and interests of an American people fighting a depression. Besides the NLRA (aiding labor), the New Dealers passed and implemented the Agricultural Adjustment Act (aiding farmers), the Emergency Banking Act (aiding banks), and the Social Security Act (aiding the elderly and incapacitated). In sum, FDR welcomed a diverse array of Americans into the polity, they responded by voting for the New Deal—voter turnout, even in off-presidential years, increased steadily during this time—and the New Dealers responded in turn by enacting and implementing legislation that thrust the national government into the economic marketplace as never before. Under the new pluralist democracy, the individual's goal, it appeared, was to participate in politics: to express one's values and interests, to have governmental officials listen to those expressions of values and interests, and to have the government, acting through experts, fulfill one's desires in a reasonable number of instances.[18]

The Theory of Pluralist Democracy

For modernist intellectual and political leaders, the only path to knowledge lay in experience: the empirical study of external reality. Among intellectuals, the commitment to empiricism ineluctably engendered an acceptance of ethical relativism; facts and values were distinct. Thus, just as an ostensible value-relativism took hold as a political reality, it took hold as a persistent intellectual outlook. If knowledge must be grounded on experience, then ethical values seemingly could not be verified. Individuals could and did assert values, but scientists could not empirically test the validity of those values. Lippmann went so far as to claim that many individuals acknowledge "that they know of no compelling reason which certifies the moral code they adhere to, and that therefore, their own preferences, when tested . . . seem to have no sure foundation of any kind."[19]

In the early 1930s, ethical relativism seemed untroubling to intellectuals. It was little more than a logical corollary to empiricism, one to be noted and then put to one side. By the end of the decade, however, it had become problematic. Because of the rise of totalitarian governments in Europe, American intellectuals recognized that they needed to justify the superiority of democracy. One could not merely describe democracy in relativistic terms, as no better and no worse than fascism, communism, or Nazism. Yet modernist intellectuals could not turn back the clock to premodern times: They were committed to empiricism, and ethical relativism clung to its coattails. Joseph Schumpeter noted that, under republican democracy, the common good had been conceptualized as objective: "[E]very [governmental] measure taken or to be taken [could] unequivocally be classed as 'good' or 'bad.'" But relativism undermined a belief in such a common good: "[T]o different individuals and groups the common good is bound to mean different things." Republican democracy now seemed impossible, but what democratic theory could replace it?[20]

Ironically, political theorists solved this conundrum by embracing relativism: The superiority of democracy, they reasoned, arose from its acceptance of a plurality of values. Totalitarian governments claimed knowledge of objective values and forcefully imposed those values and concomitant goals on their peoples. But democratic governments allowed their citizens to express multitudes of values and goals. The key to democracy lay not in the specification of supposedly objective goals, such as the common good, but rather in the following of processes that allowed all citizens to voice their particular values and interests within a free and open democratic arena. Thus, in 1939, John Dewey contrasted authoritarian methods with the "plural, partial, and experimental methods" of democracy.[21]

After World War II, numerous political theorists subscribed to and elaborated pluralist democratic theory, often accentuating the importance of groups or associations in America. Wilfred E. Binkley and Malcolm C. Moos described democracy as the best means for accommodating "our multigroup society." The only way to determine public values and goals, they explained, is "through the free competition of interest groups." By "composing or compromising" their different values and interests, the "competing groups [would] coordinate their aims in programs they can all support." Indeed, Binkley and Moos analogized democracy "to the play of mechanical forces: 'Were it possible to plot pressure groups objectively as parallelograms of forces and compute the resultant, significant predictions might be made not only as to what party platforms are likely to be, which parties will win, but also as to significant trends in public policy.'" Ultimately, they concluded, legislative decisions turn on negotiation, persuasion, and the exertion of pressure through the normal channels of the democratic process; "policies thus declared 'tend to become a series of compromises along lines of least resistance.'"[22]

No one articulated pluralist democratic theory more comprehensively than Robert A. Dahl. He began by emphasizing the crucial difference between republican and pluralist democracies. "[T]he ancient belief that citizens both could and should pursue the public good rather than their private ends became more difficult to sustain, and even impossible, as 'the public good' fragmented into individual and group interests." The pursuit of self-interest, Dahl maintained, is indefatigable: "If unrestrained by external checks, any given individual or group of individuals will tyrannize over others." Because pluralist (or polyarchal) democracy accepted the inevitable pursuit of self-interest—rather than the pursuit of an ideal substantive goal (the common good)—pluralist democracy required the institutionalization of a "process" that would allow the people to determine which interests would be at least temporarily enshrined as communal goals. A communal goal was legitimate only if the conditions for democracy were satisfied—if the proper process were followed. Thus, Dahl's primary aim was to identify conditions, such as the identical weighing of each vote and the choice of the option receiving the greatest number of votes, that were prerequisite to the operation of a democratic process. But the most important component of the democratic process, according to Dahl, is "effective participation": Citizens must have "adequate" and "equal" opportunities "for expressing their preferences . . . for placing questions on the agenda and for expressing reasons for endorsing one outcome rather than another."[23]

3

Pluralist Democracy: Dissent and Evolution

Pluralist democracy achieved hegemony during the post–World War II era as the correct theory and practice of government. Yet pluralist democracy neither went unchallenged nor remained static. The first part of this chapter focuses on Leo Strauss, a leading opponent of pluralist democracy, while the second part explains the ways in which the pluralist democratic regime changed over time.

Émigré Dissenter: Leo Strauss

European émigrés, particularly Leo Strauss, an escapee from Nazi Germany, persistently opposed pluralist democracy. By the end of the 1940s, Strauss and other émigrés, such as Hannah Arendt and Eric Voegelin, were established political philosophers within the American intellectual community.

Thus, Strauss (and the others) experienced the rise and entrenchment of pluralist democracy from both an insider perspective, living and working in the United States, and an outsider perspective, having matured intellectually in Europe. While Strauss appreciated the American constitutional system—the United States, after all, had provided the émigrés with refuge—he could not accept unbridled celebrations of American democracy. While in Europe, Strauss not only had witnessed the collapse of the democratic Weimar Republic into Nazi totalitarianism but also, as a Jew, had suffered personal hardships and dislocations because of the Nazi perversions of the state. From his vantage, American democracy was too fragile to leave unexamined.[1]

In the United States, Strauss launched a sustained critique of the interrelated intellectual components of modernity that supported pluralist democracy. Historicism, Strauss explained, "seems to show that all human thought is dependent on unique historical contexts that are preceded by more or less different contexts and that emerge out of their antecedents in a fundamentally unpredictable way." To put it in different words, historicism stresses the (historical) context of all perceptions and experiences. With everything becoming contextual and therefore contingent, historicism allows us to look constantly toward the future. Awareness of the past can liberate us from that past. To be sure, we are not guaranteed to progress in the future, epoch by epoch, but we can nonetheless aim "toward ever greater prosperity; [enabling] everyone to share in all the advantages of society or life."[2]

Yet, Strauss warned, historicism undermines the very possibility of knowledge and understanding. For example, historicism leads us to conclude that we cannot specify the content of justice because it appears to vary from society to society, from context to context. Justice means one thing in the United States, another thing in China, and another thing in Egypt—or so the historicist claims. More broadly, "[a]ll understanding, all knowledge . . ., presupposes a frame of reference . . ., a comprehensive view within which understanding and knowing take place." Thomas Kuhn would soon refer to this overarching frame of reference as a paradigm. The problem with this outlook, Strauss argued, is that "[t]he comprehensive view of the whole [or, in other words, a paradigm] cannot be validated by reasoning, since it is the basis of all reasoning." We always must choose among competing viewpoints, but we are left "without any rational guidance." Each viewpoint is "as legitimate as any other." But then, Strauss asked, is not historicism "self-contradictory"? How can historicism claim that it is a valid viewpoint itself? And even more important, when humanity is ostensibly freed of all "permanencies," such as knowing "the distinction between the noble and the base," then we are too apt to spiral into terror, as happened with Hitler and the Nazis. "It was the contempt for these permanencies which permitted the most radical historicist in 1933 [to gain power]."[3]

Strauss attacked the pretensions of modern social science with equal vigor. Social scientists claim that facts and values must be separated: "[T]he Is and the Ought" cannot be joined. They posit that all knowledge must be empirical, based on experience of facts, and that therefore social science must be "value free" and "ethically neutral." But to Strauss, modern social science is wrongheaded on several counts. Most simply, he argued that value-free social science is impossible. Values seep into any social or political analysis in numerous ways, from the choice of research questions to the definition of terms. At a deeper level, to insist on value-free social science, including political science, would be to render it meaningless: "It is impossible to study social phenomena, i.e., all important social phenomena, without making value judgments. . . . A man who refuses to distinguish between great statesmen, mediocrities, and insane impostors may be a good bibliographer; he cannot say anything relevant about politics and political history."[4]

And even if value-free social science were possible, the single-minded focus on empirical research, on facts, would necessarily preclude any knowledge of values and ends. From the modern standpoint, values, which are the sources of our goals or ends, are not subject to scientific (empirical) determination and therefore are not knowable. Modern social science leads us, then, to ethical relativism. "[T]here cannot be any genuine knowledge of the Ought. [The modern social scientist] denied to man any science, empirical or rational, any knowledge, scientific or philosophic, of the true value system: the true value system does not exist; there is a variety of values which are of the same rank, whose demands conflict with one another, and whose conflict cannot be solved by human reason. Social science or social philosophy can do no more than clarify that conflict and all its implications; the solution has to be left to the free, non-rational decision of each individual." Modern social science, with its desire to be empirical and "neutral in the conflict between good and evil," relegates us to a radical and irrational individualism—where each person acts on arbitrary preferences—and ultimately, to nihilism. Not only must we "recognize all preferences or all 'civilizations' as equally respectable," we must accept that "[i]f our principles have no other support than our blind preferences, everything a man is willing to dare will be permissible."[5]

Strauss, in sum, concluded that modernity is imploding: Its own premises inevitably cause the edifice of modernity to collapse upon itself. But as Strauss would insist, the rise of the Nazis and the ensuing Holocaust were not wrong merely from a relative perspective. We must have more than irrational individual preferences and culturally relative values that would leave us sliding toward nihilism and an acceptance of genocide. And as modernity goes, Strauss added, so goes pluralist democracy. Built on the modernist premises of historicism, empiricism, and relativism, not only is pluralist democracy indefensible from a Straussian standpoint, but it also perches us precariously on the edge of a moral abyss. But then what should we do? Strauss did not want to repudiate democracy, though he found its instantiation in the United States (at that time) to be frail and dangerous. To a degree, he sought to modify and therefore save democracy. Strauss, it seems, wanted answers. After all, Strauss criticized modernity for leaving us with only contingencies, for undermining the certainty of ostensible answers. But what solutions did Strauss propose in response to the problem of democracy and the crisis of modernity?[6]

Unfortunately, at this very point, Strauss's writings became far murkier. He turned to philosophy—specifically classical political philosophy—because, he argued, it could lead us from opinion to truth. Strauss feared that the methods of modern social science structure our understandings of politics and government by injecting the fact–value dichotomy. To avoid being led astray in this manner, we must return to a "pre-scientific understanding" of politics—"a coherent and comprehensive understanding of what is frequently called the common sense view of political things." And ancient or classical philosophy can provide us with that pre-scientific or "original form of political science," so to speak. Yet Strauss acknowledged that classical political philosophy cannot provide us with clear and direct access to solutions for our current difficulties. We cannot solve our problems by pretending to live in a Greek *polis*; a global economy, nuclear weapons, and the proliferation of nation-states present us with unique political dilemmas. Even so, we must quest after "universal knowledge" of the truth, quest for answers to our dilemmas, and ancient philosophy might guide us on our journey. But the end of the quest might never be reached—it might never become visible.[7]

In his quest for truth, Strauss insisted that we consider whether the ancients had correctly linked political philosophy with natural right. To explore this possibility, Strauss distinguished between the classical (or ancient) and modern concepts of natural right. According to the ancients, natural right could be comprehended only in connection "with a teleological view of the universe," Strauss explained. "All natural beings have a natural end, a natural destiny, which determines what kind of operation is good for them." Natural right, then, arose from the inherent end or purpose of a political regime. That is, "classic natural right doctrine . . . is identical with the doctrine of the best regime." The philosophical quest for natural right amounts to a search for "the perfect moral order." Strauss left ambiguous, it should be noted, the precise relationship between classical (or ancient) natural right and classical (or ancient) natural law. Sometimes he appeared to distinguish between natural right and natural law, but other times he appeared to use the terms interchangeably. In fact, when Strauss equated classical natural right with the best regime or perfect order, he defined natural right in a manner that resonated closely with commonplace definitions of natural law. Strauss himself referred to natural law as "an objective order." That societal order or best regime, Strauss suggested, entailed "doctrines [that] taught the duties of man." Thus, at one point, Strauss wrote, "Traditional natural law is primarily and mainly an objective 'rule and measure,' a binding order prior to, and independent of, the human will."[8]

Regardless, Strauss unequivocally stressed a break between classical natural right (and natural law) and modern natural right (and natural law). To be sure, Strauss's historical narrative is idiosyncratic: Traditional accounts tend to describe a logical movement from premodernity to modernity that links the ancient and modern notions of natural right (passing relatively smoothly from antiquity through Christianity and into secularity). But Strauss emphasized discontinuity: The sharp distinction between the ancients and the moderns helped explain, according to Strauss, the fragility of modern democracy. Machiavelli initiated modern political theory by rejecting the ideals of Plato and Aristotle for the nitty-gritty of realpolitik. Instead of describing the just or perfect republic, Machiavellian political theory guides the ruler who must maneuver through the pitfalls of reality.

Strauss argued, then, that Hobbes sought to retain Machiavelli's realism while reintroducing "moral principles" into politics—reintroducing, that is, natural right (and natural law). To do so, Hobbes focused on "the fear of death, and, more particularly, the fear of violent death at the hands of others." In Hobbesian political theory, as interpreted by Strauss, "[d]eath takes the place of the *telos*" and "natural law must be deduced from the desire for self-preservation." Thus, unlike in classical political philosophy, where natural right starts with the best political regime, which then engenders certain duties and responsibilities, Hobbes's modern political theory starts from an assertion of individual natural right—"from an absolutely justified subjective claim which, far from being dependent on any previous law, order, or obligation, is itself the origin of all law, order, or obligation." Consequently, Hobbes concluded that "[t]he state has the function, not of producing or promoting a virtuous life, but of safeguarding the natural right of each."[9]

Even further, according to Strauss, not only did the early moderns, like Hobbes, transform (and diminish) natural right, but the later moderns repudiated it altogether. Jeremy Bentham, for one, is famous for denigrating "[n]atural rights [as] simple nonsense: natural and imprescriptible rights, rhetorical nonsense,—nonsense upon stilts." Bentham's disciple John Austin rejected the concept of natural law as "ambiguous and misleading." Indeed, many critics insisted that widespread disagreements about the content of natural right demonstrated that it was inherently and hopelessly ambiguous. In the United States, the framers' generation had been firmly committed to natural right (and natural law), yet after the Civil War, numerous American jurisprudents repudiated it. According to the jurist and scholar Oliver Wendell Holmes Jr., natural law jurists suffered from a "naïve state of mind." Modernists stopped searching for universals (rights and laws) in nature and instead focused on historical changes, individual claims of right, and sovereign assertions of law.[10]

When Strauss considered whether the ancients had correctly linked political philosophy with natural right, he emphasized that the mere disagreement among individuals and societies about the content of natural right does not logically necessitate its repudiation. Because the rejection of natural right eventually leads, he argued, to the monumental modernist problems of historicism and relativism, we should demand stronger proof before jettisoning the possibility of natural right, and from Strauss's perspective, such proof is not forthcoming. Not only did Strauss, then, want to contemplate the truth and implications of natural right, but he also reconsidered the fundamental republican democratic principles. In opposition to pluralist democracy and its countenanced pursuit of self-interest, Strauss sought to resurrect the common good. "Laws are just to the extent that they are conducive to the common good. But if the just is identical with the common good," he reasoned, "the just or right cannot be conventional: the conventions of a city cannot make good for the city what is, in fact, fatal for it and vice versa. The nature of things and not convention then determines in each case what is just." Consequently, Strauss continued, the political activities of citizens and governmental officials should be virtuous, aiming for perfection and justice.[11]

* * *

Pluralist democracy might be distasteful, with its emphasis on self-interest, its grounding on ethical relativism, and its excessive reliance on process. Any governmental system, it seems, must ultimately pursue substantive goals, which implicitly if not explicitly manifest certain values. Is pluralist democracy, therefore, so bereft of foundational values that it might be unworkable and even dangerous in the long run? Strauss certainly feared as much, and he showed himself to be a careful and biting critic of the pluralist democratic system. Yet when one seeks a practical alternative to pluralist democracy, Strauss's clarity vanishes into a fog of obscurity. He turns to philosophy—especially ancient political philosophy—in the hope that it might provide potential answers to the messy political maneuverings of modernity. In doing so, he repudiates pluralist democracy and leads us on "a return to origins" that points toward a resurrected republican democracy. But can this return to republican democracy work?[12]

Regardless, Strauss wielded substantial influence in the concrete world of American politics, as numerous neoconservatives would draw sustenance from his thought. Of course, one should not mistake influence for intent: Strauss rarely wrote with the purpose of directly intervening in American political debates.[13] Even so, he was not apolitical. Despite the ambiguities in his writings, Strauss's imprimatur of the common good, virtue, and natural right manifested unmistakably conservative political leanings. He admitted that the pursuit of virtue and the common good might require the exclusion of some individuals from the polity, as well as the coercive control of others. An individual "cannot achieve the perfection of his humanity," cannot be virtuous, "except by keeping down his lower impulses." To control such lower impulses, Strauss argued, sometimes demands coercion. Hence, rather than stress the maximization of freedom and autonomy, Strauss suggested that coercion sometimes amounts to the common good. "Justice and coercion are not mutually exclusive; in fact, it is not altogether wrong to describe justice as a kind of benevolent coercion. Justice and virtue in general are necessarily a kind of power. To say that power as such is evil or corrupting would therefore amount to saying that virtue is evil or corrupting." In light of such sentiments, Strauss inclined predictably toward other conservative outlooks. He was adamantly anti-communist and was far more elitist than egalitarian, stressing that not everyone is equally virtuous. "For Strauss, a healthy politics is one in which the gentry or gentlemen rule; in which the passions of the demos are restrained by the virtues of their betters; in which enough order and freedom are present for the pursuit of philosophy; and in which philosophers can stand as potential 'umpires' over political-moral disputes."[14]

The Evolution of Pluralist Democracy

Just as republican democracy evolved during the nineteenth century—with the meanings of virtue and the common good shifting—pluralist democracy likewise evolved once it became entrenched during the twentieth century. This section examines three changes in pluralist democracy: first, its intertwinement with a mass-consumer culture; second, its spawning of a proliferation of interest groups; and third, its encouragement of sclerotic political activity.

The Mass-Consumer Culture and Democracy

Mass-consumer culture was one of the most significant forces to act on pluralist democracy. In the 1920s, the development of mass-consumerism had helped create a widely shared American culture revolving around the consumption of mass-produced items and the worship of mass-media celebrities. This mass-consumer culture, in turn, helped fuse Americans into a more encompassing polity that would serve as a springboard for pluralist democracy. But the development of the mass-consumer culture did not end in the 1920s; it continued in the 1930s and, even more so, after World War II, as the nation emerged from its prolonged economic depression.[15]

From a cultural standpoint, Americans increasingly embraced mass-consumerism after the war. Personal consumption expenditures on products such as clothing, furniture, and jewelry rose from $56.289 billion in 1935 to $121.699 billion in 1945 to $256.94 billion in 1955. The amount devoted to the purchase of new and used cars alone jumped an incredible tenfold over those two decades. Unsurprisingly, GNP increased nearly threefold from 1935 to 1945 and then nearly doubled again by 1955. Changes in commercial advertising contributed significantly to the growth of the mass-consumer culture. The very nature of advertising transformed during the twentieth century. Early in the century, product advertisements provided potential consumers with information that would allow them to assess rationally the benefits of purchasing the respective products. During the 1920s, however, advertisers began to market images and lifestyles; advertisements encouraged individuals to purchase particular products because the products symbolized certain attractive personality traits or ways of living. A particular automobile, for instance, might be marketed as conducive to a relaxed drive in the country on a Sunday afternoon. An advertisement for a cereal, Post Bran Flakes, showed a picture of an overwrought businessman and a caption that read as follows: "Too Busy to Keep Well! We Americans, what a hurly-burly race we are! Getting up by the alarm clock; racing through our meals; hurrying from this appointment to that as though our lives depended on it." The advertisement's message was clear: The "resulting poor health and constipation . . . happily could be cured by eating Post Bran Flakes regularly."[16]

Of course, advertisers continued to experiment, to quest after ever more effective means of generating sales. Advertisements could, for example, generate previously unrecognized anxieties—"Oh no! my underarms might look sweaty!"—that only a certain product could alleviate—"Thank goodness for my antiperspirant." After World War II, marketing analysts realized that they could increase sales by targeting distinct segments of the population with particularized advertisements and products—for example, marketing one deodorant for males and another for females, one beer for the wealthy and another for the middle class. Meanwhile, changes in the mass media further transformed advertising. In the early twentieth century, advertisements were placed within the print media—newspapers and magazines. The development of electronic mass media—radio in the 1920s, television in the 1950s, and the Internet in the 1990s—opened additional pathways for reaching consumers. Given these new venues and the evident success of advertising as a means of increasing profits, the amount of money devoted to commercial advertising grew astronomically. In 1900, $542 million was spent on advertising; by 1929, the amount had jumped to $3.426 billion. The volume of advertising dropped during the Great Depression but recovered during the war years so that by 1946, it had nearly reached again its 1929 volume. From that point, advertising volumes skyrocketed: In 1949, the amount had climbed to more than $5.2 billion, and by 1957, the amount was above $10.3 billion. The numbers continued their ascent: In 1990, an amazing $129.968 billion was spent on advertising, a figure that nearly doubled by 2001.[17]

The expanding mass-consumer culture fused with American law and politics in multiple ways. Pluralist democracy, emphasizing the individual pursuit of self-interest, had from its outset resonated with capitalist ideology. But during the postwar period, pluralist democracy effectively became a consumers' democracy. Politics grew increasingly like commercial consumption: Citizens followed their own values and interests, whether shopping for a product or for a candidate. In the presidential campaigns of the 1950s, New York advertising agencies successfully marketed Dwight "Ike" Eisenhower. Then, when market analysts realized the effectiveness of aiming advertisements at targeted population segments, political analysts followed close behind. Thus, the John F. Kennedy campaign was marketed to distinct segments of the political market in the 1960 election. Election campaigns became "indistinguishable in form (and often in content) from product marketing campaigns."[18]

Interest group politics, at the core of pluralist democracy, reflected the intertwining of the mass-consumer culture and democracy. Interest group leaders or entrepreneurs learned that they needed to sell potential members on the benefits of joining and remaining within their respective political organizations. Advertising became crucial. Group leaders would, of course, publicize the purposes or policy goals of their respective organizations. A leader of the National Rifle Association (NRA) would emphasize gun use and the dangers of governmental regulation; a leader of the Sierra Club would accentuate environmental issues. But interest group advertising could be far more strategic and sophisticated. Group leaders might "claim credit for policy successes even when the group's effort was of little consequence to the outcomes." Or group leaders might offer membership perks that would personally benefit individual members, even if the perks were largely unrelated to the organizations' political goals; magazines, insurance discounts, and special travel deals proved useful as "selective incentives." Moreover, realizing the effectiveness of aiming at population segments, many group leaders became "skilled at targeting their messages and appeals to exploit social organization and structure." In short, interest group leaders learned to treat group members (and potential members) as consumers.[19]

Tort reform provides a powerful illustration. Around 1980, advocates seeking to limit civil recoveries began to pursue a strategy of "pop tort reform." Regardless of empirical information, which often contravened their views, these tort reformers "articulated their case ever more through mass media to condition public attitudes and to supply to the public information that would advance tort reforms." Thus, in an effort to define the issue to their advantage—suggesting that tort lawsuits regularly bestowed exorbitant monetary awards on undeserving malcontents—tort reformers would constantly invoke inflammatory slogans such as the "litigation lottery," the "litigation explosion," the "tort crisis," and the "sue-icidal impulse." In this same vein, tort reformers encouraged the press, the sellers of "infotainment," to reinforce this sloganeering. The point was to win, to sell one's policy agenda, and if doing so required tort reformers to "encourage derision [of alternative views] rather than intelligent debate," so be it.[20]

Finally, by the end of the twentieth century, multinational corporations had come to dominate the mass-consumer culture as never before. Individuals rarely bought their mass-produced items at independent Mom and Pop stores. Instead, people shopped at Target, or SuperWalmart, or online at Amazon.com. The American economy had thoroughly transformed into a *corporate* capitalist system. With this change, pluralist democracy also shifted, as corporations exercised increasing control over democracy and government. During the late twentieth century, corporations became more resolute at using their bureaucratic organizations and accumulated wealth to intervene in the pluralist democratic marketplace. Over the last five years of the 1970s, for instance, the number of corporate political action committees zoomed from 300 to 1,200. Even more extreme, from the early

1970s to the early 1980s, the number of corporations with registered lobbyists in Washington expanded nearly fifteenfold. With ever-increasing proficiency, corporations manipulated democracy and government for their own advantage—benefiting the respective corporations as well as corporate business more generally. Today, "corporate power and its culture are no longer external forces that occasionally influence policies and legislation." Citizens still vote, but corporations exercise control over "highly managed elections" and strongly influence government between elections. Our consumers' (pluralist) democracy might now be better termed "democracy incorporated" (or Democracy, Inc.).[21]

The Proliferation of Interest Groups

While the growth of the mass-consumer culture significantly affected pluralist democracy, other forces further altered the formation and operation of interest groups. Initially, after World War II, political and constitutional theorists envisioned a fluid democratic process with flexible interest groups that would negotiate and compromise. The early pluralist democratic theorists, in other words, presented a "rosy picture" of the political process in which power fairly offset power. No theorist focused on the formation and operation of interest groups more than David B. Truman. In his book *The Governmental Process*, he defined an interest group as "any group that, on the basis of one or more shared attitudes, makes certain claims upon other groups in the society for the establishment, maintenance, or enhancement of forms of behavior that are implied by the shared attitudes." While acknowledging that particular interest groups might be either "good or bad," Truman explained that groups such as labor unions and trade associations form naturally in response to the complexity of and disturbances within society. "[L]abor unions and their federations have been the product of the increasing division of labor within industry, the growing differentiation between employer and worker, and the consequent major changes in the status and rewards of both workers and managers," he wrote. "These disturbances have been aggravated by rapid developments in transportation and communication and by the shifts in economic organization that have removed policy-makers in institutionalized economic groups from direct and intimate contact with workers. The disturbances resulting from these changes have produced the alterations in attitudes (interests) necessary for cohesive associations among workers."[22]

The competing interest groups thus exist, in the words of V. O. Key, in "a more or less unstable equilibrium." If one group "becomes discontented with the existing state of things," then "the processes of politics go into operation to produce a new equilibrium." As numerous theorists emphasized, the pluralist democratic process was "dynamic, not static; fluid, not fixed." The process was open, flowing, and balanced. Even when interest groups were defeated in legislative battle, explained Earl Latham, they possessed "the right to make new combinations of strength if they are able to do so, combinations that will support a new effort to rewrite the rules in their favor." Latham especially emphasized how legislatures were sites of interest group struggle, negotiation, and compromise. And whether in a legislature or elsewhere, "[t]oday's losers may be tomorrow's winners." The early Robert Dahl largely subscribed to this optimistic outlook, explaining that "all the active and legitimate groups in the population can make themselves heard at some crucial stage in the process of decision."[23]

To an extent, this belief in the fluidity and balance of the pluralist democratic process corresponded with political reality. Most postwar political theorists perceived a widespread American cultural agreement on the value of democracy. While pluralist democratic theorists emphasized the requisite processes for democracy, they also asserted that a democratic system would be unsustainable without a democratic culture. Democracy depended in part on the internalized commitment of Americans to the "rules of the game" for the "democratic mold," to use Truman's terminology. Thus, Dahl and, before him, Dewey argued that American culture imbued the people with a willingness to negotiate and compromise rather than to do battle over their political differences. In the economic boom years of the 1950s, Daniel Boorstin argued, the "genius" of American politics lay not in any philosophy but in a "genuine community of our values," a "common faith" in a pragmatic and pluralist democracy. Indeed, Louis Hartz worried that "America's moral unity," the cultural commitment to an "American Way of Life," was so strong that it could engender a stifling and even dangerous conformity of public opinion. Some political scientists went so far as to brood about an insufficient degree of disagreement between Democrats and Republicans: An American Political Science Association committee concluded that the two parties, in consensus on important issues, did not present the people with adequate choices. Yet the general perception was that the widespread cultural commitment to pluralist democracy was propitious. Citizens might strongly hold and pursue their preexisting interests and values, but they were always willing to accommodate the interests and values of others. If you didn't win now, don't worry: Everybody wins and loses at different times. That's (pluralist) democracy.[24]

While pluralist democracy achieved hegemony during the postwar era, numerous critics emerged to question its actual operation. Whereas the émigré dissenters, such as Strauss, questioned the very foundations of pluralist democracy, these other critics tended to accept its broad parameters while impugning the functionality of parts of the system. Some critics argued that the pluralist democratic claim to fluidity and balance was mythical. In reality, a powerful elite consistently held the levers of power. Other critics emphasized that various obstacles might hinder like-minded individuals from forming into politically effective interest groups. Mancur Olson, in particular, emphasized the "free rider" problem: "[B]ecause the costs of contributing to collective action generally outweigh the benefits, rational individuals often will refrain from acting collectively even if it is in their best interest to do so." Individuals, in other words, hope to get a free ride: Why should Jane Doe join a group when others will do so, thus allowing Jane to benefit from the group activities without contributing resources? As one political scientist trenchantly commented, "A widespread collective interest, a belief that rivers should be clean or that forests should not be razed, does not generate an interest group." If so, then certain societal groups that overcame the obstacles to organization might wield undue influence in the democratic process, practically controlling legislative and administrative agendas. And if powerful elites and privileged interest groups enjoyed a surfeit of power, then some individuals and societal groups suffered a dearth of power. The prototypical example of habitual democratic losers were African Americans, especially in the South, where numerous laws still explicitly precluded blacks (at least through the 1960s) from fully participating in public life.[25]

In short, interest groups did not necessarily form and reform as a natural and easy response to societal pressures, and of the groups that managed to organize, many did not wield power commensurate with their membership numbers. Still, the civil rights movement, led by the National Association for the Advancement of Colored People (NAACP), showed in the 1950s and early 1960s that a persistently disempowered group could gain greater access to the pluralist democratic process. The movement culminated in discrete victories, such as the passages of the Civil Rights Act of 1964 and the Voting Rights Act of 1965 (as part of President Lyndon Johnson's Great Society program). Neither sudden nor complete, these democratic breakthroughs manifested a stage in a long, difficult, and sustained struggle. Regardless, with such success, the civil rights movement provided a model and a training ground for political action. A determined and moderately organized assertion of power and claim to rights could produce political change (even though some scholars would eventually argue that civil rights advances were merely formal or theoretical, bereft of substance). The National Organization for Women (NOW), formed in 1966, explicitly modeled itself after the NAACP, while a former NAACP staff member helped organize the Mexican-American Legal Defense and Education Fund (MALDEF) in 1968.[26]

While the apparent advances of the civil rights movement inspired political activists, many other factors further contributed to the organization of numerous new interest groups. In fact, although the uncertainty of a baseline renders measurement of interest group activity somewhat problematic, political scientists widely agree that the number of organized groups increased exponentially in the 1960s and subsequent decades. The numbers, such as are available, are astounding. According to the *Encyclopedia of Associations*, there were 5,843 national nonprofit associations in 1959. By 1980, that number had nearly tripled, to 14,726, and by 1990, it had jumped to 22,289. If one goes beyond national associations to consider regional, state, and local associations as well, the total number, as of 2008, leaps to 100,000.[27]

The variety of organizations is almost as staggering as the quantity.

> [There] are groups representing business interests, such as trade associations (e.g., the Semiconductor Industry Association, American Iron and Steel Institute), peak business associations (U.S. Chamber of Commerce, National Association of Manufacturers), and the many individual corporations that maintain a political presence in Washington. Numerous groups also represent occupational interests, including labor unions (e.g., the American Postal Workers Union, American Federation of Teachers), professional associations (American Medical Association, National Bar Association), and farm groups (National Farmers Union). Non-material interests also find representation in the political process. Groups have

> organized to represent those who share common views on a set of ideological or social issues and who wish to see those views reflected in government policy. There are, for example, groups representing different views on religion (American Jewish Congress, Christian Coalition), drug and alcohol policy (Mothers Against Drunk Driving, National Organization for the Reform of Marijuana Laws), gun control (National Rifle Association, Handgun Controls, Inc.), abortion rights (National Right to Life Organization, National Abortion and Reproductive Rights Action League) . . . and a host of others.

Despite the variety, the largest number of associations, by far, fit year after year into the "trade, business, and commercial" category, though the numbers of groups in other categories are substantial. For instance, in 1990, nearly 4,000 organizations were devoted to business, while almost 1,000 were devoted to agricultural and environmental concerns.[28]

What forces or factors have produced this proliferation of interest groups? No single factor is determinative; "there are many roads to group success." The overarching message of pluralist democracy is that individuals legitimately participate in politics by seeking to satisfy their own interests and values. Interest groups form to fulfill that goal, at least in part. Thus, to illustrate, governmental regulations and programs tend to promote the creation of interest groups. If the government grants benefits to the elderly, then a group such as the American Association of Retired Persons (AARP) might form to push for continued or greater benefits. If the government regulates a particular type of commercial enterprise, then the regulated businesses might form an association to influence and monitor the governmental actions. Not coincidentally, interest groups began to proliferate in the 1960s and 1970s, when governmental expenditures and regulations expanded. Likewise, changes in technology can prompt the formation of interest groups that seek to monitor or prevent governmental regulation of the new technology. The introduction of genetic engineering sparked interest group formation, as did the introduction of personal computers. (Moreover, advanced communication technology has facilitated interest group organizational, recruitment, and mobilization activities.) And as David Truman suggested decades ago, social disturbances can generate interest group activity; an expansion in immigration might, for example, cause new interest groups to appear.[29]

These examples suggest a simple stimulus-response model: The government enacts a regulatory statute, for example, and an interest group (or groups) forms. But "the logic of collective action," to borrow a phrase from Mancur Olson—or, more precisely, the logic of pluralist democratic interest group formation—can be more complex. Free rider problems might deter individuals from joining large groups even if they share certain common or collective goals (such as preserving the wilderness), as Olson argued, yet empirical studies suggest that people will join such groups if they sense that their collective goals are threatened (e.g., the government plans to open pristine wilderness to mining or logging). More broadly, the logic of interest group formation must be understood in conjunction with a legal culture that encourages individuals to pursue "total justice." A society inclined toward total justice, according to Lawrence Friedman, is "a society that tries to offer its public many ways to express their grievances, many ways to look for satisfaction of their wrongs."[30]

Numerous forces contributed to the molding of a total justice culture. The modernist outlook, which took hold in the early twentieth century, suggested that human inventiveness could produce endless progress. Modernism thus encouraged individuals to believe that harms could be avoided and that injuries could be remedied; scientific and technological advances could protect us from the vagaries of the natural and human-made environments. Most important, pluralist democracy itself helped engender the total justice culture, even as the total justice culture contributed to the evolution of pluralist democracy. The early emergence of pluralist democracy centered on the opening of democracy to diverse Americans. In theory, with the establishment of the pluralist democratic regime, all Americans could participate by expressing and asserting their own interests and values. But this participatory urge and potential could not be limited to discrete democratic processes, such as voting. It spread to all forms of political and legal processes. The legal culture of total justice imbues each individual with the attitude that he or she has a right of access to, a right to participate in, both the political system and the legal system. Each individual has a right to vote, a right to express one's views, a right to be shielded from harm, a right to be compensated for injury—a veritable right to have one's rights protected.[31]

Eventually, the logic of pluralist democracy, driven in part by the developing total justice culture, led to the proliferation of interest groups. The basic pluralist democratic pursuit of self-interest—manifested in a fear that somebody else's actions might harm one's own interests, and the total justice desire to protect against such harm—caused interest group formation to surge. The civil rights movement and the NAACP inspired the formation of groups like NOW and MALDEF. Reacting against the operation of these and other liberal groups, conservative interest groups began to spring up in the 1970s and 1980s. The success of these groups helped provoke the formation of additional progressive (or liberal) groups (think of MoveOn.org), and so on. Organization is "its own cause, or, to put it another way, mobilization begets countermobilization."[32]

Interest Group Sclerosis

The proliferation of interest groups, spurred by the total justice drive within the parameters of pluralist democracy, affected not only the formation but also the maintenance and operation of interest groups. In fact, the logic of interest group maintenance and operation has pushed pluralist democracy along an evolutionary path toward increasing interest group "sclerosis," to borrow another term from Mancur Olson. As already discussed, the early pluralist democratic theorists, writing after World War II, asserted that interest groups would not only form naturally and readily but also operate in a spirit of openness and flexibility, seeking to negotiate and compromise with competing interest groups. But as pluralist democracy evolved in the latter twentieth century, interest group relations hardened. Openness and flexibility gave way to bilious hostility and stubbornness.[33]

Writing in 1982, Olson expanded on his earlier work articulating the logic of collective action. Because free rider problems impede the formation of interest groups, Olson reasoned that in any particular country, such as the United States, some potential groups will organize while others will not. But over time, in a stable society, an increasing number of interest groups will organize, and, once formed, these interest groups tend to endure, even if changed circumstances undermine their original purposes. Once any interest group organizes, then it will quest after advantageous governmental actions and policies: The interest group will operate to satisfy its avowed interests and values, including its own continued existence, even if doing so injures other groups or unorganized individuals. Thus, in a stable society, an increasing number of interest groups will inevitably exist and pursue their own respective interests and values. And if any interest group can benefit from a governmental action yet induce others to bear the concomitant costs, all the better. That is, the logic of collective action applies at the group (as well as at the individual) level: Even though many interest groups would benefit from society-wide economic growth and efficiency, for example, most groups would not have an incentive to sacrifice for or contribute to such communal economic goals. Just as individuals who hope to free ride will refrain from joining interest groups, an interest group will hope to free ride and will avoid contributing to the economic well-being of society. Let other interest groups pay the freight![34]

Ultimately, Olson posited that stable societies suffer from "institutional sclerosis." As the number of interest groups grows, the groups will dull economic efficiency, slow economic growth, and "make political life more divisive." The competing interest groups will consistently seek the free ride and will therefore refuse to contribute to the improvement of society.[35] Significantly, then, empirical research shows that in a political world with a multitude of interest groups, such as the United States over the past four decades, Olson's sclerosis thesis is correct in its pertinent parts. Once our stable American society embraced pluralist democracy, increasing numbers of interest groups have emerged and, in their struggles to survive, these groups have clogged the political flow of democratic negotiation and compromise. Already by 1970, even before Olson posited his sclerosis thesis, research suggested that interest groups were cooperating less than pluralist democratic theorists had hypothesized. Alignments of interests tended to be "persistent" rather than fluid and "shifting."[36]

For purposes of my argument, the crux of the sclerosis thesis is not only that, over the past several decades, interest groups have proliferated but also that the multitudinous groups now must fight to survive in order to continue their existence. Whereas the postwar pluralist theorists described cooperating interest groups, fused harmoniously in a cultural consensus, we instead find conflict-ridden struggle. Sometime during the 1960s, the ostensible consensus of the 1950s fell to pieces with a shattering crash, audible far and wide. With the emergence of a women's movement, a consumers' movement, an environmental movement, a black power movement, and of course, a protest movement against the Vietnam War, one would have been hard-pressed to maintain even a veneer of cultural consensus. Then, in the 1970s and 1980s, as conservative Christians became a predominant and aggressive interest group, all pretenses toward societal harmony were discarded. Numerous social and political commentators talked openly of the "culture wars."[37]

Thus, in this world of multitudinous organizations, the logic of interest group relations dictates that interest groups must battle to survive. Any interest group that does not aim in part to maintain its operations will cease to exist, supplanted by more aggressive organizations. The simple stimulus-response model, suggested by David Truman's argument, captures some of this social reality. Once the government funds a program, for example, the beneficiaries are likely to be motivated to lobby for continued (or more) funding. Partly for this reason, interest groups tend to persist once they have formed, as Olson emphasized. Individuals form or join an interest group to pursue or protect their interests and values. They are not likely to relinquish their benefits or renounce their desires, even if other societal problems might grow more momentous. The Humane Society, for instance, will continue to advocate for the safe treatment of stray dogs even if the number of homeless people has increased (and I do not intend to denigrate the Humane Society with this example).[38]

But the battle for survival is just that: a battle. Interest groups might want to persevere, but survival does not merely happen as a matter of course. Interest group leaders who want to keep their jobs must think strategically about how to maximize the lifespans of their respective organizations. The provision of selective benefits, like magazines or travel discounts, might matter more than the organization's avowed purposes and policy goals.[39] Most important, many interest group leaders have concluded in recent decades that political extremism is beneficial. Rather than state their positions in nuanced detail, interest group leaders are more likely to fulminate in overblown rants that appear to preclude negotiation and compromise. For example, I recently received a letter that contained an NRA membership card and invited me to join the organization. Using language that became increasingly incendiary in naming the "enemies of gun rights," the letter began by emphasizing the urgent policy goals of the organization: "Your constitutional right to own a gun is under attack by hundreds of anti-gun politicians, global gun ban diplomats at the U.N., militant anti-hunting extremists, radical billionaires and the freedom-hating Hollywood elite. . . . If you want to protect your guns and your precious freedoms—for you and your children—please act NOW. Please accept this card and join NRA today." Then, after this pugnacious policy-oriented introduction, the letter moved on, of course, to underscore (literally, with underlined and bold-faced type) the additional perks I would receive if I joined promptly: "And if you join NRA in the next 30 days, you can join at low, introductory new member rates. That's right. If you join NRA today, you'll get a full year of NRA membership for just $25 (normally $35). . . . Join NRA today at these savings and I'll send you three special benefits: The first benefit I'll send you: NRA's heavy-duty duffel bag. . . . The second benefit I'll send you: Your choice of NRA magazines. . . . The third benefit I'll send you: Your NRA member credentials package with your personalized membership card and a guide to all the NRA benefits—insurance, Friends of NRA events, competitions, safety training, FREE admission to NRA's annual Guns, Gear and Outfitter Show, and special savings on goods and gear worth hundreds."[40]

Throw in a Ginsu knife and I might join, even if I oppose the NRA's policy goals![41]

The emergence of extremism as a political ploy goes hand-in-hand with the much-discussed phenomenon of political polarization. *Polarization* often refers to the separation of Democrats and Republicans into two strongly opposed camps, but it can more broadly refer to the identification of Democrats, Republicans, and other groups with distinct and often seemingly irreconcilable political interests and values; think of polarization that is not necessarily bipolar. Systemic polarization initially arose among political leaders rather than voters. Thus, for instance, members of Congress led the way in expressing their viewpoints with extreme and acrimonious rhetoric. Through much of the 1960s, Republicans and Democrats in Congress were civil to and even friendly with each other. Congressional voting often crossed party lines, and bipartisan coalitions often contributed to policies and bills. In short, for the first couple of decades after World War II, partisanship in Congress was passionless. To be sure, congressional Republicans and Democrats had occasionally been polarized in the past, but those periods of polarization tended to focus "on only one major issue at a time (for example, slavery and civil rights)." But starting in the 1970s and accelerating in the 1980s, polarization between the parties grew increasingly intense and widespread, reaching across sundry issues. By the 1990s, "party antagonism" had become the rule, with each party accusing the other of depravity and venality. The Republicans and Democrats both demonstrated enhanced institutional strength, thus engendering ideological homogeneity within each party. Congressional members were pressured to demonstrate party loyalty, with the result that voting consistently followed party lines. The Clinton impeachment imbroglio of 1998–99 epitomized this polarization: The House vote to impeach and the Senate vote to acquit tracked party lines almost exactly. Needless to say, with such dramatic polarization, "political compromise often remains elusive." In many instances, "there is virtually no communication between" the two sides, rendering the negotiation of a "consensus solution" nearly impossible.[42]

The causes of increased polarization among political leaders, including congressional members, are numerous yet obscure. For instance, different researchers have argued that factors as diverse as rising income inequality, shifts in immigration patterns, and changes in internal congressional procedures have contributed to the transition. Most researchers agree, though, that the civil rights movement, which led to the political realignment of the South, was an important causal factor. In the wake of the Supreme Court's 1954 *Brown v. Board of Education* decision, most southern Democrats initially opposed school integration. The national Democratic Party, however, had already decided to support civil rights. As early as 1948, in their party platform, the Democrats pledged themselves "to eradicate all racial, religious and economic discrimination." The 1956 Democratic Party platform reiterated: "We will continue our efforts to eradicate discrimination based on race, religion or national origin." Meanwhile, the Republican Party in 1964 nominated for president Barry Goldwater, an arch-conservative opponent of the Civil Rights Act. The stage was now set for massive party shifting. Southern white conservative Democrats began to rush to the Republican side, enhancing Republican conservative forces and simultaneously leaving a more homogeneous set of liberals on the Democratic side. An increasing number of African Americans began to vote (Democratic) after the passage of the Voting Rights Act of 1965, not only intensifying partisan racial divisions but also magnifying the geographical realignment of the parties. Thus, for instance, "[i]n the 85th Congress (1957–1958), Southerners made up 45 percent of the Democrats in the Senate; by 1983 they made up just 23 percent. During roughly the same period, the percentage of Republican senators from New England and the Mid-Atlantic States dropped from 37 to 19 percent."[43]

Concomitant with this geographical shifting, tied to race, an interrelated cultural divide between the parties began to widen. The Supreme Court's

1973 *Roe v. Wade* decision catapulted abortion to the forefront of national political issues. Republican conservatism grew more vigorous as the party emphasized abortion and other cultural issues along with racial separation. "'Racial and cultural concerns, which used to divide parties internally more than externally, now have joined economic and social welfare issues as clear sources of interparty cleavage and intraparty homogeneity.' The parties have polarized over race, abortion, school prayer, [and] the rights of gay men and lesbians." Significantly, many of these emerging wedge issues seemed more symbolic than material, and such symbolic issues often seemed intractable. A disagreement over the allocation of economic resources would likely be more amenable to compromise than would a disagreement over homosexual rights. If anything, then, polarization seemed to snowball among elites; one extreme pronouncement would trigger a venomous reply, which would in turn produce an even more vituperative response, and so forth. Democratic politics transformed into a series of grand postures, gridlocks, and rounds of the "blame game," with each party portraying "the other as the real extremists." It's fair to say "[t]he old norm of political discourse that encourages one 'to disagree without being disagreeable' seems to have been replaced by [congressional] members who are 'disagreeable even when they don't disagree.'"[44]

In sum, American pluralist democracy has developed a serious case of sclerosis. Hostility and stubbornness have replaced free-flowing negotiation and compromise. Nowadays, we should not say that the pluralist democratic process is infected because of invidious prejudices; rather, the process *is* the confrontation among persistent groups constituted chiefly by their invidious prejudices against others. Indeed, some commentators argue that the political process has changed so much that the term *pluralism* should be replaced (by, for instance, *neopluralism*). Perhaps in the past, venomous intransigence was exceptional, but it has become normal, as evidenced by the incredible number of single-issue interest groups. Single-interest organizations began to multiply in the late 1970s and early 1980s. Quite evidently, "in a complex society with a remote government, groups that espouse simple answers to difficult questions have great appeal." Commentators have described these single-issue groups as "'passionate blocs' of voters" who "'will vote against any legislator who votes the 'wrong' way on a particular issue.'" And in fact, advanced communication technology, especially the Internet, expedites the sharing of information among like-minded individuals and thus facilitates the mobilization of single-issue groups. Nevertheless, many single-issue organizations exist only as pseudo–interest groups. They maintain the external shell of an interest group—funding and leadership—but they lack the substance: namely, members. Even such a pseudo–interest group, though, can perform many standard interest group functions, such as sending mass mailings, distributing information to legislators, and feeding acrimonious pronouncements to the media.[45]

The "quintessential" single-issue interest groups have arisen in the political context of abortion. A national pro-life (or anti-abortion) leader explained, "Our issue is totally and absolutely different than any other issue. . . . We're not talking about dollars or cotton; we're talking about human life. When you abort it, you kill it. You can't compromise with human life. . . . Compromise is the name of the game for many issues because unfortunately, it's the only way to get things done. If I compromise with someone over the size of the budget, I'm not bothering anyone. But if I compromise on abortion, the compromise harms human life. And life is sacred." As the abortion controversy exemplifies, the modus operandi of single-issue organizations is zealotry (whether the respective organization is a true or pseudo–interest group). Single-issue groups exist, in theory, for one and only one reason: to advocate for a particular position on a particular issue. Consequently, single-issue interest groups emblematize sclerotic processes. Whatever an organization's chosen issue, compromise is unacceptable. Other "more mundane questions" might be negotiable, interest group members would assert, but their issue is not. Their cause is too fundamental, "so central, it is often claimed, that negotiation would be a kind of moral betrayal." Trading votes is anathema; one does not bargain away a moral absolute. "The candidate who promises to support their cause gets their vote; the candidate who either does not promise to do so or hedges is being opposed. Nothing else counts."[46]

4

On Neoconservatism

The Rise of the Neocons

The typical neoconservative grew up in New York City in a "lower-middle-class or working-class" family. Many (though not all) were Jewish and attended City College of New York (CCNY), often because, at the time, other schools followed antisemitic admission policies. In the 1920s, numerous colleges, including Ivy League schools, began to require that entering classes display "geographical diversity," exactly because such a requirement would curtail the number of Jewish applicants admitted from New York and other Eastern urban centers. During the 1930s, in the midst of the Great Depression, many of the CCNY students gravitated toward leftist politics. They split, however, in their sentiments: Trotskyites congregated in one cafeteria alcove, while Stalinists congregated in another. The Trotskyites, many of whom would eventually become neoconservative, distrusted utopian communist theories that could be translated into the dystopian practices of Stalinist terror and violence.

Irving Kristol, one of the Trotskyites who would later help start the neoconservative movement, remembers cutting his teeth on political argument while jousting with his fellow CCNY students.[1]

Many of these students, however, were so focused on their debates against the Stalinists that they were slow to recognize the Nazi danger in Europe. When other Americans had begun to call for aggressive U.S. action against Germany, the Trotskyite students were still "preoccupied with debating the fine points of Marxist dogma." Perhaps partly because of their dilatoriness in this regard, they were among the first to take a strong anticommunist stance after World War II, at the outset of the Cold War. Kristol and others became staunchly anticommunist and would remain so through the 1950s and into the 1960s; appeasement was unacceptable.[2]

Still, Kristol and like-minded cohorts remained liberal and Democrat; for example, in a 1963 essay on race relations, another founder of neoconservativism, Norman Podhoretz, unabashedly labeled himself a "liberal." But two factors caused Kristol, Podhoretz, and others to begin moving rightward in the 1960s. First, they reacted against what they saw as the excesses and delusions of Lyndon Johnson's Great Society programs. In a 1963 essay that Podhoretz published in *Commentary*, a journal he edited for more than thirty years, Podhoretz doubted the appropriateness of white liberal guilt for black misfortunes in America. More important, just as these budding neoconservatives, when young Trotskyites, had questioned the implementation of communist theory in the Soviet Union, they now questioned the effectiveness of LBJ's attempts at "social engineering." Even a leading Democrat such as Daniel Patrick Moynihan suggested that, while liberalism might be appealing in theory, its implementation in practice might prove futile and even counterproductive. Kristol and Daniel Bell founded *The Public Interest* in 1965 partly because, with their working-class backgrounds, they could not accept the Great Society premise that political mobilization would somehow alleviate poverty. Work, they believed, not politics, would help the poor.[3]

Second, Kristol, Podhoretz, and other incipient neoconservatives reacted against the student counterculture that emerged in the 1960s. When the apparent cultural consensus of the 1950s shattered in the 1960s, college students led the way. Not only did they protest against the Vietnam War, they also questioned the truths and values that their professors had been teaching for decades. Many students rebelled, in particular, against the so-called

Great Books courses. Required at numerous colleges and universities, these courses taught the canon of Western civilization, typically including works by Plato, Aristotle, Aquinas, Shakespeare, and so forth. According to Podhoretz, the student protesters "condemned such courses politically as lacking 'relevance' to the problems of the contemporary world, and culturally as 'elitist' in promoting the kind of works traditionally preferred by the upper reaches of society while contemptuously dismissing anything that appealed to popular taste." Great Books courses, students insisted, were "marked by a 'European-Western and male bias' (or to use the tag that would later become so familiar, 'Dead White European Males') and by 'sexist and racist stereotypes.'" And what were the results of such student protests? Much to the chagrin of Podhoretz and other neoconservatives, many colleges and universities eliminated their Great Books courses. The universities, which had taught truth and value, now capitulated to populist relativism, or so complained Podhoretz, who gave this example: "[A]n eminent professor of literature at a major university declared that to choose between Shakespeare and Jacqueline Susann was 'no different from choosing between a hoagie and a pizza.'"[4]

As described by the neoconservative Jeane Kirkpatrick, the counterculture considered the United States to be "immoral—a 'sick society' guilty of racism, materialism, imperialism, and murder of Third World people." But this viewpoint was wrongheaded, explained Kirkpatrick: The United States was not "essentially immoral" or "deeply flawed." Moreover, not all values were relative: Some ethical propositions were right, and some were wrong. There is a difference between "good and evil." Thus, to give a core illustration, Kirkpatrick emphasized that "there were important differences between democracy and dictatorship." But merely teaching the right and the wrong, the good and the evil, was no longer sufficient. The student protesters had triggered war: The battles over the Great Books were merely the opening bursts of the "culture wars." And from the neoconservative standpoint, the winners in these wars were not necessarily correct; they were simply more powerful. Ideas mattered, to be certain, but good did not always vanquish evil by the force of the best argument.[5]

Indeed, some former Trotskyites who had become college professors during the postwar years now literally faced the student protesters on their shared university turfs. Allan Bloom, a former student of Leo Strauss's, was teaching at Cornell in the 1960s. In late 1968 and early 1969, black students, acting under the auspices of a student group, the Afro-American Society, sought curriculum changes at Cornell and the creation of a "separate 'black college.'" The students protested that the current "curriculum was inherently white, middle-class and racist." These protests sparked a series of diverse "incidents," including the initiation of disciplinary proceedings against five black students and the burning of a cross in front of a black students' residence. Then, early on April 20, 1969, approximately one hundred African American students, some of whom were armed with rifles and shotguns, seized the student union. After a thirty-six-hour standoff, the students agreed to vacate the union in exchange for the withdrawal of all disciplinary proceedings against them. The faculty soon rejected this agreement, but when the dean of faculty threatened to resign, the faculty revoted and reversed its decision, nullifying at least the original disciplinary charges.[6]

From Bloom's perspective, the Cornell faculty had capitulated to "outrageous demands." They had, in effect, expressed "their willingness to change the university's goals and the content of what they taught." The university had succumbed to relativism, he maintained, abandoning "all claim to study or inform about value—undermining the sense of the value of what it taught, while turning over the decision about values to the folk [or students]." Bloom feared that the university had acted as if there were no longer any standards of right and wrong; "the very distinction between educated and uneducated in America had been leveled." In reaction, Bloom and the former Trotskyites moved rightward, becoming neoconservatives. If there were any remaining doubts, the Democratic Party's 1972 nomination of George McGovern for president put them to rest. To the neoconservatives, McGovern represented the counterculture itself, so his nomination forced them to admit that they no longer fit in the Democratic Party. Thenceforth they would more openly adopt conservative positions and gradually align themselves with the Republicans.[7]

In short, the incipient neoconservatives were liberals reacting against perceived problems with liberalism, especially as recently implemented by Democrats. Many of these former liberals were intellectuals, and as such, they quested for an intellectual foundation to support their increasingly conservative inclinations. They found that foundation in the writings of Strauss, a teacher and scholar of extraordinary renown. Kristol exclaimed, "Encountering Strauss's work produced the kind of intellectual shock that is a once-in-a-lifetime experience. He turned one's intellectual universe upside down." Strauss proved appealing to the erstwhile liberals for many reasons, not least of which was his emphasis on the American founders' principles of political philosophy. Strauss began *Natural Right and History*, perhaps his most important book, by quoting from the Declaration of Independence. The American founders, Strauss argued, had aimed to build a nation on principles of justice, in the spirit of ancient political philosophy, rather than on Machiavellian and Hobbesian notions of realpolitik. But the nation today had accepted historicism, empiricism, and value-relativism, the building blocks for modernity and pluralist democracy that Strauss vigorously criticized. Thus, Strauss asked the crucial question: Could the United States still live up to its founding principles?[8]

And now, Kristol, Podhoretz, Kirkpatrick, and other former liberals were asking the same question. In the American founding, Strauss saw elements of the fundamental principles of classical political philosophy, the fundamental principles of a republican democratic regime. Contrary to modernist relativism, Strauss argued, human reason could discern right and wrong, good and evil. Universals existed. The average person might lack the perspicacity or determination to discover the universal truths, but a virtuous elite could draw on tradition and religion to help inculcate the proper values in the populace. When the people and their leaders were sufficiently imbued with virtue, with the desire for human excellence, then the political community would naturally strive to become the best regime possible, to pursue the common good and attain a moral order commensurate with natural right.[9]

The former liberals, disgruntled with the state of pluralist (liberal) democracy, welcomed these Straussian propositions as foundational for their new form of conservatism—for their neoconservatism. These neoconservatives could embrace both elements of the Straussian intellectual persona: Strauss the pessimist, a caustic and precise critic of our current circumstances, and Strauss the optimist, an obscure yet inspirational advocate for natural right and republican democracy. Indeed, Strauss's ambiguities could be appealing to the neocons. Strauss viewed himself as a friend to democracy, but he believed that its current American instantiation in a pluralist democratic regime was inherently fragile and dangerous. Yet we could not turn back the clock and pretend to live in a Greek *polis*. We somehow needed to learn from the past and, with that knowledge, save democracy by resuscitating republican democratic principles within our present political circumstances. Unlike traditionalist conservatives, Strauss did not aim to reinvigorate tradition merely because it was tradition; rather, he aimed for the good (and the common good). Beyond such nebulous pronouncements, though, Strauss rarely attempted to articulate specific prescriptions for political or governmental action (though he occasionally did so). Thus, the budding neocons could draw on Strauss, develop his principles, and then explain how those principles led to certain preferred political stances, without worrying about what Strauss himself might have uttered about the particular topic. Aim for the good regime that pursued the common good—that was what Strauss counseled—and the neoconservatives could wholeheartedly follow that advice. After all, the neocons were more political commentators than philosophers: They were seeking invigoration and general direction, not aiming for rigorous analyses of Strauss's texts.[10]

So, with the Straussian foundation for support, neoconservatism began to crystallize as a political ideology, as an intellectual movement. Still, though, neoconservatives wielded little political clout through the early 1970s. Kristol, Podhoretz, and others published a continual flow of essays in *The Public Interest*, *Commentary*, and other journals exploring the ramifications of neoconservatism for domestic and foreign policies. For example, they wrote numerous "broadsides" attacking President Richard Nixon and Henry Kissinger's efforts to accommodate the Soviet Union through peaceful negotiations. As these neoconservative critiques of the Nixon administration demonstrate, the neocons did not all dash wildly into Republican arms at the end of the 1960s. Many supported Senator Henry "Scoop" Jackson's bid for the Democratic presidential nomination in 1976 (he had briefly sought the nomination in 1972 as well). In fact, Jackson could be fairly characterized as a neoconservative himself, given his opposition to détente with the Soviets, his skepticism toward the United Nations, and his vigorous support for Israel.[11]

In any event, neocon political fortunes shifted when they were swept up into the Ronald Reagan whirlwind. While initially wary of Reagan as a national politician, the neocons embraced him by the end of the 1970s, largely because of their disgust with President Jimmy Carter's foreign policies. Before long, the neoconservatives were claiming Reagan as one of their own, "a genuine neocon." And he had, at least roughly, the appropriate background: After a long history of strong anticommunism, he converted from the Democratic to the Republican Party in 1962. During his presidency, *Commentary* was the "White House's favorite political journal."[12]

Reagan and the neoconservatives mutually benefited from their joining of forces. In 1964, the Republicans had nominated Barry Goldwater for president, but his arch-conservatism had seemed unpalatable to the vast majority of Americans. He received less than 40 percent of the popular vote and lost in a landslide; Johnson garnered 486 Electoral College votes to Goldwater's 52. But between the Goldwater debacle and Reagan's rise in 1980, the neoconservative intellectual movement helped imbue conservatism with respectability. Some neocons were university professors, and others published not only in neocon journals like *The Public Interest* but also in "prestige magazines [like] the *Atlantic Monthly, Harpers*, and the *New York Times Sunday Magazine*." Meanwhile, the Republicans successfully built political power in the 1970s and 1980s by mobilizing the Christian right and by invoking racial divisions to consolidate their gains from the southern realignment of the 1960s. To be sure, "given post–civil rights movement norms against overt racism," Republican strategists could not explicitly appeal to white resentment against black civil rights advances. Instead, Republicans insistently proclaimed their commitment to colorblindness, governmental policies that ostensibly disregarded race. Nonetheless, the Republicans created "a narrative that portrayed the Democrats as the party of intellectual elites and undeserving rabble." Race was implicit in this narrative: The elites were white, and the rabble were black. The Republicans then supposedly represented a large "virtuous middle" that was unmistakably white. The most (in)famous manifestation of this Republican racial narrative was Reagan's repeated tellings of the "story of the Cadillac-driving welfare queen." Ultimately, Reagan and neoconservatism, united together, became a potent political force. Neoconservative intellectual strength and reputability bolstered Reagan's political standing, while Reagan's successful runs for president allowed neocons to gain official positions of political power and to see their policy recommendations implemented.[13]

Thus, under the charismatic succor of Reagan's big tent, neoconservatism cross-pollinated with other forms of conservatism. These were halcyon days for conservatives of all stripes. New conservative organizations such as the Federalist Society, think tanks such as the Heritage Foundation, and journals such as *The National Interest* emerged and flourished in the 1980s, with neoconservatives often leading the way. Kristol, for instance, joined the American Enterprise Institute (AEI) and helped transform it into a neoconservative hotbed.[14]

Near the end of Reagan's second term, he deflected those who proclaimed that he had led a conservative revolution. Instead, he said, it had been a "Great Rediscovery: a rediscovery of our values and our common sense." But without Reagan, the conservative movement wavered, as evidenced by Bill Clinton's presidency. The differences among competing conservative outlooks seemed to intensify, with some commentators suggesting in the late 1990s that neoconservatism, in particular, had lost its vitality. Yet, most neocons, including a new generation—for instance, Kristol's son, William Kristol—never slowed in their ongoing efforts to develop the neoconservative outlook. And then neocons once again gained prominent positions of influence and power in President George W. Bush's administration. From the outset, Bush's campaign pledge to implement "compassionate conservatism" was rooted in the work of a neocon, Gertrude Himmelfarb, whose book *Poverty and Compassion* was published in 1991. Regardless, partly because of the cross-pollination among the varieties of conservatism that occurred during the 1980s, categorizing particular conservatives as one type or another could be difficult. But many individuals who could fairly be characterized as neoconservative held positions of significant power during the Reagan and Bush II administrations. Besides Reagan and Bush themselves, a partial list would include the following: Jeane Kirkpatrick, William Kristol, Eugene V. Rostow, William Bennett, Elliott Abrams, Paul Wolfowitz, Morris Abram, and Richard Perle. Some would add key Bush II officials like Dick Cheney, Condoleezza Rice, and Donald Rumsfeld to the list. Finally, of great significance, as will be discussed later, with Republicans occupying the White House for so many years since 1980, numerous Supreme Court as well as other federal judicial appointees were unequivocally conservative. If anything, though, categorizing Supreme Court justices as specific types of conservative, whether neoconservative or otherwise, is even more treacherous than categorizing other officials because jurists rarely flaunt their political opinions on specific issues (though their general political outlooks are usually clear).[15]

Neoconservative Principles and Policies

Some neoconservatives maintain that they never truly constituted a political movement. Rather, they shared (and continue to share) "a way of looking at the world" or a "persuasion," composed of certain overarching principles. A thorough description of neoconservatism should begin with the core principles and then move into more specific policies and theories.[16]

The Inherent Instability of Pluralist (Liberal) Democracy

Like Strauss, neoconservatives argued that debilitating inherent tensions riddle modernism and pluralist (liberal) democracy. Daniel Bell elaborated this theme in his 1976 book, *The Cultural Contradictions of Capitalism*. Bell divided society into three realms: the techno-economic (or social), the cultural, and the political. The three realms, he suggested, will contribute to a stable society if they either remain separate or operate in ways that reinforce one another. For instance, early in the development of capitalism, a culture of hard work, self-discipline, and self-denial—characterized by Max Weber as the Protestant ethic—bolstered the capitalist economy by encouraging individuals to devote themselves to employment in bureaucratically organized workplaces. By the second half of the twentieth century, however, the three realms overlapped and intersected in ways that were not mutually reinforcing; rather, they contradicted one another, causing societal instability. The main contradiction of modern life, according to Bell, was between the capitalist economy and the modernist culture, which imbued individuals with a hedonistic desire for self-gratification. "In the world of capitalist enterprise, the nominal ethos in the spheres of production and organization is still one of work, delayed gratification, career orientation, devotion to the enterprise. Yet, on the marketing side, the sale of goods, packaged in the glossy images of glamour and sex, promotes a hedonistic way of life whose promise is the voluptuous gratification of the lineaments of desire. The consequence of this contradiction . . . is that a corporation finds its people being straight [read: upright and disciplined] by day and swingers [read: pleasure seekers] by night."[17]

Bell also accentuated tensions between the economic and political realms. The operative principle of the capitalist economy was efficiency, maximizing one's benefits while minimizing costs, while the operative principle of the pluralist democratic polity in post–World War II America was equality, requiring that all individuals be "able to participate fully" as citizens. If the two realms had remained distinct, each could successfully fulfill its respective principle. But the two realms bled into each other, Bell argued, thus producing discordance: Capitalism, aiming for efficiency, relied on hierarchically structured bureaucratic organizations that collided with the political desire for participatory equality. Moreover, as the two realms intermingled, an increasing number of issues, previously settled in the capitalist marketplace, shifted into the political realm. Consequently, instead of being decided pursuant to "technocratic rationality" leading to economic efficiency, they were (and are) resolved through a political "bargaining" process that facilitates participation. Economic decisions, therefore, were (and are) made for the wrong reasons. This problem was greatly exacerbated, according to Bell, because the modernist culture of self-gratification induced individuals and societal groups to express an ever-increasing number of excessive demands within the political realm. Demands for equal participation gave way to demands for "rising entitlements," including "a basic minimum family income," a minimal "standard of living," and so on. These never-ending demands then generated group conflict and societal instability.[18]

Bell sent an unequivocial message: Problems emanated from all three realms, but America's most serious societal difficulties arose from the modernist culture. Bell reserved his most caustic denunciations, in particular, for the counterculture that had emerged in the 1960s. The counterculture, Bell wrote, "announced a strident opposition to bourgeois values and to the traditional codes of American life." But to Bell, the counterculture was a mere manifestation of modernism; despite its pretensions, the counterculture was neither "daring" nor "revolutionary." Bell's personal disgust was evident: "The counter-culture proved to be a conceit. It was an effort, largely a product of the youth movement, to transform a liberal life-style into a world of immediate gratification and exhibitionistic display. In the end, it produced little culture and countered nothing."[19]

The Attack on Relativism

A wide array of neoconservatives, consistent with Strauss, maintained that one source of liberal instability was value-relativism. In the words of Douglas Murray, relativism is "the predominant thought-disease" infecting American society. No neoconservative has explored and critiqued relativism as extensively as Allan Bloom in his book *The Closing of the American Mind*. Relativists, according to Bloom, claim that "[v]alues are not discovered by reason, and it is fruitless to seek them, to find the truth or the good life." Relativism, Bloom claimed, is necessary for tolerance of other individuals and openness to other cultural outlooks: "[I]t [is] the only plausible stance in the face of various claims to truth and various ways of life and kinds of human beings." Relativism thus becomes the springboard for the type of pluralist (liberal) democracy articulated by Robert Dahl.[20]

But Bloom was no less critical of relativism than Strauss had been. Relativists cannot prove relativism, Bloom emphasized. Instead, ironically, the American commitment to relativism is a product of our educational culture. We teach students, both before and after they enter college, that "truth is relative." In fact, Bloom added, students learn that relativism is equivalent to "a moral postulate, the condition of a free society." If we were to abandon relativism, students are taught, then we would sacrifice tolerant peacefulness and be doomed to war. For it is the "true believer," the relativist asserts, who "is the real danger"; the true believer will fight to crush all apostates. But from Bloom's perspective, these arguments are perverse. Similar to Strauss, Bloom reasoned that "the fact that there have been different opinions about good and bad in different times and places in no way proves that none is true or superior to others." But relativism forces us to doubt reason itself. We question whether we can differentiate right from wrong, good from evil. We become indiscriminate because we supposedly lack any ground for discriminating other than our prejudices. Ultimately, Bloom concluded, relativism will lead us to nihilism and then war: When we can no longer reason with others, then our disagreements can be settled only in battle.[21]

Relativism, neocons stressed, is not merely a troubling intellectual conundrum. From the neoconservative standpoint, ideas matter. Fukuyama talked of "the autonomous power of ideas." We go astray when we attribute societal developments solely to material forces. The "realm of consciousness and culture" affects even the spread of market capitalism. Thus, Murray went so far as to argue that the idea of relativism can cause Americans to lose wars, including the war on terrorism and the war in Iraq. "[Relativism] starts by encouraging the perception that America and her allies have no moral authority over terrorists, tyrants, and genocidal dictatorships. It continues by excusing, then supporting, the terrorists and tyrants. It finishes by saying why the terrorists and tyrants have the right to win over us, trying to persuade us that they will win over us because the West does not have the right to conquer or destroy evil. Relativism culminates by helping terrorists to win and evil to triumph."[22]

Relativism has other dangerous implications, according to the neocons. Again like Strauss, neoconservatives linked it with social science empiricism. According to the fact–value dichotomy, only facts can be objectively known, while values are necessarily subjective. Given the neoconservatives' animosity toward relativism, they unsurprisingly were also skeptical of social science. Whereas the pluralist democratic regime relies on social science experts to guide regulatory and administrative programs, neocons worried that expert-created and -led social programs often produce unanticipated and detrimental results. Bloom declared that "the fact–value distinction" is "the suicide of science," much less social science.[23]

What is the solution for relativism? In one way or another, all neocons have argued for "moral clarity." Virtues and universal values exist, and contrary to the fact–value dichotomy, we can objectively know them. Bloom, for instance, asserted that not only is there a human nature but that reasoning about human nature can lead us to appreciate the difference between good and evil, between right and wrong. Daniel Bell, meanwhile, sought to reinvigorate our commitment to religion and the sacred. Religion had been in the past and could be again in the future the source of "character," a concern for morality and discipline. As such, "religion can restore . . . the continuity of generations, returning us to the existential predicaments which are the ground of humility and care for others." Without religion, Bell lamented, "we are left with the shambles of appetite and self-interest and the destruction of the moral circle which engirds mankind. Can we—must we not—reestablish that which is sacred and that which is profane?" Yet, it should be noted, Bell did not emphasize religion because of his own unshakable faith. Rather, he believed that religion could be instrumentally useful: It could help correct for the excesses of modernist culture and inject a degree of stability into American society.[24]

Resuscitating Republican Democracy

The critique of pluralist (liberal) democracy, the repudiation of relativism, and the commitment to moral clarity all lead to an overarching neoconservative goal: the resuscitation of republican democracy. Once again, the neoconservative debt to Strauss is unmistakable. Bloom might have been drawing from his days studying at Strauss's feet when he wrote, "The United States is one of the highest and most extreme achievements of the rational quest for the good life according to nature. What makes its political structure possible is the use of the rational principles of natural right to found a people, thus uniting the good with one's own. Or, to put it otherwise, the regime established here promised untrammeled freedom to reason—not to everything indiscriminately, but [nonetheless] to reason." When Bloom referred to "the regime established here," he clearly was not referring to the post–World War II pluralist democratic regime built on relativism, historicism, and social science empiricism. He was looking back to the republican democratic regime, which he equated with Strauss's concept of the "best regime."[25]

In this vein, Irving Kristol repeatedly invoked republican democratic principles. In one essay, he encouraged Americans to recollect the nation's original "revolutionary message." The "founding fathers," Kristol explained, "understood that republican self-government could not exist if humanity did not possess—at some moments, and to a fair degree—the traditional 'republican virtues' of self-control, self-reliance, and a distinterested concern for the public good." But how can Americans cultivate civic republican virtue? We do so "through the shaping influence of religion, education, and [our] own daily experience." That is, we must teach or inculcate virtue and then allow people to practice "self-government."[26]

From the neoconservative standpoint, a democratic regime that fails to attend to the inculcation of virtue is one that will "degenerate into a libertinism." For this reason, Kristol argued for the governmental regulation of pornography. To be sure, under pluralist democracy, pornography is constitutionally protected free expression, but according to Kristol, this asserted First Amendment freedom only underscores the inherent weakness of pluralist democracy. Kristol denounced a "'managerial' conception of democracy" that reduces to no more than "a set of rules and procedures." As Kristol phrased it, "[t]he purpose of democracy cannot possibly be the endless functioning of its own political machinery."[27]

Thus, Kristol emphasized his preferred political regime, a republican democracy, the purpose of which "is to achieve some version of the good life and the good society." In such a regime, the focus is not on the proper democratic processes but "on the character of the people." Kristol elaborated, "This idea starts from the proposition that democracy is a form of self-government, and that if you want to be a meritorious polity, you have to care about what kind of people govern it." The government, from this standpoint, must attend to societal values, to the education of a virtuous people. Pornography contravenes this goal. If a government allows the unrestrained production and distribution of pornography and obscenity, if the government disregards "the quality of public life," then the people will lack virtue and the government itself will become "vicious, mean, squalid, and debased." Consequently, as Kristol concluded, in the republican democratic regime of the nineteenth and early twentieth centuries, the government persistently censored pornography and obscenity, "and it did so with a perfect clarity of mind and a perfectly clear conscience." Under republican democracy, the government could restrict any speech or writing, pornography included, that had bad tendencies or would otherwise contravene the common good. In sum, neocons were confident and aggressive: They believed they had identified the best form of American government; they believed they knew the values or virtues that would support such a government; and they believed they could design domestic and foreign policies that would cultivate the desired values and form of government.[28]

Neoconservative Domestic Policy

Confident of their own views, neoconservatives brought a renewed skepticism to *liberal* domestic policies by questioning whether programs engendered by good intentions nonetheless brought negative results. Irving Kristol criticized welfare programs on this ground: "A liberal and compassionate social policy has bred all sorts of unanticipated and perverse consequences." The so-called War on Poverty of the 1960s unexpectedly caused a "welfare explosion" because higher and more readily available governmental payments induced people to accept welfare rather than work at low-paying jobs. In 1971, Kristol brooded about how welfare programs had produced "the disorganization and demoralization" of African American families. "It used to be thought that a generous welfare program, liberally administered, would help poor families stick together," Kristol wrote. "We now find that as many poor black families are breaking up *after* they get on welfare as before they got on; and that, in general, the prospect of welfare does nothing to hold a poor family together." Years later, in 1993, Kristol worried more about the growth of a "self-perpetuating 'underclass.'" Despite lofty intentions, the welfare "system breeds social pathologies—crime, juvenile delinquency, illegitimacy, drug addiction, and alcoholism, along with the destruction of a once functioning public school system."[29]

Nathan Glazer argued similarly against affirmative action programs. He insisted that the government, in the fields of employment, education, and housing, should guarantee equal opportunity and remedy personal discrimination but should not enforce set statistical distributions based on group memberships. In short, Glazer argued against any affirmative action programs that smacked of quotas. The problem with such programs, Glazer reasoned, is that they produce unanticipated and detrimental societal consequences. First, affirmative action proponents maintain that such programs are necessary to improve the employment, educational, and housing conditions of impoverished inner-city blacks. Yet in reality, such programs rarely benefit such individuals. Instead, professional and middle-class blacks reap the advantages. In other words, those who do not need assistance are helped, while those desperate for assistance gain nothing. Second, according to Glazer, affirmative action programs encourage a culture of victimhood. Individuals begin to accentuate their "group affiliation" because membership in a victimized group justifies governmental assistance. "New lines of conflict are created, by government action," wrote Glazer. "New resentments are created; new turfs are to be protected; new angers arise; and one sees them on both sides of the line that divides protected and affected from nonprotected and nonaffected." Although Glazer did not phrase his argument in such terms, he implicitly suggested that affirmative action programs contribute to interest group sclerosis. Finally, Glazer argued that affirmative action engenders white resentment and backlash, especially among white ethnics. Many whites believed that they had earned their jobs, education, and housing without governmental assistance, and they did not understand why racial minorities, particularly African Americans, should be treated any differently. In a word, whites thought affirmative action programs to be inequitable. Glazer admitted that such white perceptions were based on a "crude and unfair comparison" because, unlike white immigrants, blacks had been forced to come to America as slaves and then purposefully and legally subjugated for centuries. Even so, from Glazer's perspective, the white resentment and backlash was both real and understandable and therefore needed to be accounted for when assessing the costs and benefits of affirmative action. Ultimately, as other neocons would declare, governmental actions and policies must be colorblind.[30]

While neocons were skeptical about whether various domestic programs could achieve their professed liberal goals, they confidently asserted an alternative and overarching goal: to imbue such programs with a newfound degree of moral clarity. Domestic programs should cultivate the virtues necessary for a republican democratic regime dedicated to the common good. This emphasis on morality and virtue became paramount in debates about education. Liberal educators stressed that Americans voice a plurality of competing and equally worthy values. From their standpoint, then, schools should avoid choosing to favor and cultivate specific values and instead should teach the skills needed to function in a pluralist democratic society—skills such as communicating with people of diverse backgrounds. But former Secretary of Education William J. Bennett disagreed. A neocon, he repudiated "moral relativism" as a basis for education. "We must care about our public schools; and we must care about the values taught in them." Children must be educated to be good citizens, and citizens are judged by their "character, their virtue, and their interest in the common good."[31]

To promote virtue and to avoid unintended negative consequences, neocons insisted that we need to "get the incentives right," regardless of whether we are discussing welfare, affirmative action, or any other domestic policy. Thus, when it came to the policing of urban neighborhoods, neoconservatives articulated a "broken windows" approach: The police should work to maintain social order and uphold community values and not merely fight crime. "The essence of the police role . . . is to reinforce the informal control mechanisms of the community itself." If one broken window is left unfixed, neocons argued, then community values and controls will begin to weaken and, before long, all of the windows in the neighborhood will be shattered. Even when it came to economic policy, neoconservatives claimed to support supply-side economics (Reaganomics)—"cutting tax rates in order to stimulate steady economic growth"—more because of values than because of economic efficiency. Kristol stressed that an unfettered free market capitalism promotes the overarching values of democracy and liberty, while Himmelfarb argued that capitalism both reinforces and relies upon Victorian virtues (or values): "[hard] work, thrift, prudence, temperance, [and] above all self-reliance and personal responsibility." Partly for this reason (and sometimes in tension with libertarian conservatives), Kristol and other neocons generally tended to temper their laissez-faire leanings by suggesting that desires for economic profits should not obliterate moral sentiments.[32]

This neoconservative emphasis on moral clarity was most prominent in the debates about welfare. Neocons argued that, despite our best intentions, welfare programs generated moral decay. Himmelfarb, in particular, emphasized that the social science experts who constructed and administered the welfare system had failed to account sufficiently for the moral dimension. "After making the most arduous attempt to objectify the problem of poverty, to divorce poverty from any moral assumptions and conditions, we are learning how inseparable the moral and material dimensions of that problem are. And after trying to devise social policies that are scrupulously neutral and 'value-free,' we are finding these policies fraught with moral implications that have grave material and social consequences." Neocons were willing to "accept the welfare state," but they sought to "return it to its Victorian roots by concentrating resources on the deserving poor." Spurred by Himmelfarb's historical writings on Victorian values, Kristol explained how a redesigned welfare system could be "consistent with the basic moral principles of our civilization and the basic political principles of our nation." Under Kristol's proposed plan, "able-bodied men and mentally healthy men would have no entitlement whatever to welfare. If they are alcoholics or drug addicts or just allergic to responsibilities, they can rely on private charities." Meanwhile, women who married and had children but were then "divorced or widowed or abandoned by their husbands" still frequently followed "family values," according to Kristol, and therefore should be eligible for welfare. Young unmarried women, though, should be discouraged from having children. Such women who nonetheless "permit themselves to get pregnant" because they view going on welfare to be an attractive alternative to their current circumstances should receive diminished payments. For instance, they "should receive no housing allowance," Kristol elaborated. "Having your own apartment, in which you can raise your child, can be seen as 'fun.' Living with your child in your parents' home is a lot less alluring."[33]

Neoconservative Foreign Policy

While theorists categorize approaches to foreign policy (or international relations) in a variety of ways, neoconservatism can be usefully contrasted with three alternatives. First, realists, such as Henry Kissinger, emphasize the pursuit of national interests and maintain that power determines the international order. For that reason, realists care more about the actions than the avowed principles of other nations. Second, liberal internationalists bring a degree of idealism to foreign affairs; they "hope to transcend power politics altogether and move to an international order based on law and institutions." Finally, isolationists advocate for minimal involvement with other nations. Basically, an American isolationist believes the United States should seek its internal perfection while leaving other nations to deal with their own problems.[34]

Just as the bedrock of moral clarity generated confident and aggressive neoconservative domestic policies, so, too, with foreign policy. Neocons believed that democracy unequivocally was (and is) the best form of government. Thus, not only should Americans be proud of their country, they also should clearly "distinguish friends from enemies." Communist and other authoritarian governments were the enemy. Moreover, this moral clarity should engender a healthy skepticism toward international institutions, such as the UN, that might deviate from true moral principles. The nation, therefore, must be willing to take unilateral action if necessary to fulfill its moral mission. Neocons could fairly be said to entertain a "moralistic, Wilsonian . . . dream of exporting democracy."[35]

The neoconservative commitment to moral clarity and the concomitant antipathy to relativism moved into the spotlight on November 10, 1975. Speaking before the UN General Assembly, Ugandan President Idi Amin advocated for the "extinction" of Israel and the passage of Resolution 3379: "The General Assembly . . . determines that Zionism is a form of racism." Over the protests of the United States and other nations, the General Assembly adopted the resolution by more than a two-to-one vote. Daniel Patrick Moynihan, the U.S. ambassador to the UN at the time, delivered a speech that condemned Resolution 3379 on neoconservative principles. More than anything, Moynihan emphasized a difference between right and wrong, between truth and lies. The resolution equating Zionism with racism was categorically wrong: It was an "obscenity" and an "infamous act." The resolution was a "political lie" that itself amounted to antisemitism. And because ideas and words matter in the world, this "terrible lie . . . will have terrible consequences." The resolution, Moynihan said, will undermine the UN itself because the institution no longer will appear to uphold the truth, and it will harm the cause of human rights "because it will strip from racism the precise and abhorrent meaning that it still precariously holds today." Neocon Jeane

Kirkpatrick, ambassador to the UN from 1981 to 1985, expressed similar disgust: She questioned whether the United States could rely on an international institution that accorded "moral parity" to democracies and dictatorships alike.[36]

This steadfast moral clarity defined the neoconservative foreign policy agenda during the Cold War. It animated Reagan's speech condemning the Soviet Union as an "evil empire," delivered on March 8, 1983, at an annual convention of the National Association of Evangelicals: "I urge you to beware the temptation of pride—the temptation of blithely declaring yourselves above it all and [labeling] both sides equally at fault, to ignore the facts of history and the aggressive impulses of an evil empire, to simply call the arms race a giant misunderstanding and thereby remove yourself from the struggle between right and wrong and good and evil." From the neoconservative perspective, the United States was and is exceptional: Our national commitment to liberty and democracy was right and good as a matter of absolute and universal moral principles. The United States, therefore, must not retreat to the realist position accommodating those evil regimes that appeared to behave acceptably vis-à-vis the United States. The fundamental values and ideas predicating any national regime were of the utmost importance. Indeed, as a moral exemplar for the world, the United States was obligated to use its military power to confront evil, particularly the evil of Soviet communism. The moral impoverishment of international institutions like the UN should not sway the United States from fulfilling this mission.[37]

Following this neoconservative agenda in the early 1980s, Reagan pushed for a massive arms buildup to increase the American threat to the Soviet military and economy. When the Soviet Union collapsed and the Cold War ended in the late 1980s and early 1990s, neoconservatives declared not only an American victory but also the vindication of their views. Fukuyama published in 1989 an essay (later expanded into a book) that declared the "end of history." "What we may be witnessing is not just the end of the Cold War, or the passing of a particular period of postwar history," Fukuyama explained, "but the end of history as such: that is, the end point of mankind's ideological evolution and the universalization of Western liberal democracy as the final form of human government." Fukuyama did not, of course, mean that no historically meaningful events would ever again happen. Rather, he meant that, in a loosely Hegelian sense, the dialectical evolution of political ideologies had ended. According to the philosopher G. W. F. Hegel, ideas develop dialectally: One idea (the thesis) produces a conflicting idea (the antithesis), and then the two conflicting ideas generate a new idea (the synthesis). Plus, from the Hegelian perspective, such ideas manifest themselves in the historical (material) conditions of the world; political ideas or ideologies engender political communities. Fukuyama argued that, during the twentieth century, democracy had been locked in a dialectical battle with communism and fascism, and that, now, democracy had won. American (Western) democracy was the climax, the culminating synthesis of political ideologies.[38]

Indeed, with this declaration of victory, neoconservatives were momentarily nonplussed: Where do we go from here, they wondered? The battle against communism had always defined neoconservative foreign policy. Now that the battle was won, now that Soviet communism had been defeated, what could be the point or purpose of a neoconservative outlook? Before long, neoconservatives had found an answer. They had never advocated merely for the destruction of communism, they reasoned; rather, they had always aimed for the victory of democracy. To be sure, Soviet communism had been the primary foe of democracy, but even with its eradication, much work remained if democracy was to assume its rightful place as the ruling ideology for the entire world. In a 1996 article, *Toward a Neo-Reaganite Foreign Policy*, William Kristol and Robert Kagan called for a reassertion of American exceptionalism through a policy of "[b]enevolent global hegemony": "The first objective of U.S. foreign policy should be to preserve and enhance [the nation's strategic and ideological] predominance by strengthening America's security, supporting its friends, advancing its interests, and standing up for its principles around the world." To achieve that objective, Kristol and Kagan recommended taking three steps. First, expand the defense budget. Second, remind citizens of their responsibilities for the defense of the nation and emphasize the connections between the civilian population and the military. Finally, and perhaps most important, reemphasize the need for "moral clarity." Given that America's "moral goals and its fundamental national interests are almost always in harmony," the nation should actively promote "American principles of governance abroad—democracy, free markets, respect for liberty." Such an approach would not only require the United States to support "friendly regimes that are trying to carry out democratic and free market reforms" but would also sometimes require "actively pursuing policies . . . ultimately intended to bring about a change of regime."[39]

These policy steps became hallmarks of neoconservative foreign policy during the next few years. A new generation of neocons, led by William Kristol, founded a think tank, the Project for the New American Century (PNAC), which declared its intent "to make the case and rally support for American global leadership." Its founding *Statement of Principles* reiterated the call for "moral clarity" and the need "to challenge regimes hostile to our interests and values." Such an approach, emphasizing regime change, required an "American leadership" that would be willing to launch preemptive strikes: "The history of the 20th century should have taught us that it is important to shape circumstances before crises emerge, and to meet threats before they become dire." The neocons, in fact, unequivocally advocated for regime change in Iraq well before the terrorist attacks of September 11, 2001. In fall 2000, for instance, Kristol and Kagan wrote, "[I]n the post–Cold War era a principal aim of American foreign policy should be to bring about a change of regime in hostile nations—in Baghdad and Belgrade, in Pyongyang and Beijing, and wherever tyrannical governments acquire the military power to threaten their neighbors, our allies, and the United States itself."[40]

After 9/11, these neoconservative views served as the foundation for the Bush Doctrine, encapsulating the foreign policy agenda of Bush II's administration. Bush articulated the main elements of his foreign policy in a June 1, 2002, graduation speech at West Point. He stressed moral clarity: "Some worry that it is somehow undiplomatic or impolite to speak the language of right and wrong. I disagree. Different circumstances require different methods, but not different moralities. Moral truth is the same in every culture, in every time, and in every place." This "moral clarity was essential to our victory in the Cold War," and Bush underscored the American victory by echoing Fukuyama's end-of-history thesis: "The 20th century ended with a single surviving model of human progress, based on non-negotiable demands of human dignity, the rule of law, limits on the power of the state, respect for women and private property and free speech and equal justice and religious tolerance." Yet, the need for "firm moral purpose" was no less today, Bush declared, in fighting the war on terror. And such firm convictions sometimes require "preemptive action": "We must take the battle to the enemy, disrupt his plans, and confront the worst threats before they emerge." And as the Iraq War would underscore, the Bush Doctrine anticipated that preemptive actions sometimes would focus on regime change and would proceed regardless of the UN's positions.[41]

In fact, the Bush administration's blind pursuit of regime change in Iraq generated divisions among neoconservatives themselves. Some neocons, most prominently Fukuyama, argued that Bush had forgotten an elementary lesson of neoconservatism: that we should be skeptical of expert-led social engineering. While such skepticism typically animated neoconservative domestic policy—or at least neoconservative criticisms of *liberal* domestic programs—these neocons now brought it to bear in foreign policy. The Bush administration's failure to retain a healthy skepticism led it to forget that, from the Straussian and neoconservative standpoint, a regime was never a mere framework of rules and procedures. Rather, a regime was constituted in part by the underlying culture: A political community would strive to become the best regime possible only if the people and their leaders were sufficiently virtuous. A vibrant democracy would not necessarily fill the void left by a toppled dicatorship, and the United States could not impose a democracy on another country merely by handing it a new (democratically structured) constitution.[42]

Neoconservative Constitutional Theory

An important manifestation of neoconservative thought arose in the realm of constitutional theory. As was true of much of neoconservativism, the ideas slowly emerged, eventually spread, then became intertwined with other strands of conservative thought. Judicial review in the republican democratic regime had revolved around the principles of virtue and the common good. Courts, including the Supreme Court, sought to uphold governmental actions that supposedly promoted virtue and the common good while invalidating governmental actions that failed to do so. As it was frequently explained, courts were to invalidate "class legislation"—legislation that furthered partial or private (or factional) interests rather than the public good. In exercising the power of judicial review, the justices usually applied an a priori formalism that assumed the existence of readily discernible objective categories (or dichotomies), whether the common good versus partial or private interests, or otherwise. For example, in *Lochner v. New York*, decided in 1905, the Court invalidated a state law that restricted the number of hours employees could work in bakeries (ten per day and sixty per week). The state argued that the law furthered the common good, justifying any interference with employer or employee liberty to enter into contracts. In fact, the state presented substantial evidence showing that the law was an effective health measure: Long hours of toil in a bakery were dangerous because of flour dust. Nonetheless, the Court reasoned that "[t]o the common understanding the trade of a baker has never been regarded as an unhealthy one." In other words, the justices formalistically discerned the border between the common good and partial and private interests, despite the evidence. The Court therefore concluded that the statute constituted impermissible class legislation favoring employees over employers. "It seems to us that the real object and purpose were simply to regulate the hours of labor between the master and his employees (all being men, *sui juris*), in a private business, not dangerous in any degree to morals, or in any real and substantial degree to the health of the employees."[43]

Once pluralist democracy had supplanted the republican democratic regime during the 1930s, the Supreme Court came under increasing pressure to accept the parameters of the new democracy. The persistent resistance of the Court's conservative justices was the impetus for FDR's proposed Court-packing plan, a blatant political effort to pressure the justices to accept New Deal legislation. Regardless of whether the justices were responding to this political pressure, they turned in 1937, accepting the practices of pluralist democracy. Given this transition, the Court's exercise of its power of judicial review became a conundrum. After all, the structure of judicial review could no longer logically follow from the republican democratic opposition between the common good and partial or private interests. Under pluralist democracy, the Court could not condemn a statute as class legislation because all legislation was a product of competing interests, pressed by opposed groups. So, what was the Court to do?[44]

Over the next few years, the justices hashed out several approaches to pluralist democratic judicial review. When it came to economic and social welfare legislation—typified by New Deal statutes often invalidated earlier in the 1930s under republican democratic judicial review—the Court consistently deferred to the democratic process. As the Court explained in a 1942 case adjudicating the scope of congressional power, the "effective restraints" on legislative power arose "from political rather than from judicial processes." The Court also eschewed the a priori formalism that it had applied during the republican democratic regime and instead began, in many cases, to balance competing interests, as if the justices themselves were legislators reweighing the claims of various interest groups. In some cases, the Court examined whether the proper democratic processes had been followed, while in others the Court held that certain rights and liberties, so-called preferred freedoms such as free expression and religious freedom, were beyond the reach of pluralist democratic majorities, even if the proper processes had been followed.[45]

After World War II, constitutional theorists became increasingly focused on the puzzle of pluralist democratic judicial review. During this time, legal scholars so closely followed the pluralist democratic focus on process that the predominant postwar jurisprudential approach became known as "legal process." Some constitutional theorists, like John Hart Ely, argued that the Court should do no more than "police" the pluralist democratic process to ensure that all citizens could fairly and equally participate. From this perspective, constitutional adjudication could be pure process-based and therefore value-free; any judicial reliance on substantive values or principles, whether the common good or otherwise, would contravene the tenets of ethical relativism. According to Ely, the Court could invalidate a legislative action if the process had been defective—for instance, if a relevant societal group (a discrete and insular minority) had not been allowed to vote for the legislators—but the Court was otherwise to defer to the legislature, even if the justices disagreed with the substance or content of the legislative action. Other legal process theorists admitted that the justices might occasionally refer to values or principles, but only in the narrowest fashion. For example, Alexander Bickel asked what role the Supreme Court could play in a constitutional system where values were relative and legislative decisions arose from unprincipled battles among self-interested political actors. He theorized that the Court could articulate and enforce enduring American principles, so long as such principles were neutral, thus supposedly remaining consistent with relativism.[46]

Meanwhile, the transition from republican to pluralist democracy profoundly affected the constitutional doctrine of free expression. Under republican democracy, free expression had been important, but no more so than other constitutional rights: Free expression had always remained subordinate to the overarching republican democratic concerns with virtue and the common good. In particular, courts delineated the scope of free expression pursuant to a bad tendency test. The government could not impose prior restraints on expression, but it could impose criminal penalties for speech or writing that had bad tendencies or likely harmful consequences. Thus, the government could (and did) punish any expression that might be deemed antithetical to a virtuous citizenry or the common good. For example, in an 1879 federal prosecution for mailing obscene materials, the trial court held that the government could restrict expression having "a tendency to suggest impure and libidinous thoughts in the minds of those open to the influence of such thoughts, and thus deprave and corrupt their morals, if they should read such matter."[47]

Nevertheless, once the Supreme Court accepted pluralist democracy, starting in 1937, the doctrinal approach to free expression changed dramatically. The crux of pluralist democracy was free and open citizen participation; if citizens could not express their interests and values, then such participation was impossible. Free expression appeared to be a precondition for the pluralist democratic process itself. Thus, while the Court had not even arguably upheld any free-expression claims until 1931, the Court consistently upheld such claims after 1937. In the pluralist democratic regime, the Court, in effect, created a presumption favoring free expression: Any governmental action burdening speech or writing was presumed invalid. During the post–World War II years, most scholars and jurists agreed that free expression had become a constitutional "lodestar." Justices Hugo Black and William O. Douglas became renowned as First Amendment absolutists. "[T]he First Amendment does not speak equivocally," wrote Black. "It prohibits any law 'abridging the freedom of speech, or of the press.' It must be taken as a command of the broadest scope that explicit language, read in the context of a liberty-loving society, will allow."[48]

In this context, Walter Berns's writings provide a helpful introduction to neoconservative constitutional theory. A political scientist who studied under Strauss, as well as Bloom's faculty colleague at Cornell during the student uprisings, Berns wrote extensively about the First Amendment and democracy. In 1957, when Berns published his first book, *Freedom, Virtue, and the First Amendment*, he introduced several Straussian themes into constitutional theory that he continued to elaborate in future publications. Berns emphasized that, at the time, the predominant free-expression doctrine was the "clear and present danger" test: "The question in every case is whether the words used are used in such circumstances and are of such a nature as to create a clear and present danger that they will bring about the substantive evils that Congress has a right to prevent." According to Berns, the justices interpreted the "clear and present danger" test in the pluralist democratic regime to preclude courts, for the most part, from considering the content of speech and writing for purposes of First Amendment analysis. Except for cases involving national security, "speech of almost any character, true or false, good or bad, enjoys a favored status before the Court." This approach supposedly followed from the modernist liberal (and social science) commitment to the fact–value dichotomy, which asserted that "all judgments of better and worse are arbitrary."[49]

Berns denounced as dangerously misguided this judicial attempt to eschew value judgments regarding the content of expression. The "problem of free speech," Berns explained, was really "the problem of virtue." In resolving free-expression cases, the Court should attempt to "promote the virtue of citizens" and to pursue the "general welfare," or, in other words, the common good. Hence, Berns recommended the following: "Congress shall make no law abridging the freedom of *good* speech. The basic point is that the purpose of law is and must be to promote virtue, not to guarantee rights of *any* description." And, of course, this approach was the correlative equivalent, from a doctrinal standpoint, of the bad tendency test. The Court should allow the government to punish harmful or bad expression but should proscribe the government from punishing virtuous or good expression. In other words, Berns advocated for a return to a republican democratic approach to free expression. The Court must distinguish between "good and evil," then must allow the government to censor the licentious while shaping or educating citizens to be of "good character." Otherwise, the United States would be unable to protect "against dangers to civility" and would no longer be a "decent society." Berns quoted Justice Robert Jackson in emphasizing that the Bill of Rights should not be interpreted to become a societal "'suicide pact.'" Thus, Berns unequivocally concluded that the government should be permitted to prevent not only the spread of Nazi and communist ideologies but also the preachings of Jehovah's Witnesses who denounced the Catholic Church. The republican democratic focus on virtue and the common good was, to Berns, far more important than the pluralist democratic focus on the proper process: "The right [moral] education is ultimately much more decisive for good government, for free government, than any of the mechanical arrangements, such as the separation of powers, in which we Americans have traditionally placed our trust."[50]

Just under twenty years later, Berns would explicitly castigate the leading postwar proponent of pluralist democracy, Robert Dahl. Dahl might recognize the importance of the American cultural commitment to democracy, but according to Berns, he failed to understand that political and legal institutions engendered and reinforced the democratic culture. Moreover, Berns argued that the Court's First Amendment decisions, on both free expression and religious freedom, reflected the same failure. To elaborate his interrelated critiques of Dahl and the Court, Berns explained the connections among societal institutions, cultural values, and law. "Whether [the Court's decisions] will conduce to a decent self-governing country of the sort the Founders hoped for depends . . . on the character of the people constituting the many; and that character depends on the condition of religion, the family, the schools, and on the strength of the people's attachment to republican principles. The Court in its First Amendment decisions has proceeded in blissful ignorance of this, promoting pornography in the name of freedom of expression; casting aside, as so many irrational encumbrances, the conventions of decency that used to govern public discourse; refusing to permit financial support to religious education; and subtly undermining the venerable character of the Constitution itself." In sum, Berns insisted that not all ideas are equivalent and that not all values are relative. Despite the pretentions of pluralist democratic theorists, a civilized society cannot function if human relationships are based on nothing more than "calculating self-interest." As citizens, we must proclaim our standards—we must distinguish good from evil—and we must then cultivate a good and virtuous society. And the justices need to do the same. At a bare minimum, Berns sighed, the Court must interpret the First Amendment to allow the public to label "vice as vice."[51]

Alexander Bickel reacted more circumspectly to the problems of pluralist democracy. Like many neocons, Bickel began his career supporting pluralist democracy and liberalism, then gravitated rightward, articulating neoconservative positions. But even the more mature Bickel never repudiated pluralist democracy and never became a full-fledged neocon, though his conservative drift might have continued if he had not died prematurely in 1974. While still affirming pluralist democracy, the later Bickel worried about the implications of its underlying ethical relativism. By necessity, democracy in America might need to accept a plurality of values, but democracy and civil society could not survive without "a foundation of moral values." "A valueless politics and valueless institutions are shameful and shameless and, what is more, man's nature is such that he finds them, and life with and under them, insupportable." Bickel, here, went beyond the typical pluralist democratic declaration that America sustained a democratic culture. He referred to a "vision of good and evil." But where do Americans find this vision? Where do they discover their moral values? We must "find our visions of good and evil," Bickel asserted, "in the experience of the past, in our tradition, in the secular religion of the American republic." Thus, like Allan Bloom, Bickel denounced the empty rationalism, supposedly bereft of values, of the multiculturalist university professors who, when "being confronted with various demands for instant change, found that they believed nothing and could not judge any change as better or worse than another."[52]

More important for purposes of constitutional theory, Bickel argued that his neoconservative-tinged notion of pluralist democracy engendered certain implications for judicial review. He had earlier argued that the Court should decide cases based on neutral principles, but he now questioned the feasibility of such an approach. After all, how could a principle (or value) have any substantive content yet be neutral? Furthermore, in an argument that resonated with mainstream neoconservative criticisms of domestic programs, Bickel insisted that the Court should not attempt to craft cases that would chart the course of societal "progress." According to Bickel, numerous Warren Court decisions, including *Brown v. Board of Education*, were failing to achieve their social engineering goals. Instead, the decisions were "heading toward obsolescence, and in large measure abandonment." Societal change was necessarily slow—tradition evolved gradually—and small adjustments to social values and policies were to be made through "the political process" rather than through the courts. Ultimately, then, Bickel called for judicial restraint: In most circumstances, the Court should defer to "the political institutions" and allow them to engage in "policy-making." When the Burger Court decided *Roe v. Wade*, holding that a constitutional right of privacy protected a woman's interest in choosing whether to have an abortion, Bickel unsurprisingly agreed with the dissenting view: The decision was illegitimate because it was "legislative rather than judicial action." In rare circumstances, the Court could proceed "cautiously and with some skepticism" to articulate principles, but even then, the justices should be wary, communicating the principles "more as cautions than as rules."[53]

Bickel, it should be added, moved rightward during an era when constitutional theory itself appeared to become politicized. Before the 1960s, constitutional theorists often claimed political neutrality. Herbert Wechsler, for example, claimed to agree with the political aim of *Brown*, holding *de jure* segregrated public schools to be unconstitutional, but Wechsler nonetheless argued that legal reasoning could not adequately justify the result. He would not allow his political desires to influence his legal theory, or at least so he declared. Yet, when the ostensible societal consensus of the 1950s crumbled into the jagged shards of the 1960s, the political fragmentation seemed to trigger a boom not only in the volume but also in the political openness of constitutional theory. Everybody knew that Frank Michelman and Ronald Dworkin were liberals while Robert Bork and Lino Graglia were conservatives.[54]

Indeed, Bork, in his early writings, closely followed the later Bickel, his friend and colleague on the Yale Law School faculty. The early Bork accepted Bickel's acquiescence in pluralist democracy and ethical relativism and even cited approvingly to Dahl. Given this acceptance, Bork insisted that the Court's exercise of judicial power, which needed to reconcile majority rule with minority rights, could be legitimate only if the justices applied neutral principles. But the concept of neutrality must be pushed to its logical extreme. "[I]f a neutral judge must demonstrate why principle X applies to cases A and B but not to case C," Bork wrote, "he must, by the same token, also explain why the principle is defined as X rather than as X minus, which would cover A but not cases B and C, or as X plus, which would cover all cases, A, B and C." The crux of the matter, according to Bork, was that the Court could never satisfy this demand for neutrality without violating the tenets of relativism. "There is no principled way to decide that one man's gratifications are more deserving of respect than another's or that one form of gratification is more worthy than another. Why is sexual gratification more worthy than moral gratification? Why is sexual gratification nobler than economic gratification? There is no way of deciding these matters other than by reference to some system of moral or ethical values that has no objective or intrinsic validity of its own and about which men can and do differ. Where the Constitution does not embody the moral or ethical choice, the judge has no basis other than his own values upon which to set aside the community judgment embodied in the statute. That, by definition, is an inadequate basis for judicial supremacy."[55] For that reason, Bork insisted that the Court should defer to the value choices derived through the pluralist democratic process. The early Bork became one of the most vigorous advocates for judicial restraint: The Court should never *choose* "fundamental values." Such choices should be left to the legislatures. The Court could legitimately invalidate a legislative choice or action only if it conflicted with a constitutionally protected value or right, of which there were only two types. First, the Court should enforce any "specific values" or "specified rights" that "text or history [shows] the framers actually to have intended [to protect] and which are capable of being translated into principled rules." Second, the Court should enforce "secondary or derived individual rights" that were necessary to preserve the constitutionally established "governmental process." If the justices were to follow this originalist approach, enforcing only these two types of rights, they would never personally choose what to enforce. Rather, Bork emphasized, they would necessarily "stick close to the text and the history, and their fair implications."[56]

Thus, Bork argued that the Court had unjustifiably expanded the First Amendment protection of free expression. Categorizing free expression within the second type of rights—as a prerequisitie for democratic government—Bork insisted that only "explicitly political" speech and writing should be constitutionally protected. Other expression is not integral to the governmental process. Thus, "[t]here is no basis for judicial intervention to protect . . . scientific, literary or that variety of expression we call obscene or pornographic." Speech or writing should not be constitutionally protected merely because it contributed to one's self-fulfillment. Thus, quoting from Walter Berns, Bork underscored that the community should be permitted to restrict pornography, even if some individuals wanted to possess it. Pornography should be "seen as a problem of pollution of the moral and aesthetic atmosphere precisely analogous to smoke pollution," Bork explained. "A majority of the community may foresee that continued availability of pornography to those who want it will inevitably affect the quality of life for those who do not want it, altering, for example, attitudes toward love and sex, the tone of private and public discourse and views of social institutions such as marriage and the family." Finally, Bork added that even expression that might otherwise be designated as political should be unprotected if it is potentially harmful to the community because it "advocates forcible overthrow of the government or the violation of any law."[57]

* * *

While the early Bork already leaned toward neoconservatism—given his criticisms of liberal Supreme Court jurisprudence and his emphasis on allowing legislatures to enforce moral values—the later Bork fit more comfortably into the neocon camp. He joined the American Enterprise Institute, began citing frequently to Himmelfarb and Irving Kristol, and published in neoconservative journals. The largest change between the early and later Bork lay in his atttitude toward ethical relativism. The early Bork acquiesced in the widespread acceptance of relativism and built his theory of judicial review upon it. The later Bork displayed unmitigated hostility toward relativism.[58]

The later Bork continued to argue that the Court, in exercising its power of judicial review, must reconcile majority rule with the protection of minority rights. To do so, the judiciary must articulate and rely on a constitutional theory that produces politically neutral results. The only such theory, according to Bork, is originalism. As now modified by Bork, originalism demands that the justices uphold the original public meaning of the Constitution rather than the subjective intentions of the constitutional framers. "All that counts is how the words used in the Constitution would have been understood at the time." Ever since 1937, however, when the Court switched from a republican to a pluralist democratic approach, the justices have consistently refused to be bound by originalism. Instead, Bork maintained, the justices have imposed a modern liberal cultural agenda that simultaneously encompasses both "radical egalitarianism (the equality of outcomes rather than of opportunities) and radical individualism (the drastic reduction of limits to personal gratification)." In typical neoconservative fashion, Bork rued the 1960s counterculture for promoting these hallmarks of liberal culture, which together engender moral relativism. Because egalitarianism "is hostile to hierarchies and distinctions," it produces a relativist acceptance of diverse ideas and moral values. Likewise, because individualism entails "the privatization of morality," it engenders relativism: "One person's morality being as good as another's, the community may not adopt moral standards in legislation." According to Bork, these aspects of modern liberalism have caused America's "cultural degeneration"—indeed, Bork depicted a cultural disaster. "Sometimes the impulses of radical individualism and radical egalitarianism cooperate. Both, for example, are antagonistic to society's traditional morality—the individualist because his pleasures can be maximized only by freedom from authority, the egalitarian because he resents any distinction among people or forms of behavior that suggests superiority in one or the other. When egalitarianism reinforces individualism, denying the possibility that one culture or moral view can be superior to another, the result is cultural or moral chaos, both prominent and destructive features of our time."[59]

To be clear, the later Bork insisted that various societal institutions, including legislatures, churches, and schools, could uphold the moral values that prevent "rootless hedonism." And in fact, these societal institutions sometimes attempted to do just that. The problem was that the Court used its power of judicial review to invalidate these attempts: The Court imposed relativism on the rest of society. To Bork, almost all of the justices (even most Republican-appointed justices) were members of a liberal cultural elite, and as such, they enforced the relativist tenets of liberalism, encompassing radical egalitarianism and individualism. "[T]he judge who looks outside the historic Constitution always looks inside himself and nowhere else. And when he looks inside himself he sees an intellectual, with, as often as not, some measure of intellectual class attitudes." Again, Bork turned to free expression to illustrate the Court's errors, this time the judicial enforcement of relativism. Rather than defer to legislative attempts to cultivate communal values, the Court protected only "self-expression, personal autonomy, or individual gratification." In *Cohen v. California*, the Court invalidated the conviction of a defendant for disturbing the peace; the defendant had worn in a courthouse a jacket inscribed with the message "Fuck the Draft." Bork expressed his disgust: "The majority opinion by Justice [Lewis] Powell asked 'How is one to distinguish this from any other offensive word?' and answered that no distinction could be made since 'one man's vulgarity is another's lyric.'" Well, not to Bork, who recognized vulgarity for what it is—and it's not lyric. Rather than interpret the First Amendment to impose an individualist relativism, the Court should have allowed the community to protect itself from offensive language.[60]

Bork argued that the Court should comprehend that "in a republican form of government where the people rule, it is crucial that the character of the citizenry not be debased." In elaborating this position, he explicitly invoked a broken-windows type of neoconservative argument. If one broken window is left unfixed, then community values and controls will begin to weaken, and, before long, all of the windows in the neighborhood will be shattered. An unfixed broken window conveys "the message," in Bork's words, "that nobody cares much." Before long, "[a]uthority is marginalized." Consequently, "*Cohen* was just the beginning"; the Court soon held that the First Amendment protected offensive speech uttered in other situations: during a school board meeting, in a university chapel, and in a confrontation with police officers. And *Cohen* itself, Bork suggested, arose because of earlier broken (moral) windows that manifested an acceptance of relativism and degradation. "The relativism of these [Supreme Court] decisions seems to reflect a loss of will to maintain conventional standards. The Court refused to allow punishment for the same obscene and assaultive speech that was tolerated by supine university faculties and administrators in the late 1960s and early 1970s. When the faculties collapsed, the universities were corrupted; when the Supreme Court gave way, the national culture was defiled. Now, of course, such language is routine on television and in motion pictures."[61]

Despite his neoconservative arguments, Bork could also be categorized as a traditionalist conservative. His concerns about upholding moral values harmonized with traditionalism; thus, he unsurprisingly brooded in one essay about "the prospects for the survival of traditional American culture." In fact, conservative constitutional theorists might be split roughly into two groups, neither of which is explicitly neoconservative. One group advocates for judicial restraint, seeking to limit the Court's power so that other societal institutions can be venues for the exercise of democracy and the sustenance of moral values. This traditionalist group includes Bork and Graglia. The second group advocates for judicial aggressiveness, so long as the Court acts to constrain Congress and other governmental institutions for the purpose of maximizing individual liberty. This libertarian group includes Richard Epstein and Randy Barnett. Questioning the effectiveness of governmental programs, these latter theorists believe that most programs diminish individual autonomy.[62]

Even so, traditionalist and libertarian conservative constitutional theories both overlap considerably with neoconservatism. Traditionalists, like neoconservatives, emphasize moral clarity and the cultivation of values. Libertarians, also like neoconservatives, doubt the worthiness of governmental programs that attempt to implement various social engineering visions. But, most important, neoconservatism unites with both traditionalism and libertarianism in one overarching theme: a desire to resurrect a pre-1937 republican democratic approach to judicial review. Many conservatives, in both the traditionalist and libertarian camps, advocate for a return to republican democratic judicial review through the interpretive method of originalism. In fact, in 1988, the U.S. Department of Justice, under Reagan's attorney general Edwin Meese, issued two reports intended to guide government attorneys in the proper (conservative) mode of constitutional interpretation: originalism. Originalists initially interpreted the Constitution in accord with its text and the intentions of its framers, but in response to criticisms, many originalists modified their approach. Instead of looking to the framers' subjective intentions, they began to focus on the original public meaning of the Constitution. On the traditionalist side, Bork now clearly follows this "new originalism" or original-meaning approach, while on the libertarian side, Barnett does so. Bork, for instance, admitted that one can usually discern the text's public meaning by focusing on "the ratifiers' original understanding," yet he insisted that the ultimate standard remains public meaning. "[W]hat the ratifiers understood themselves to be enacting must be taken to be what the public of that time would have understood the words to mean. . . . The search is not for a subjective intention. . . . When lawmakers use words, the law that results is what those words ordinarily mean." Barnett explained similarly. "[T]he words of the Constitution should be interpreted according to the meaning they had at the time they were enacted," Barnett wrote. "'[O]riginal meaning' originalism seeks the public or objective meaning that a reasonable listener would place on the words used in the constitutional provision at the time of its enactment."[63]

While most (if not all) conservative theorists tend to stress originalism, they find that it has different implications depending on whether they lean toward traditionalism or libertarianism. Traditionalist-oriented conservatives, with their concern for moral clarity and values, tend to see originalism as leading to an emphasis on the republican democratic concept of virtue. Bork, for one, intertwined originalism and judicial restraint with a stress on morality (or virtue): Courts should defer to legislatures and other societal institutions when they articulate and impose moral values. Libertarian-oriented conservatives, meanwhile, with their concern for limitations on government, tend to see originalism as leading to an emphasis on the republican democratic concept of the common good. As the libertarians interpret history, the requirement that governmental action be for the common good constrains the government within narrow realms of action and therefore maximizes individual liberty. Barnett, for instance, argued that the original meaning of the Constitution connoted a particular conception of justice encompassing the protection of liberty. In fact, Barnett went so far as to argue that respect for a natural right to liberty equates with the common good itself. Thus, courts should actively protect liberty: If a governmental action infringes on protected liberty, then the government, by definition, has contravened the common good. Thus, from Barnett's perspective, the Court correctly decided both *Lochner*, protecting a liberty to enter contracts, and *Roe v. Wade*, protecting a woman's liberty to choose whether to have an abortion.[64]

But, to reiterate a key point, traditionalists and libertarians ultimately coincide in advocating for neoconservative themes. Indeed, partly because of the cross-pollination that occurred among the various types of conservatism, many conservative constitutional theorists do not rest neatly in one category or another. Thus, while the later Bork still leaned toward traditionalism, he unquestionably manifested the neoconservative persuasion. He castigated the '60s counterculture and blamed it for promoting moral relativism. Like Strauss himself, Bork worried that relativism could ultimately provoke a desperate populace to turn to an authoritarian Nazi-like demagogue; as society spiraled downward into hedonism and nihilism, people would be willing to sacrifice freedom for security. Bork assumed the existence of clear moral values that societal institutions could regenerate, if only the Supreme Court would allow them to do so. And the Court could clear the path for other institutions if only the justices would return to the "actual Constitution." To use different terminology, Bork sought a return to a Constitution that liberal post-1937 justices had sent into exile. But if the Court were to stop "making up the Constitution" to correspond with liberal culture, then the justices could return "to fundamental republican principles." They could revive the true or exiled pre-1937 (republican democratic) Constitution merely by upholding the original meaning of the text.[65]

In short, the crux of neoconservative constitutional theory is the restoration of the so-called Constitution-in-exile, to use conservative Judge Douglas H. Ginsburg's controversial phrase, introduced in 1995. To be sure, some conservative theorists resist this label partly because it obscures their numerous disagreements. Nevertheless, conservatives oriented to libertarianism (like Barnett) as well as those oriented to traditionalism (like Bork) often advocate for a return to republican democratic judicial review in some significant respects. For instance, while Barnett championed the protection of liberty, he also explicitly distinguished between liberty and license, a distinction that numerous jurists emphasized during the republican democratic era. Barnett argued that the Constitution protects liberty, which is "bounded freedom," but does not protect license, which is "unbounded freedom." More overtly, while Barnett did not expressly use the term *Constitution-in-exile*, he entitled his recent book *Restoring the Lost Constitution*, unambiguously denoting his goal of resurrecting the pre-1937 (republican democratic) Constitution.[66]

A common libertarian strategy is to argue that a return to republican democratic judicial review would entail restrictions on congressional power. When Epstein published his book *Takings* in 1985, he established himself as a champion of libertarianism. Starting with a Lockean state of nature, Epstein argued that individuals are imbued with natural rights to liberty and property. Whenever property is taken from an individual, Epstein explained, "he must receive from the state (that is, from the persons who take it) some equivalent or greater benefit as part of the same transaction." Moreover, according to Epstein, the Constitution adopted this especial concern for protecting property rights, as demonstrated in the Eminent Domain or Takings Clause: "Nor shall private property be taken for public use, without just compensation." Insisting that the Constitution be interpreted in accord with its original meaning, Epstein reasoned that every governmental *regulation* of property amounted to a taking that required the payment of just compensation. Any such takings that were uncompensated (or not for a public purpose) would be unconstitutional. Following this reasoning, most of our current economic and social welfare laws, including those rooted in the New Deal, would be invalid. And Epstein did not hesitate to encourage judicial aggressiveness: Courts should sweep away "many of the heralded reforms and institutions of the twentieth century: zoning, rent control, workers' compensation laws, transfer payments, progressive taxation." For Epstein, then, a restoration of the pre-1937 republican democratic Constitution would entail the judicial imposition of libertarianism. In fact, in a subsequent book, Epstein explicitly argued that the vigorous protection of liberty and property equates with the promotion of the republican democratic principles of virtue and the common good.[67]

Epstein's renown within conservative circles led Reagan's attorney general Edwin Meese to ask Epstein to investigate the scope of Congress's power under the Commerce Clause. Epstein's research led to the publication of an article, *The Proper Scope of the Commerce Power*, which questioned the post-1937 (pluralist democratic) judicial interpretation of the congressional commerce power: "The labor statutes, the civil rights statutes, the farm and agricultural statutes, and countless others rest on the commerce power, or more accurately on a construction of the commerce clause that grants the federal government jurisdiction so long as it can show (as it always can) that the regulated activity burdens, obstructs, or affects interstate commerce, however indirectly. Is this underlying interpretation of the commerce clause correct?"[68]

Epstein's answer was, in his words, "clear enough": The Court should return to its pre-1937 position that limited Congress's commerce power. This resolution manifested the overlap between libertarianism and neoconservatism: Skeptical of governmental programs, Epstein maintained that congressional power should be severely curtailed. He reached this conclusion by ostensibly following an original-meaning approach to constitutional interpretation. As he discerned "the overall constitutional structure," Congress was to pursue the "common good," but that pursuit alone was insufficient to justify the exercise of congressional power. Instead, Congress was "to be limited by specific jurisdictional grants." That is, Congress could (and always must) pursue the common good, but it could do so only if it was also exercising one of its expressly enumerated powers, such as the commerce power. Yet, as Epstein explained the original meaning, the post-1937 Court had turned the Commerce Clause "upon its head." Before 1937, the Court had distinguished between, on the one hand, commerce, and on the other hand, production, including manufacture and agriculture. Congress could regulate commerce but, in most instances, could not regulate production. After the 1937 switch, however, the Court eliminated this limitation on congressional power. The justices now allowed Congress to regulate any activity that had "a substantial effect upon interstate commerce." Based on this standard, the commerce power was transformed from a carefully circumscribed grant into a comprehensive police power that allowed Congress to regulate all aspects of production as well as commerce.[69]

Epstein thus urged the Court to return to "the original constitutional understanding" of the Commerce Clause. He acknowledged that such a resurrection of the pre-1937 Constitution would be "radical" insofar as it would require the Court to overturn fifty years of its own Commerce Clause precedents and demolish most congressionally created New Deal and Great Society programs. Yet, from Epstein's perspective, his argument "from principle" demanded this judicial aggression. As he would write in another article, the Court should reverse "the mistakes of 1937"—when it repudiated republican democratic judicial review and accepted pluralist democracy—and should begin again invalidating "class legislation" that fails to promote virtue and the common good. Numerous other conservative scholars have argued for a return to pre-1937 judicial restrictions on congressional power. Barnett cited approvingly to Epstein and reached similar conclusions concerning Congress's commerce power, though he admitted that the original meaning of the Commerce Clause was somewhat ambiguous. More generally, proponents of a law and economics approach to legal scholarship often conclude that courts should limit all governmental power in order to promote economic efficiency.[70]

In any event, regardless of whether focused on liberty, traditional values, or economic efficiency, a vast array of conservative constitutional theorists have converged on a neoconservative theme: The Court blundered when it accepted pluralist democracy in 1937 and, therefore, the Court should resurrect its pre-1937 republican democratic methods of judicial review. To be sure, depending on their respective conservative orientations, theorists differ about the implications of a return to a pre-1937 Constitution. Yet, despite these sometimes sharp differences, a unity has animated conservative constitutional theory because of the neoconservative emphasis on looking backward for guidance, an emphasis rooted in Straussian political philosophy. Unsurprisingly, this neoconservative orientation was nowhere clearer than in the writings of Walter Berns, perhaps the most unambiguous proponent of an explicitly neoconservative constitutional theory. "[T]he constitutional law of the [post-1937] First Amendment has not been built on the precedents and principles of the past," Berns wrote. "One looks almost in vain for references in the Court's opinions to what the great [nineteenth century] commentators—Story, Kent, and Cooley, for example—have written on freedom of speech and religion, or to what the Founders intended with the First Amendment." From Berns's perspective, shared by so many other conservative theorists, a look backward would usefully guide the Court as it approaches cases in the present and the future.[71]

Neoconservative Successes and Failures

The neoconservative movement achieved multiple successes. Neocons gained substantial influence within the conservative coalition that largely dominated American politics for more than twenty-five years. They filled numerous positions within the Reagan and Bush II administrations and shaped Republican policies during those times. Partly in response to neoconservative arguments, affirmative action has been severely curtailed. The neocons pushed so successfully for welfare reform that it was implemented during a Democratic administration. And the neoconservative advocacy for tort reform produced changes in tort law. Moreover, neoconservatives have influenced the appointment of federal judges, including Supreme Court justices, which has led, of course, to the appointment of numerous neocons themselves as judges and justices. These judges and justices have shaped the development of the law and will continue to do so in the future.

There have been failures, too. Many would argue that the Iraq War manifested a neocon disaster. Many would also argue that some domestic policy victories were only partial. Tort reform, for instance, might be deemed more rhetorical than substantive because the major contours of tort law remained intact. In terms of the overarching aims of neoconservatism, though, the largest neocon defeat by far was the failure to displace pluralist democracy with a resurrected republican democracy. Many of the neocons' specific policy recommendations arose from their disdain for pluralist democracy and their desire to return America to a republican democratic regime—a goal rooted in Straussian thought. They confidently and aggressively aimed to reinstitute a government that promoted certain American virtues or values and that pursued the common good rather than partial or private interests. But whereas the neocons successfully implemented some of their desired policies and programs, they never even approached their goal of toppling pluralist democracy. In fact, they never had a chance to do so. They were doomed to fail from the outset.[72]

Even while the neocons castigated the pluralist democratic regime, they necessarily operated within its parameters. They acted as if they were an interest group trapped in sclerotic political battles against the multitudes of other interest groups. And they had little choice but to do so if they wished to aggrandize their power rather than to fade into insignificance. Thus, they self-consciously followed political entrepreneurs who cultivated patrons, formed organizations, and then strategically acted to maximize their political sway. Neocons spread their ideas in journals like *The Public Interest* and *Commentary*; they networked in organizations like the AEI and the Federalist Society; and they worked at public interest law firms that successfully advocated for the judicial adoption of neoconservative policies. They often explained and applied (or manipulated) originalism as a constitutional theory so that it promoted their specific political goals. Like any aggressive interest group in the era of pluralist democratic sclerosis, they lambasted their opponents while proclaiming their own righteousness. Consequently, they denounced liberals for practicing a "politics of victimhood," then turned around and declared that they, too, were victims. Irwin Stelzer complained, for instance, that neocons had been unfairly characterized as a "cabal" and as "ideologues," while Douglas Murray protested that "numerous enemies" had described neoconservatism "dishonestly."[73]

In short, neoconservatives never transcended pluralist democracy in their own practices, much less transformed the entire democratic system. Why? The primary obstacle blocking the neoconservative resurrection of republican democracy always remained the entrenched pluralist democratic regime itself. Republican democracy collapsed in the 1920s and 1930s after decades of pressure from multiple forces including industrialization, urbanization, and immigration. The practices of a republican democratic regime, which had fit a nineteenth-century society that was largely agrarian, rural, and ethnically and religiously homogeneous, could no longer be sustained in the America of the early 1930s. Thus, the antecedent cause of the rise of pluralist democracy in the 1930s was not some scholarly proposal for a new and better theory of democratic government. Rather, a variety of social and cultural forces undermined republican democracy and generated the practices of pluralist democracy. For the most part, pluralist democratic practices came first and then pluralist democratic theory followed, as intellectuals in the mid- to late 1930s struggled to make sense of the new democratic forms. To be sure, a few intellectuals in the 1920s and early 1930s had questioned republican democratic practices and had wondered about alternative governmental systems. Moreover, for decades the intelligentsia had been rearranging the intellectual furniture and, in effect, setting the stage for a potential transition in democracy. The ushering in of the empirical social sciences and the repudiation of natural law, for instance, facilitated the eventual regime change. Indeed, one can reasonably categorize these intellectual developments as an aspect of the cultural forces that pressed against the faltering republican democratic regime in the early twentieth century. But still, the intellectual developments were no more than one factor among many that contributed to the democratic transition. No single theoretical insight, or even a multitude of theoretical insights, produced the regime change. And no scholar even approached developing a full-scale theory of pluralist democracy until the late 1930s and early 1940s.[74]

Regardless, theorists of pluralist democracy would dominate political science and constitutional law after World War II. Consequently, when neoconservatives eventually began writing essays and books during the postwar era, they argued that republican democracy was preferable to the then-prevailing pluralist democracy. A democracy based on virtue and the common good was, according to the neocons, better than a democracy bereft of foundational values and dedicated to the unmitigated pursuit of self-interest. Naturally, from a social and cultural standpoint, neocons could not return the nation to a time when it was agrarian, rural, and ethnically and religiously homogeneous. That could never happen. In fact, many of the neocons were among the societal outsiders whose immigrant parents or grandparents had contributed to the transition to pluralist democracy. Partly for this reason—that the neocons' ancestors were the immigrants who had helped undermine the republican democratic regime in the first place—paleoconservatives often questioned the neocons' conservative credentials. Paleos often seemed to regard neocons as unwelcome interlopers. Regardless, under the circumstances, the neocons unsurprisingly argued at the level of theory, and they were comfortable doing so. Neocons always emphasized that ideas mattered. Many of them were intellectuals who articulated abstract and elaborate arguments insisting that a republican democratic government based on virtue and the common good was preferable to a pluralist democratic government based on self-interest.[75]

But partly because pluralist democracy had developed first as a practice and only later as a theory, neoconservative theory-arguments only dinged the outer body without reconstructing the inner motor of the pluralist democratic regime. An argument at the level of theory might be interesting—indeed, the neocons might have presented a superior theory of government—but such a theory-argument would nonetheless be futile vis-à-vis the ultimate goal of resurrecting republican democracy. A powerful theory might persuade some people to change their political views and might lead to a few policy reforms—for instance, a change in the welfare laws. Yet without some momentous changes in the underlying social structures and predominant cultural forces, such a theory would be unlikely to lead to a revolutionary change in democratic regimes (from pluralist to republican democracy). And such momentous social and cultural changes were not forthcoming. The nation had become irretrievably heterogeneous; it had become urban, suburban, and exurban; and it had become post-industrial and informational. In short, in the late twentieth and early twenty-first centuries, regardless of neoconservative arguments, republican democracy no longer fit the American society and culture.

The neocons should have anticipated this problem. Strauss himself doubted the worthiness of modern political theories (especially pluralist democratic theory). Like the ancients, he had sought to describe the perfect or best regime rather than develop a theory to control a realpolitik world of self-interested individuals grasping for power. Thus, most Straussian neoconservatives understood (or should have understood) that a regime was more than the implementation of a theory of government, more than a well-designed framework of rules and procedures. A regime always remained integrally connected to the underlying culture: Only a virtuous people would strive to realize the best regime possible. But all too often, when the neocons argued for the resurrection of a republican democratic regime, their enthusiam for abstract ideas overcame their concern for the cultural supports of a regime. True, a neoconservative theorist might argue that republican democracy surpassed pluralist democracy as a governmental system, but such a theory-argument would not by itself produce a change in actual regimes. Some neocons might have hoped that the ostensible weaknesses of pluralist democracy, such as ethical relativism, would lead it to implode, to collapse upon itself, opening a pathway for the return of republican democracy. But again, the neoconservative arguments about the inherent weaknesses of pluralist democracy were highly abstract; the social and cultural foundations for the pluralist democratic regime always remained intact.[76]

Were not, though, many of the neoconservative domestic policy recommendations aimed at changing those social and cultural foundations? Neocons suggested that certain domestic programs had produced unintended consequences that undermined virtue and the people's commitment to the common good. The welfare system, for instance, supposedly provided incentives that weakened commitments to family values. Therefore, change the welfare system, neocons argued, so that it would instead promote the proper values. In other words, neocons imagined that if Americans implemented enough of these piecemeal domestic reforms, emphasizing and encouraging the proper values, then the people would once again become sufficiently virtuous to pursue the common good. But the neocons overlooked that, during the republican democratic era, the accepted conceptions of virtue and the common good were grounded on homogeneity. The rural and agrarian character of the nation went largely unquestioned during much of the nineteenth century, and the cultural dominance of white Protestants could hardly be gainsaid. Thus, throughout most of the republican democratic era, virtue and the common good reflected the rural, agrarian, and white Protestant society. Challenges to the prevailing societal and cultural tenets occasionally arose—for example, when nearly one million Irish Catholics immigrated to the United States during the 1840s. Old-stock Americans, however, generally met such challenges with forceful reassertions of dominance, such as the common school movement, which strove to Americanize (acculturate) Catholic children so that they, too, would share Protestant interests and values. Eventually, though, industrialization, urbanization, and immigration undermined American homogeneity, thus twisting and straining the republican democratic concepts of virtue and the common good until they broke. Given this, a neoconservative argument to proscribe pornography, let's say, almost seems beside the point; even if successful, such advocacy could not bring back the homogenous social and cultural foundation that had sustained the old republican democratic regime.[77]

Again, the neocons, with their energetic confidence, strayed from Strauss's guidance. On the one hand, Strauss ultimately sought to resuscitate republican democratic principles—thus inspiring the neocons in that direction—but on the other hand, Strauss always remained guarded in his methods. "The return to classical political philosophy," he wrote, "is both necessary and tentative or experimental." We should not pretend to be living in antiquity, as if we could then readily reinstate republican principles. Rather, we should learn from the past and use that knowledge, if possible, to help revive republican democracy in our contemporary world. "Only we living today can possibly find a solution to the problems of today." Yet, Strauss never forgot that all governmental regimes were inevitably rooted in the societal and cultural soils of their respective eras. No prior regime, republican democratic or otherwise, could be readily replanted in a new era, in a different society and culture. Thus, Strauss left obscure the details of his revivified republican democracy. Of course, the neocons' departure from Strauss's teachings in this respect—their ardent advocacy of numerous detailed policy prescriptions—might stem from their different purposes. Strauss sought to contribute primarily to political philosophy, while the neoconservatives, however theoretical they might be, sought to contribute largely to political debates. Given these distinct goals, one might expect Strauss to be more circumspect, to be the wise philosopher, whereas the neocons would be more enthusiastic, the aggressive political advocates.[78]

Nevertheless, if one focuses on the difficulties that Strauss as well as other émigré political philosophers of the post–World War II era shared when confronting the perceived problems of pluralist democracy, then the neocons' dilemma in challenging pluralist democracy becomes more perspicuous. Strauss and other émigrés, particularly Eric Voegelin and Hannah Arendt, vigorously criticized the pluralist democratic regime that they encountered in the United States, but they then proceeded in different directions. When Strauss turned from his biting criticisms to proposed solutions, his caution rendered his writings exceedingly vague. He quested after the truth and sought guidance from ancient philosophy, but his journey never reached a lucid outcome. Ultimately, he recommended that we resuscitate republican democratic principles, but the means of doing so remained elusive. Voegelin, too, looked to the past: His exhaustive and erudite explorations led him to emphasize a resurrected spiritual Christian order, which rendered his philosophical conclusions not only abstruse but unappealing to most twentieth-century Americans. Meanwhile, Arendt refused to turn back to either republican democracy or a religious order. Instead, she tried to imagine a pure politics that was neither republican nor pluralist in any ordinary sense. Individuals engage in political action, according to Arendt, solely for the purpose of creating and disclosing their meaningful identities to other individuals. Her concept of politics, though, was so pure, so refined, that it appeared to have no connection to social reality. Indeed, Arendt insisted that when politics attempts to deal with social reality—to solve economic disputes, for instance—then the political realm is necessarily corrupted. Such a purified politics, it would seem, could exist in only one place: utopia—small solace for people living in the real world.[79]

Strauss's, Voegelin's, and Arendt's difficulties leave us wondering: If one repudiates pluralist democracy, then what are the alternatives? The neoconservatives, from this perspective, might be understood as attempting to articulate another option, though more in the concrete realm of political advocacy than in the abstractions of political philosophy. Of course, the neocons theorized as well: Indeed, in the world of political commentators and advocates, they leaned heavily toward the abstract. But compared with Strauss and the other émigrés, they were far more focused on the nitty-gritty problems of everyday political life. And in seeking guidance, as they tackled those nitty-gritty problems, they found Strauss, among the various émigré dissenters to pluralist democracy, the most engaging, the most inspirational, politically and intellectually. Thus, the neocons largely followed Strauss in advocating for a return to republican democracy, but whereas Strauss moved hesitantly because of his philosophical prudence, they advanced more aggressively because of their political aims. Ultimately, though, the neocons encountered the same predicament that Strauss, Voegelin, and Arendt had faced: They could repudiate pluralist democracy, but they could not offer a coherent and workable alternative. If anything, the neocons confronted a more difficult task than the one facing the émigrés. As philosophers, Strauss, Voegelin, and Arendt could be satisfied with abstract and even obscure solutions that might not translate readily into the everyday world. But the neocons were political commentators and advocates. They needed solutions that could be politically implemented. What did they, then, discover? They could criticize pluralist democracy, but they could not escape it.

The neocons might advocate for a return to republican democracy, but as political advocates, they could wield political power within the pluralist democratic regime only by operating pursuant to the norms of pluralist democracy itself. Thus, starting in the 1960s, neoconservatives contributed, like thousands of other interest groups, to the sclerosis that seeped through the pluralist democratic regime. Post–World War II theorists of pluralist democracy had presumed that interest groups would fluidly form and re-form and that competing interest groups would freely negotiate and compromise. As the years passed, however, interest groups proliferated and sclerosis developed and thickened: Interest group leaders adopted extreme and rigid political positions, issued inflammatory pronouncements, and avoided negotiation and compromise. Naturally, the degree to which individual neocons contributed to this ideological rancor and conflict varied. Allan Bloom and Robert Bork, for example, heaped especially bitter denunciations on their opponents' heads. Regardless, the key point is that some neocons contributed to sclerosis, which pushed America even further away from its republican democratic past. If republican democracy demanded that virtuous citizens deliberate about the common good rather than pursue their own interests, then sclerosis manifested an evolved and intensified form of pluralist democracy. Individuals and multitudinous groups would no longer even negotiate about their conflicting interests; instead, they used any means available to manipulate and bully their opponents as well as governmental officials. Ironically, then, even as neocons argued for the resuscitation of republican democracy, they simultaneously acted to reinforce the sclerotic pluralist democratic regime.[80]

5

The Supreme Court and Neoconservatism

In the 2008 election, the American people largely banished neoconservatives from the executive and legislative branches of the national government. Naturally, with periodic congressional and presidential elections, the ratio of conservative Republicans and liberal Democrats in positions of official power will vary depending on the most recent electoral results. Regardless, neocons will continue to wield considerable power from entrenched positions within the national government: namely, as judges on the federal courts and, most particularly, as Supreme Court justices. Although Alexander Hamilton disparaged the judiciary as the "least dangerous" branch because it controlled neither sword nor purse, Supreme Court justices, as the final interpreters of the Constitution, brandish authority over our entire governmental system.[1]

To be sure, neoconservatives insist that judicial decision making, even at the Supreme Court level, can be apolitical. They argue that if only the justices followed an originalist approach, then the Court would necessarily return to the true Constitution, the pre-1937 Constitution, the republican democratic Constitution that liberal (progressive) justices have forcefully rejected. But, even putting aside the problematic neoconservative argument that the United States can resurrect republican democracy, the claim that constitutional adjudication can be apolitical is highly controversial. Numerous scholars in political science and law disagree. Indeed, the predominant political science methodology, the attitudinal model, describes many Supreme Court decisions as being purely political, with legal doctrine being irrelevant. One does not need to accept this extreme political science viewpoint to recognize that politics at least influences constitutional decisions, as an increasing number of legal scholars acknowledge. Scholars as diverse as the liberal philosopher Ronald Dworkin and the conservative jurist Richard Posner emphasize the political component of constitutional adjudication.[2]

Unsurprisingly, then, one can reasonably conclude that conservatives, such as Robert Bork and Edwin Meese, advocated for originalism at least partly as a political strategy. By arguing that liberal justices politicized adjudication while disregarding the original meaning of the Constitution, conservatives (including neocons) sought to gain the political upper hand. Conservatives could denounce liberals as corrupting constitutional decision making for political purposes while claiming that they (conservatives) stayed above the political fray. But, of course, even as conservatives advanced these arguments—insisting that originalism produced politically neutral results—they applied originalism to constitutional issues and found that it consistently produced results harmonizing with the Republican Party agenda. What an uncanny coincidence!

One should not be too quick, however, to criticize conservatives for this display of political alchemy. Like everyone else, they acted within the constraints of a pluralist democratic regime that depicted (and structured) government as a realm of constant political struggle: Either one fought to the top of the political heap by whatever means possible—whether by avowing one's political neutrality or otherwise—or one sank quickly to the bottom.[3]

Finally, even if it were true that apolitical constitutional adjudication is possible, neocons would undoubtedly admit that the Supreme Court today is the situs of political battles and has been so for decades (at least since the 1937 turn). On the one side is the conservative outlook—which conservatives sometimes label as neutral or apolitical—and on the other side is the liberal or progressive outlook—which conservatives sometimes label as corrupt and activist. Regardless of the labels, though, Supreme Court justices can seemingly follow either the conservative or liberal outlook: There is a (political) choice. And after all, the apparent importance of politics to constitutional adjudication is the reason that presidents and members of Congress devote so much energy to the political vetting of Supreme Court appointees. Does anyone truly doubt whether Thurgood Marshall's and Antonin Scalia's different political orientations would produce different judicial results—even if both justices claimed to apply the original meaning of the Constitution? Meese's 1988 Justice Department Report, *The Constitution in the Year 2000*, though claiming that originalism is apolitical, emphasized that the selection of Supreme Court justices greatly affects "the public policy realm." In fact, given how pluralist democracy has evolved, the political stakes in Supreme Court cases can appear toweringly high. Consider a case challenging an affirmative action program in higher education, or a case involving a woman's interest in choosing whether to have an abortion. In such cases, the Court often appears to choose between irreconcilable political positions, though a judicial decision is not necessarily the last word—exactly because the legal issues are also political issues. When the Court handed down *Roe v. Wade* in 1973, concluding that a constitutional right of privacy protected a woman's interest in reproductive choice, the judicial victory for the women's movement provoked in response an energetic anti-abortion (or pro-life) political movement.[4]

What, then, are the political preferences of the Supreme Court justices? Few observers deny that, over all, the early John Roberts and William Rehnquist Courts were conservative; Republican presidents appointed seven of the nine justices sitting at the end of the October 2008 term (in reverse chronological order of appointment: Samuel Alito, John Roberts, Clarence Thomas, David Souter, Anthony Kennedy, Antonin Scalia, and John Paul Stevens). In fact, the four appointees preceding Stevens (William Rehnquist, Lewis Powell, Harry Blackmun, and Warren Burger) were all Republicans, as was Sandra Day O'Connor, appointed after Stevens. The political scientists Jeffrey Segal and Albert Cover have empirically scored Supreme Court nominees' perceived political ideologies at the time of nomination, with .000 being most conservative (e.g., Scalia) and

1.000 being most liberal (e.g., LBJ's confidant Abe Fortas). Just before the recent appointments of Justices Sonia Sotomayor and Elena Kagan, the average score for the then-nine justices was remarkably conservative, .275, with only Ruth Bader Ginsburg scoring on the liberal end (.680). Stephen Breyer, the sole other Democratic appointee at the time, scored as a moderate conservative (.475). The two Republican appointees who were considered liberal, Souter and Stevens, scored as solid conservatives: .325 and .250 respectively. Thus, as expected, during Souter's first term on the Court, he voted consistently with the conservative stalwarts, Rehnquist and Scalia. The two most recent Republican appointees, Roberts and Alito, scored .120 and .100 respectively. Significantly, the retirements of Souter and Stevens and the appointments of Sotomayor, sporting a solid liberal .78 score, and Kagan, with a .73 score, are unlikely to affect the political alignment of the Court: Quite simply, two liberals (or progressives) replaced two others (because Souter moved leftward during his tenure). And if President Barack Obama (or a different Democratic president) has the opportunity to appoint another (Democratic) justice, he (or she) will almost certainly again be replacing a liberal, as Ginsburg currently appears to be the justice most likely to retire soon. Consequently, for the foreseeable future, the Court is likely to retain its current alignment, with five conservatives and four liberals, and of course, the fact that conservatives hold a majority is crucial. As for Kennedy, the conservative now considered most likely to swing his vote on occasion to the progressive side, Segal and Cover scored him at .365 (more conservative than O'Connor's .415). Needless to say, if a Republican president were to have the opportunity to replace Ginsburg, then the Court would move even further to the right.[5]

Given that the majority of the current (Roberts Court) justices share Republican pedigrees and parade such low Segal–Cover political ideology scores, the early Roberts Court has predictably produced a steady stream of conservative decisions. Here is one description of the Court's first two terms:

> [T]he Court . . . resolved [seven antitrust cases] all in favor of the corporate defendants and in the process overruled an almost 100-year-old precedent holding minimum price restraints to be per se anticompetitive. Consumers lost when the Court held that regulatory action by a federal agency preempted a state tort action against an allegedly defective medical

> product in one case, and in another when the Court afforded insurance companies a good-faith defense for a mistaken reading of a regulatory statute. The Court has continued to protect corporate defendants against large punitive damage awards. . . . In a sharp departure from a decision just seven years earlier, the Court upheld a law criminalizing abortion by means of intact dilation and evacuation, despite the fact that the statute made no exception for the need to protect the health of the mother. Important decisions on the Fourth Amendment have run against criminal defendants. The Court held voluntarily adopted school integration efforts in Seattle, Washington, and Louisville, Kentucky, to be unconstitutional, over a passionate dissent by the moderate Justices. In a failure to follow what was arguably a controlling precedent, the Court held that taxpayers had no standing to bring an Establishment Clause challenge to a federal agency's use of federal money to fund conferences to promote the President's faith-based initiatives.[6]

Not only is the Roberts Court unequivocally conservative, it can reasonably be categorized as predominantly neoconservative. Three justices—Scalia, Thomas, and Alito—are members of the Federalist Society, while Roberts has been listed on the organization's leadership directory. Numerous commentators have explicitly labeled four of the justices as neoconservatives or Straussians: Scalia, Thomas, Alito, and Roberts (despite Roberts's professed dedication to judicial restraint, uttered during his confirmation hearings). Neocons tend to score extremely low (i.e., conservative) in the Segal–Cover political ideology rankings. For instance, going back to the 1930s, the only nominees to score zeros (.000) were Scalia and Douglas H. Ginsburg (who coined the term *Constitution-in-exile*), while Bork scored a .095. Given Rehnquist's political ideology score, .045—lower or more conservative than Bork's—as well as his voting record, Rehnquist could fairly be categorized as a neocon, too. If so, then the Court has been imbued with a strong neoconservative presence since at least the beginning of the 1990s (Thomas was appointed in 1991).[7]

Even so, for several reasons, the identification of particular decisions as specifically neoconservative, traditionalist, or libertarian might often be difficult, if not impossible. Partly because of cross-pollination, the overlaps among the various forms of conservatism are so substantial in some areas that distinctions are beside the point. Particular legal and political viewpoints might fall simultaneously into multiple conservative categories. This blurring of the boundaries among the forms of conservatism is, as already discussed, especially severe in the realm of constitutional theory; neoconservative theorists share views with traditionalists and libertarians. Consequently, some theorists fit easily into multiple categories. One can, for instance, label Bork as both neoconservative and traditionalist. The same is true for the Supreme Court justices. Scalia might sometimes seem both neoconservative and traditionalist (and even libertarian). Moreover, partly because of their lifetime appointments, justices can diverge from partisan positions more readily than can other governmental officials. Republicans might criticize but cannot seriously punish a conservative justice who votes progressive in a certain case, much less punish a neocon justice for voting libertarian (or vice versa). Thus, the labels that might stick tightly to governmental officials (and political commentators)—liberal or conservative? neocon, traditionalist, or libertarian?—can slide off the robes of some Supreme Court justices. Perhaps partly for this reason, some commentators have divided the justices into different conservative categories, distinguishing arch-conservatives, who combine economic and social conservatism, from "country-club Republicans," who are economically conservative but indifferent or moderate on many social issues. Among current and former justices, Scalia and Thomas would be arch-conservatives, while O'Connor, Kennedy, Blackmun, and Powell would be moderate or country-club conservatives (and the justices most often identified as swing voters). Of course, from this perspective, the alternative categorizations of *neo*conservative and *arch*-conservative strongly overlap (neoconservative justices tend to be arch-conservatives, and vice versa).[8]

The nature of judicial opinion writing only compounds this categorization problem. In practice, any justice writing an opinion might temper his or her strongest views in order to garner the votes of other justices. Thomas might wish to write a majority opinion focused solely on original meaning, but if he cannot retain the votes of at least four other justices, he would need to modify his reasoning (or he would no longer be writing the majority opinion). Moreover, when the justices write their opinions, they couch them in acceptable modes of legal argument rather than in overt political terms. For instance, in an equal protection case focused on affirmative action, the majority opinion will likely discuss the relevant legal doctrine (the so-called strict scrutiny test), the Court's earlier equal protection precedents, and the history of the framing of the Fourteenth Amendment (including the Equal Protection Clause). The opinion will not declare that it must invalidate (or uphold) the disputed affirmative action program because it is inconsistent (or consistent) with the Republican Party platform. A dissenting opinion would reason similarly: It might argue that the majority either applied the wrong doctrinal test, applied the correct doctrine but did so improperly, or perhaps misunderstood the history.[9]

To be clear, I do not mean to suggest that the justices' legal arguments are mere pretexts for bald political decisions. On the contrary, the justices' legal arguments are most often sincere, but even so, their legal arguments manifest the justices' respective political outlooks. Law (or more precisely, legal interpretation) and politics are integrally and thoroughly intertwined. A justice ordinarily interprets legal texts consistently with his or her politics because politics is part of and shapes interpretation (which explains why Thurgood Marshall and Antonin Scalia could sincerely interpret the same precedents and apply the same legal doctrines but reach opposite results). Sometimes, though, a justice's choice of particular legal arguments reflects his or her political orientation. If a majority opinion, for instance, dwells on the original meaning of a constitutional provision, then one might surmise that the Court was deciding the case in accord with neoconservative constitutional theory. Such would be true of *District of Columbia v. Heller*, in which Scalia's opinion analyzed the original public meaning of the Second Amendment and held that a restriction on handgun possession was unconstitutional. But despite *Heller*, in many other cases, this surmise might be warranted—or unwarranted: Even neoconservatives such as Scalia and Thomas do not always apply an originalist approach, while liberal-progressive justices will readily discuss original meaning and the framers' intentions, as Stevens did in his *Heller* dissent. Indeed, because the justices articulate their positions in acceptable legal rather than overt political terms, one can never know with certainty a justice's (political) motivations for applying even explicitly neoconservative methods (or reaching neoconservative conclusions). Scalia, for instance, claims to apply original-meaning originalism for two reasons: Not only is it, from a normative standpoint, the proper "way of construing a democratically adopted text," but it also is the only reasonable interpretive method. In other words, if one accepts Scalia's self-explanation, he is drawn to originalism partly because he does not recognize any feasible alternative; non-originalists, he insists, cannot agree on a "guiding principle for evolution" for their so-called Living Constitution. From Scalia's perspective, having some interpretive method or rule (originalism) is better than having no method or rule (non-originalism).[10]

Given such uncertainties, one should consider at least three factors when attempting to categorize specific decisions as neoconservative or otherwise. First, what is the result in the case? Does it harmonize generally with neoconservative political positions? Second, when focusing on an opinion—majority, concurring, or dissenting—what is the method of reasoning? Does the justice, for instance, invoke arguments that were more common before rather than after 1937? Third, who wrote the opinion? Based on the individual justice's background and history, is he or she likely to view the world from a neoconservative perspective?

Congressional Power Cases

Recent cases adjudicating Congress's power under the Commerce Clause demonstrate the Court's neoconservative direction. During the republican democratic regime, the Court enforced two substantive constraints on Congress. First, the Court required that congressional actions promote the common good rather than partial and private interests, and second, the Court demanded that Congress act pursuant to one of its specifically enumerated powers. In applying these limitations, the justices confidently implemented a formal conceptualism that assumed the existence of readily discernible objective categories (or dichotomies), such as the common good versus partial or private interests, and commerce versus production. For instance, in *Railroad Retirement Board v. Alton Railroad Company*, decided in 1935, the Court invalidated the Railroad Retirement Act as class legislation contravening the common good and thus beyond Congress's commerce power. The Court reasoned that the legislation promoted only "the social welfare of the worker" rather than fostering "the railroads' duty to serve the public [good] in interstate transportation." The next year, in *Carter v. Carter Coal Company*, the Court distinguished national and local activities as if they were preexisting a priori categories. Mining, like manufacturing, growing crops, and other types of production, was "a purely local activity," the Court explained, and therefore beyond Congress's power to regulate interstate commerce. Meanwhile, in other cases plumbing the limits of Congress's enumerated powers, the Court sometimes emphasized that the Tenth Amendment precluded Congress from using any of its powers to intrude into a judicially protected realm of state sovereignty. Thus, in *Hammer v. Dagenhart*, the Court invalidated a federal statute proscribing the shipment in interstate commerce of goods produced in factories employing child labor. If the Court were to uphold this statute, the majority reasoned, it "would sanction an invasion by the federal power of the control of a matter purely local in its character, and over which no authority has been delegated to Congress." In effect, the Court itself demarcated and enforced a line separating congressional power and state sovereignty as the crux of our federalist system.[11]

Ever since the Court switched to a pluralist democratic approach to judicial review in 1937, however, the justices eschewed imposing such judicial limitations on congressional power. Under pluralist democracy, Congress was no longer limited to acting for the common good; Congress might legitimately legislate for no better reason than that well-placed interest groups wanted a statute. The Court, therefore, would police the pluralist democratic *process* but would not define and enforce substantive limitations on congressional power, whether rooted in the Commerce Clause, the Tenth Amendment, or elsewhere (though the Court would enforce limits arising from preferred freedoms or individual rights, such as free speech). In adopting this approach, deferential to Congress, the Court repudiated the formal conceptualism that had led to bold judicial proclamations of a priori categories; even the definition of interstate commerce would be determined through the pluralist democratic process. As the Court explained in 1942, "[Q]uestions of the power of Congress are not to be decided by reference to any formula which would give controlling force to nomenclature such as 'production' and 'indirect' and foreclose consideration of the actual effects of the activity in question upon interstate commerce." Hence, the scope of Congress's commerce power would be prescribed politically rather than judicially. From this perspective, the Tenth Amendment was nothing but a "truism," neither adding to nor subtracting from congressional power.[12]

The Court still entertained cases challenging Congress's exercise of its commerce power, but the justices resolved such cases pursuant to a rational basis test: "A court may invalidate legislation enacted under the Commerce Clause only if it is clear that there is no rational basis for a congressional finding that the regulated activity affects interstate commerce, or that there is no reasonable connection between the regulatory means selected and the asserted ends." In application, this rational basis test became a rubber stamp: From 1937 until 1995, the Court invalidated only one exercise of Congress's commerce power. In that case, *National League of Cities v. Usery*, the Court (with Rehnquist writing for a five-justice majority) held that Congress, by requiring state governments to pay a minimum wage and overtime rates to its employees, had unconstitutionally intruded into a protected realm of "traditional governmental functions" integral to state sovereignty. But within a decade, in 1985, the Court overruled this one instance of a judicially imposed limitation on congressional power and once again declared that the line separating congressional power and state sovereignty could (and would) shift in response to the political desires of the people. The pluralist democratic process would determine the scope of congressional power (and would define the realm of state sovereignty).[13]

By the early 1990s, however, with new Republican-appointed justices on board, the Court was ready to implement neoconservative visions of congressional power. In *New York v. United States*, decided in 1992, the Court invalidated a federal statute requiring state governments either to regulate the disposal of low-level radioactive waste pursuant to congressional directives or to take title to the waste and then pay for any subsequent damages. O'Connor's majority opinion, joined by Rehnquist, Scalia, Thomas, Souter, and Kennedy, reasoned that the Tenth Amendment prescribed a judicially enforceable limit on Congress's commerce power. Specifically, Congress could not commandeer state legislatures and force them to do Congress's bidding. The case manifested neoconservatism in three interrelated ways. First, the Court claimed that an originalist interpretive approach mandated the conclusion. Thus, when it came to federalism, the Court was not concerned with "devising our preferred system of government, but of understanding and applying the framework set forth in the Constitution." The Court even quoted from *United States v. Butler*, a 1936 case renowned for its ostensible adherence to mechanistic formalism: "'The question is not what power the Federal Government ought to have but what powers in fact have been given by the people.'" Second, the Court returned to a central component of pre-1937 jurisprudence: The Constitution raised judicially enforceable limits on congressional power. Displaying a neoconservative wariness toward legislative power, the Court would not readily defer to the pluralist democratic process. Third, in terms of the precise limit on congressional power, the Court resurrected the Tenth Amendment, a barrier that the pre-1937 Court had relied upon. According to O'Connor, the judicial enforcement of the federalist system was of the utmost importance because it indirectly promoted individual liberty. "State sovereignty is not just an end in itself: 'Rather, federalism secures to citizens the liberties that derive from the diffusion of sovereign power.'"[14]

The *New York* Court reasoned that its decision, precluding Congress from commandeering state legislatures, did not necessarily diminish Congress's commerce power to enact generally applicable laws. But the latter issue soon arose, and the Court concluded otherwise in the landmark case *United States v. Lopez*. Decided in 1995, *Lopez* held that Congress had exceeded its commerce power when it enacted the Gun-Free School Zones Act (GFSZA), a generally applicable law that proscribed the possession of firearms at school. Rehnquist's majority opinion, joined by Scalia, Thomas, Kennedy, and O'Connor, began by asserting that the Court would apply the rational basis test, but the Court now reformulated it to impose judicially enforceable limits on Congress. Under this new or modified rational basis test, as the Court explained, Congress can regulate "three broad categories of activity." "First, Congress may regulate the use of the channels of interstate commerce. Second, Congress is empowered to regulate and protect the instrumentalities of interstate commerce, or persons or things in interstate commerce, even though the threat may come only from intrastate activities. Finally, Congress' commerce authority includes the power to regulate those activities having a substantial relation to interstate commerce, *i.e.*, those activities that substantially affect interstate commerce."[15]

The Court quickly concluded that the GFSZA did not fit into the first two categories: By restricting the possession of firearms at schools, the law targeted neither the channels nor the instrumentalities of interstate commerce. Consequently, the Court focused on the third and potentially broadest category: activities substantially affecting interstate commerce. The Court, however, reached the neoconservative result, holding explicitly for the first time since 1937 that Congress had exceeded its commerce power (the *New York* and *Usery* Courts had relied primarily on the Tenth Amendment rather than the Commerce Clause). In concluding that the possession of firearms at schools did not substantially affect interstate commerce, Rehnquist's majority opinion discussed three factors—a distinction between economic and non-economic activities; a distinction between national and local concerns; and a judicial desire for congressional findings—all of which spotlighted the Court's neoconservative leanings. Rehnquist began by reasoning that gun possession at schools is a non-economic enterprise that "has nothing to do with 'commerce.'" By thus demarcating an ostensible dichotomy separating economic from non-economic activities, Rehnquist relied on a formal conceptualism that resonated with pre-1937 Supreme Court commerce power decisions. To Rehnquist, "economic" and "non-economic" were a priori categories, and gun possession could readily be placed in one (non-economic) rather than the other (economic). Breyer's dissent emphasized that, from a practical standpoint, educational activities closely intertwine with economic (commercial) development. "Schools that teach reading, writing, mathematics, and related basic skills serve *both* social and commercial purposes, and one cannot easily separate the one from the other." Disregarding this criticism, Rehnquist used similar pre-1937 formalism when he reasoned that gun possession at schools is a local rather than a national matter and thus falls outside Congress's commerce power. Indeed, his distinction between "what is truly national and what is truly local" echoed the Court's 1918 language in *Hammer v. Dagenhart*, distinguishing "a purely federal matter" from "a matter purely local in its character."[16]

The majority's neoconservative orientation was nowhere clearer than in its discussion of congressional findings. As the Court acknowledged, Congress in the pluralist democratic regime is generally not required to deliberate or "to make formal findings" when enacting legislation. After all, Congress acts legitimately under pluralist democracy when responding to interest group pressures without claiming to pursue some higher goal (such as the common good). Even so, Rehnquist wrote: "But to the extent that congressional findings would enable us to evaluate the legislative judgment that the activity in question substantially affected interstate commerce, even though no such substantial effect was visible to the naked eye, they are lacking here." In other words, the *Lopez* Court displayed a neoconservative skepticism toward Congress's ability to get things right, especially when passing this (perhaps) progressive statute, regulating guns at schools. If Congress deliberated and made specific and relevant findings, the Court seemed to suggest, then Congress would be less likely to pass a law that might produce unforeseen detrimental consequences. Moreover, by asking Congress to make findings, the Court specifically reintroduced another judicial review mechanism that had facilitated the judicial imposition of substantive limitations on congressional power during the republican democratic era. For example, in *Hill v. Wallace*, decided in 1922, the Court invalidated a statute as beyond the commerce power partly because Congress had failed to find that the evidence showed the regulated activities burdened interstate commerce. While the *Lopez* Court ultimately did not appear to rest its decision on the lack of congressional findings, it refused even to admit that Congress had "accumulated institutional expertise regarding the regulation of firearms through previous enactments." In short, Rehnquist and his majority colleagues showed no respect for, no deference to, Congress. Instead, the Court declared: Prove it to me!—prove that you (Congress) are not misfiring once again, despite ostensibly good intentions.[17]

While the *Lopez* Court's holding and Rehnquist's majority opinion manifested neoconservative elements, the Court, quite clearly, neither repudiated pluralist democracy nor resurrected a fully realized republican democratic judicial review. To the chagrin of numerous neocons, pluralist democracy endured. Rehnquist acknowledged that the post-1937 Court, by expanding Congress's commerce power, had reasonably responded to "the great changes that had occurred in the way business was carried on in this country." Partly for that reason, Rehnquist maintained in *Lopez* that he was applying the rational basis test, which had become the Court's primary doctrinal standard in commerce power cases only when the Court switched to pluralist democratic review in 1937. After reformulating the rational basis test, Rehnquist then concentrated on determining whether Congress had sought to regulate an activity that had substantial effects on interstate commerce.[18]

Meanwhile, Thomas wrote a concurrence in *Lopez* that more nearly fulfilled neoconservative ideals. Thomas explicitly declared that the Court took a "wrong turn" in 1937. If the Court continued to apply a "substantial effects" component as part of a rational basis standard, Thomas lamented, then Congress's commerce power would necessarily be transformed into a comprehensive police power. Thomas's concurrence, in fact, closely paralleled Richard Epstein's neoconservative (libertarian) article arguing for a return to a pre-1937 concept of Congress's commerce power. Most important, like Epstein, Thomas argued that the Court should interpret the Commerce Clause pursuant to its original meaning. Thus, Thomas began his analysis by discussing the definitions of commerce that could be found in dictionaries contemporaneous with the constitutional framing. Based on these sources, Thomas endorsed the pre-1937 judicial distinction between commerce and production, where commerce did not encompass manufacturing and farming. He bolstered this conclusion by arguing that "exchanges during the [constitutional] ratification campaign" revealed that "[e]arly Americans" understood commerce in this narrow manner. In sum, Thomas maintained that the Court should follow an originalist approach and that doing so would confine Congress to a limited commerce power, as supposedly reflected in *Carter Coal* and other pre-1937 Supreme Court decisions that Thomas countenanced.[19]

If Thomas's concurrence manifested a more robust judicial neoconservatism, then one might wonder why Rehnquist's majority opinion accepted only certain neoconservative elements. Most important, Rehnquist wrote for a five-justice majority in *Lopez* that included not only the solid neocons, Thomas and Scalia, but also the moderate (country-club) conservatives, Kennedy and O'Connor. Indeed, Kennedy wrote a concurrence joined by O'Connor stressing that *Lopez* should not be interpreted too radically, that it had a "limited holding." Kennedy refused to characterize the Court's 1937 turn as an unequivocal mistake. Instead, he recognized that the post-1937 Court had struggled "to interpret the Commerce Clause during the transition from the economic system [of local markets] the Founders knew to the single, national market still emergent in our own era." Given Kennedy's and O'Connor's (moderately conservative) prudence, Rehnquist needed to temper any desire to write a more aggressive and confident neoconservative opinion. If he had opted to write an opinion more similar to Thomas's concurrence, he probably would have lost Kennedy's and O'Connor's votes.[20]

Even so, the Court continued to follow its neoconservative inclinations in subsequent cases adjudicating the scope of congressional power. For example, in *City of Boerne v. Flores*, the Court narrowed Congress's power to act under the Fourteenth Amendment, section five. Holding that Congress had overreached when it enacted a statute largely protecting religious minorities, the Court again suggested, as in *Lopez*, that Congress had failed to deliberate adequately. Then, in *United States v. Morrison*, the Court applied the new doctrinal tests articulated in *Lopez* and *Boerne* and held that Congress had exceeded its powers under both the Commerce Clause and the Fourteenth Amendment, section five, when it enacted the

Violence Against Women Act (VAWA), protecting women from gender-motivated violence. Acknowledging that Congress, in this instance, had made voluminous findings, the *Morrison* Court nonetheless disparaged the congressional conclusions because they would "obliterate" the Court's formalist distinction between national and local activities. The strange case of *Gonzales v. Raich* serves only to underscore the degree to which politics, whether neocon or otherwise, permeates the Court's decision making. Kennedy flipped his vote and joined the (progressive) dissenters from *Lopez* and *Morrison* (Stevens, Ginsburg, Breyer, and Souter) to uphold a congressional action. But what was the congressional statute? A law proscribing the possession of marijuana. Thus, *Raich* presented conservatives (and progressives) with a paradox. The conservative justices would lean toward restricting congressional power, as they had done in *Lopez* and other cases, but some of those same conservative justices might simultaneously wish to allow the government to impose moral values by restricting the use of drugs. In the end, Kennedy joined a majority opinion written by Stevens that retained the *Lopez* reformulated rational basis framework but reasoned that marijuana possession substantially affected interstate commerce. Even Scalia, too, voted to uphold this statute, though he refused to join Stevens's opinion. Instead, Scalia's concurrence (in the judgment) emphasized that this case raised a factually unique situation in which the Necessary and Proper Clause empowered Congress to regulate drug possession. In sum, despite *Raich* and despite the occasional temporizing in majority opinions, needed to hold moderate-conservative votes (such as those of Kennedy and O'Connor), the Rehnquist and Roberts Courts' congressional power decisions have displayed a confident and aggressive righteousness characteristic of neoconservativism in general. Those Courts have set forth on one of the "most notable binges of congressional-law striking in history." In fact, the Rehnquist Court invalidated more congressional acts than had any previous Court; from 1995 to 2001 alone, the Court struck down thirty federal laws, more than the Warren Court invalidated from 1953 to 1969.[21]

Equal Protection Cases

Equal protection challenges to affirmative action programs presented the Supreme Court with a constitutional conundrum. During the post–World

War II era, the Court developed relatively straightforward equal protection doctrine for resolving cases of racial discrimination. If a law discriminated on its face against a suspect class, including any racial minority, then the Court would apply strict scrutiny: The law would be held unconstitutional unless the government could prove that its action was necessary to achieve a compelling purpose. If a law was facially neutral, the Court would apply rational basis review, the lowest level of judicial scrutiny, unless the challenger proved that the government had intentionally discriminated against a suspect class, in which case the Court would apply strict scrutiny. The Court formulated this doctrine to protect "discrete and insular minorities" (suspect classes) who had been historically subjugated in American society (thus, African Americans constituted the prototypical suspect class). Moreover, for sixty years, whenever the Court deemed strict scrutiny to be the appropriate level of judicial scrutiny for an equal protection claim, the Court always held the governmental action to be unconstitutional. This judicial consistency spawned the maxim that strict scrutiny was strict in theory but fatal in fact. But, then, what would happen when governmental institutions voluntarily adopted affirmative action programs designed to favor racial minorities as a means of remedying the harms of past societal discrimination? When whites challenged such programs as creating unconstitutional racial classifications, would the Court apply strict scrutiny and hold the programs to be unconstitutional?[22]

In the first Supreme Court case raising the constitutionality of affirmative action, the justices resolved the dispute without settling the larger constitutional issues. *University of California Regents v. Bakke*, decided in 1978, arose when a white applicant to a state-supported medical school challenged the school's program allocating racial minorities a minimum number of entry-class positions. Four justices (with an opinion written by Stevens) ruled for the white applicant based on a statutory claim; these justices did not reach the equal protection issue. Four justices (with an opinion by William J. Brennan) reached the constitutional claim, reasoned that an intermediate level of scrutiny was appropriate for an affirmative action program, and concluded that the state satisfied this standard. From Brennan's perspective, while the affirmative action program created a racial classification, its benign rather than invidious purpose constitutionally distinguished this state action from a Jim Crow law. Finally, the ninth justice (Powell) reached the constitutional claim, reasoned that strict scrutiny was appropriate, and ruled in favor of the white applicant because the state could not satisfy this rigorous standard. Significantly, even Powell, applying strict scrutiny, reasoned that an alternative form of affirmative action, used by Harvard College, which gave racial minorities a "plus" in the admissions process without creating a quota, could pass constitutional muster.[23]

For the next several years, the Court continued to move uncertainly in the area of affirmative action. The justices, for example, suggested that Congress, because of its power under the Fourteenth Amendment, section five, might be subject to a lesser degree of judicial scrutiny than state and local governments when mandating an affirmative action program. But in the late 1980s and early 1990s, with new conservative appointees on board, the Court turned rightward. In *City of Richmond v. J. A. Croson Company*, decided in 1989, Richmond instituted a plan mandating that contractors with the city subcontract at least 30 percent of the dollar amount of any prime contract to minority business enterprises. In invalidating this city action, a majority of justices (Scalia, O'Connor, Rehnquist, Byron R. White, and Kennedy) for the first time agreed on a standard of judicial review for affirmative action programs: strict scrutiny. Even so, O'Connor's plurality opinion left sufficient wiggle room to allow the Court to retreat to a lower level of scrutiny in the future, if a majority so desired. O'Connor suggested that strict scrutiny might not necessarily be appropriate for *all* affirmative action programs and that, even if strict scrutiny was applied in subsequent cases, governments might sometimes be able to satisfy this most rigorous judicial standard. In fact, Scalia refused to join O'Connor's opinion because, from his perspective, state and local governments could never constitutionally use race-conscious affirmative action programs: Strict scrutiny should still be strict in theory but fatal in fact.[24]

After *Croson*, the Court wiggled one more time, in *Metro Broadcasting, Inc. v. Federal Communications Commission*, when a five-justice majority applied an intermediate level of scrutiny to uphold a congressionally approved affirmative action program. Before the Court decided its next major affirmative action case, however, four of the justices in the *Metro Broadcasting* majority had resigned; most notably, Thomas replaced Marshall. Thus, in *Adarand Constructors, Inc. v. Pena*, decided in 1995, Thomas joined the *Metro Broadcasting* dissenters (O'Connor, Kennedy, Scalia, and Rehnquist) to create a solid bloc of conservative justices incontrovertibly supporting the application of strict scrutiny in all cases of affirmative action. Despite articulating this unequivocal position, O'Connor, writing the majority opinion, again asserted that strict scrutiny was not fatal in fact. She reasoned that the government, in the right circumstances, might be able to adopt an affirmative action program that would pass constitutional muster: Specifically, the redress of past invidious discrimination could possibly amount to a purpose compelling enough to satisfy the strict scrutiny test. As in all previous cases, though, O'Connor ultimately concluded that, based on the facts, the government had not satisfied strict scrutiny. Scalia, once again, disagreed with O'Connor's qualification of strict scrutiny, even if, in application, it was purely theoretical rather than practical. "In my view, government can never have a 'compelling interest' in discriminating on the basis of race in order to 'make up' for past racial discrimination in the opposite direction," Scalia explained in a concurring opinion. "Individuals who have been wronged by unlawful racial discrimination should be made whole; but under our Constitution there can be no such thing as either a creditor or a debtor race." Thomas, too, wrote a concurring opinion, but while Scalia worried about the niceties of the strict scrutiny test, Thomas perfectly encapsulated neoconservative arguments opposing affirmative action, especially quota-driven programs. Echoing Nathan Glazer's mid-1970s book, which had emphasized the unforeseen consequences of affirmative action, including the promotion of victimhood and the provocation of white backlash, Thomas argued for a colorblind Constitution.

> [T]here can be no doubt that racial paternalism and its unintended consequences can be as poisonous and pernicious as any other form of discrimination. So-called "benign" discrimination teaches many that because of chronic and apparently immutable handicaps, minorities cannot compete with them without their patronizing indulgence. Inevitably, such programs engender attitudes of superiority or, alternatively, provoke resentment among those who believe that they have been wronged by the government's use of race. These programs stamp minorities with a badge of inferiority and may cause them to develop dependencies or to adopt an attitude that they are "entitled" to preferences. . . . In my mind, government-sponsored racial discrimination based on benign prejudice is just as noxious as discrimination inspired by malicious prejudice. In each instance, it is racial discrimination, plain and simple.[25]

In 2003, the Court decided a pair of cases involving affirmative action in higher education, specifically at the University of Michigan. *Grutter v. Bollinger* challenged the law school's affirmative action admission program, while *Gratz v. Bollinger* challenged the university's undergraduate affirmative action program. Under the law school program, applicants who belonged to underrepresented racial minorities, including African Americans, would receive an unspecified advantage or "plus." Thus, the law school program resembled the Harvard College plan that a majority of justices had approved in *Bakke*. Meanwhile, the undergraduate program awarded minority individuals a precise quantity, twenty points, in an admissions system that numerically ranked the applicants. Given the Court's history in applying strict scrutiny in equal protection cases, *Gratz* predictably held the undergraduate program unconstitutional, but a majority of justices in *Grutter* surprisingly upheld the law school program, with O'Connor flipping sides, providing a crucial fifth vote and writing the Court's opinion.[26]

O'Connor, in a sense, proved she had sincerely declared in earlier cases that, at least for her, strict scrutiny was not strict in theory but fatal in fact. While she reached the typical result in *Gratz*, she refused to do so in *Grutter*. Indeed, the *Grutter* result was so anomalous that one might wonder whether the majority truly applied strict scrutiny. After all, despite O'Connor's declarations, the Court for sixty years always had reached the same result in equal protection strict scrutiny cases: The governmental program was unconstitutional. Thus, one might fairly characterize O'Connor's *Grutter* approach to be "strict scrutiny lite" rather than traditional (strict-in-theory-but-fatal-in-fact) strict scrutiny. In traditional strict scrutiny cases, the Court had never deferred to the government's articulation of a compelling purpose, yet in *Grutter*, O'Connor wrote: "The Law School's educational judgment that [student-body] diversity is essential to its educational mission is one to which we defer." Thomas and Rehnquist, each dissenting, expressed outrage at, in Thomas's words, this "[d]eference antithetical to strict scrutiny." From their neoconservative vantage, the Court should not dilute the rigor of strict scrutiny to facilitate upholding any governmental policy, least of all an affirmative action program. Thomas and Scalia then questioned another aspect of O'Connor's application of strict scrutiny (lite). When O'Connor framed the strict scrutiny test in *Grutter*, she stated that the government must prove that its program was "narrowly tailored" rather than necessary to achieve its (compelling) purpose. In previous equal protection cases, the Court had used the terms *narrowly tailored* and *necessity* interchangeably, but not in *Grutter*. The Court had never before deemed a governmental program "narrowly tailored"—or "necessary"—if the government could achieve its purpose through some less invidious means. In *Grutter*, though, when Thomas pointed out that the law school could have achieved its goal of student-body diversity by reducing the admission standards for all applicants, O'Connor reasoned that "[n]arrow tailoring does not require exhaustion of every conceivable race-neutral alternative."[27]

After *Grutter* and *Gratz*, the Court seemed firmly committed to adjudicating the constitutionality of affirmative action programs pursuant to strict scrutiny. In any particular case, though, would it be strict scrutiny traditional or lite? Apparently O'Connor's swing vote would resolve that crucial question, and her voting record demonstrated that, in the vast majority of cases, it would be traditional (strict-in-theory-but-fatal-in-fact) strict scrutiny. Certainly, any affirmative action program smacking of a quota system would be held unconstitutional—O'Connor could not accept in *Gratz* the numerical precision of the undergraduate admission program that awarded an additional twenty points to minority applicants.[28]

By 2007, when the Court decided its next major affirmative action case, *Parents Involved in Community Schools v. Seattle School District No. 1*, Roberts had replaced Rehnquist as chief justice and, more important, Alito had replaced O'Connor, thus solidifying the Court's neoconservative base. Under the *Parents Involved* programs (in Seattle and Louisville), school officials maintained racially integrated public schools by considering race when assigning students to elementary and high schools. Roberts, writing for a five-justice majority (joined by Scalia, Thomas, Alito, and Kennedy), applied traditional strict scrutiny and invalidated the programs, while Breyer (joined by Stevens, Souter, and Ginsburg) wrote a dissent applying strict scrutiny lite. Forewarning of future decisions, Roberts stressed that *Grutter* should be interpreted narrowly. *Grutter* was unique, according to Roberts, in three ways: The Michigan law school affirmative action program did not impose any type of racial quota; it allowed each applicant to be evaluated individually rather than categorized solely as a member of a racial group; and it applied only to higher education. Because the affirmative action programs challenged in *Parents Involved* differed from the Michigan law school program in all these respects, *Grutter* was inapposite.

Finally, in a plurality section of his opinion (which Kennedy did not join), Roberts concluded that equal protection required the government to be colorblind: The Constitution recognizes no difference between affirmative action programs and Jim Crow laws. The principle of equality embodied in *Brown v. Board of Education*, Roberts reasoned, mandated the invalidation of the *Parents Involved* affirmative action programs. "The way to stop discrimination on the basis of race is to stop discriminating on the basis of race."[29]

Indeed, this neoconservative stress on constitutional colorblindness became a flash point of dispute among the justices. Stevens and Breyer each wrote dissents that emphatically denounced Roberts's equating of *Brown* and *Parents Involved*. In Stevens's words: "There is a cruel irony in the Chief Justice's reliance on our decision in *Brown v. Board of Education*. The first sentence in the concluding paragraph of his opinion states: 'Before *Brown*, schoolchildren were told where they could and could not go to school based on the color of their skin.' This sentence reminds me of Anatole France's observation: '[T]he majestic equality of the la[w], forbid[s] rich and poor alike to sleep under bridges, to beg in the streets, and to steal their bread.' The Chief Justice fails to note that it was only black schoolchildren who were so ordered; indeed, the history books do not tell stories of white children struggling to attend black schools. In this and other ways, the Chief Justice rewrites the history of one of this Court's most important decisions." Meanwhile, Thomas concurred in *Parents Involved* to emphasize the importance of colorblindness. "Disfavoring a color-blind interpretation of the Constitution," Thomas wrote, Justice Breyer's "dissent would give school boards a free hand to make decisions on the basis of race—an approach reminiscent of that advocated by the segregationists in *Brown v. Board of Education*. This approach is just as wrong today as it was a half-century ago." Finally, Kennedy wrote a concurrence that explained his refusal to join the section of Roberts's *Parents Involved* opinion emphasizing colorblindness. Kennedy insisted that the government, at least in some contexts, should be allowed to take race "into account"; therefore, colorblindness "cannot be a universal constitutional principle." Thus, significantly, although Kennedy joined Roberts's opinion where it stressed the narrowness of the *Grutter* holding, Kennedy's concurrence nonetheless suggested that *Grutter* might retain some precedential value. In fact, Kennedy acknowledged that, following from *Grutter*, racial diversity might in some circumstances constitute a compelling purpose for a public school district (rather than only for higher education).[30]

In sum, even after *Parents Involved*, the neoconservative agenda for affirmative action remained only partially fulfilled. Uncertainties lingered in this key realm of equal protection law largely because of Kennedy's moderate conservatism. As in the cases dealing with congressional power, Kennedy's country-club Republicanism—moderate on many social issues and generally accepting of the status quo—dampened his enthusiasm for his neoconservative colleagues' aggressive righteousness. Still, as a general matter, Kennedy strongly favors the application of traditional (strict-in-theory-but-fatal-in-fact) strict scrutiny to affirmative action issues, despite his irresoluteness in *Parents Involved*. Inevitably, Kennedy reaches the same conclusion as the more unequivocal neoconservative justices: The government's affirmative action program violates equal protection (consequently, Kennedy dissented in *Grutter*). Thus, in his *Parents Involved* concurrence, Kennedy rigorously applied the "narrow tailoring" prong of strict scrutiny and concluded that the Louisville and Seattle school districts failed to satisfy the standard. Moreover, Kennedy was not sated by reaching this conclusion: He also explicitly criticized Breyer's endorsement and application of strict scrutiny lite. Kennedy warned that strict scrutiny lite would "have no principled limit and would result in the broad acceptance of governmental racial classifications," a possibility that Kennedy could not abide. Kennedy might not be an unmitigated neoconservative, but he is unquestionably conservative and consistently votes with the neocon justices.[31]

First Amendment Cases

The congressional power and affirmative action cases shared a specific neoconservative orientation: a distrust of government's ability to get things right. Regardless of intentions, national, state, and local governmental programs were likely to produce unintended and detrimental consequences. While this view has been central to numerous neoconservative policy prescriptions, neocon commentators often also emphasized another concern: a need for moral clarity. Neocons encouraged governmental and nongovernmental institutions to promote the articulation and teaching of "traditional" and often religious values. How has this neoconservative concern influenced the Supreme Court?

Free Expression and Education

The seminal case focusing on the free-expression rights of students was *Tinker v. Des Moines Independent Community School District*, decided in 1969. Conceptualizing public school as a training ground for pluralist democratic participation, *Tinker* articulated broad free-expression rights for students. The case arose when a high school and a junior high school suspended students for wearing black armbands in protest against the Vietnam War. Writing for a seven-justice majority, Justice Abe Fortas began by categorizing the armbands as "pure speech" rather than conduct and, therefore, as deserving of "comprehensive protection under the First Amendment." Fortas emphasized that "[i]t can hardly be argued that either students or teachers shed their constitutional rights to freedom of speech or expression at the schoolhouse gate." Fortas acknowledged that the school environment might diminish the scope of First Amendment rights, so he articulated a doctrinal rule specific for educational institutions. Even so, beginning with a presumption of constitutional protection, the Court adopted a highly speech-protective doctrine: Student expression would be constitutionally protected unless it caused "material and substantial interference with schoolwork or discipline." In this case, the evidence did not show "that the school authorities had reason to anticipate that the wearing of the armbands would substantially interfere with the work of the school or impinge upon the rights of other students." To the contrary, the officials appeared to want merely to avoid a political controversy.[32]

The Court stressed that free expression in the public schools was especially important to American constitutional government. Quoting Justice William Brennan, Fortas wrote, "'The vigilant protection of constitutional freedoms is nowhere more vital than in the community of American schools.'" Why so? Because public schools provide the training grounds where students learn the skills prerequisite for participation in pluralist democracy—the skills needed to become citizens and leaders. "The classroom is peculiarly the 'marketplace of ideas.' The Nation's future depends upon leaders trained through wide exposure to that robust exchange of ideas which discovers truth 'out of a multitude of tongues, (rather) than through any kind of authoritative selection.'" In pluralist democracy, citizens need to be able to reason, to negotiate, to compromise, and to accept (or at least tolerate) a multitude (or plurality) of values—in short, they need to communicate with diverse other citizens—and schools are "dedicated" to teaching, among other things, "personal intercommunication." In sum, *Tinker* was a prototypical pluralist democratic free-expression decision. The Court not only interpreted the First Amendment broadly, but it also seemed oblivious to considerations of virtue, values, and civility that had loomed prominently under republican democracy. Instead, Fortas emphasized, "[I]n our system, undifferentiated fear or apprehension of disturbance is not enough to overcome the right to freedom of expression. Any departure from absolute regimentation may cause trouble. Any variation from the majority's opinion may inspire fear. Any word spoken, in class, in the lunchroom, or on the campus, that deviates from the views of another person may start an argument or cause a disturbance. But our Constitution says we must take this risk, and our history says that it is this sort of hazardous freedom—this kind of openness—that is the basis of our national strength and of the independence and vigor of Americans who grow up and live in this relatively permissive, often disputatious, society."[33]

While *Tinker* involved high school (and junior high school) students, *Healy v. James*, decided in 1972, involved college students. A state college refused to accord "official recognition" to students who sought to form a chapter of Students for a Democratic Society (SDS), an organization renowned for its protests against the Vietnam War. "Denial of official recognition posed serious problems for the organization's existence and growth," the Court explained. The group's "members were deprived of the opportunity to place announcements regarding meetings, rallies, or other activities in the student newspaper; they were precluded from using various campus bulletin boards; and [they were barred] from using campus facilities for holding meetings." Reversing and remanding for further development of the facts, the *Healy* Court unequivocally applied *Tinker* in the college context. Justice Lewis F. Powell, writing for an eight-justice majority (Justice William H. Rehnquist concurred in the result only), elaborated the *Tinker* doctrine—student expression would be protected unless it "posed a substantial threat of material disruption"—by linking it to *Brandenburg v. Ohio*, a landmark of expansive First Amendment protection. Like *Brandenburg*, *Healy* pronounced a dichotomy: advocacy versus incitement. In the college context, the expression of ideas is always constitutionally protected, while expression urging (or inciting) imminent disruptive conduct is unprotected. Thus, students could advocate with impunity for changing or eliminating campus rules—including reasonable time, place, and manner restrictions on expression—but students could neither violate nor incite imminent violations of those same rules without risking punishment.[34]

Once again, as in *Tinker*, the *Healy* Court's opinion resonated with pluralist democracy. "[T]he precedents of this Court leave no room for the view that, because of the acknowledged need for order, First Amendment protections should apply with less force on college campuses than in the community at large." To the contrary, higher education should epitomize the operations of free expression in a pluralist democratic society: "The college classroom with its surrounding environs is peculiarly the 'marketplace of ideas,' and we break no new constitutional ground in reaffirming this Nation's dedication to safeguarding academic freedom." In fact, the evolution of pluralist democracy increasingly rendered political dialogue more like a pitched battle than a coldly rational marketplace exchange, and the *Healy* Court acknowledged that incivility could therefore appear "on the campus" as it did elsewhere. "[T]he wide latitude accorded by the Constitution to the freedoms of expression and association is not without its costs in terms of the risk to the maintenance of civility and an ordered society." Yet, the Court reasoned, we must abide uncivil speech and writing and the bitter clashes of opposed political groups if we are to maintain "our vigorous and free society" and to realize the advantages of pluralist democracy.[35]

By 1986, when the Court decided *Bethel School District No. 403 v. Fraser*, the nation was in the midst of the Reagan era, and the Court had swung rightward, showing neoconservative influences. *Bethel* arose when a high school suspended a student who had delivered an allegedly lewd speech at an assembly. Chief Justice Burger's majority opinion began by acknowledging that *Tinker* held that students retain First Amendment rights, but the Court then retreated from the *Tinker* doctrine. Rather than protect student expression unless it caused material and substantial interference with schoolwork or discipline, the *Bethel* Court emphasized school officials' discretion to determine whether expression "would undermine the school's basic educational mission." Based on this deferential stance, the Court found the student's expression unprotected and upheld the punishment.[36]

As in the earlier cases, the Court emphasized the intertwinement of education and democracy, but this time the Court characterized democracy in more republican terms. "The role and purpose of the American public school system were well described by two historians," the *Bethel*

Court explained, citing and quoting Charles Beard and Mary Beard's *New Basic History of the United States*, first published in 1944. "'[P]ublic education must prepare pupils for citizenship in the Republic. . . . It must inculcate the habits and manners of civility as values in themselves conducive to happiness and as indispensable to the practice of self-government in the community and the nation.'" The *Bethel* Court lifted this quotation from a section of the Beards' *New Basic History* discussing the development of democracy during the Jacksonian age of the nineteenth century. Given the era being discussed, the Beards conceptualized education in republican democratic terms. Worried about the combination of widespread male suffrage and heavy immigration, Jacksonian-era "philosophers of educational progress [believed] public education must prepare pupils for citizenship in the Republic," wrote the Beards. After emphasizing the educational inculcation of "the habits and manners of civility as values . . . indispensable to the practice of self-government," the Beards quoted Horace Mann, the "indefatigable leader in the public-school movement," who stated that the purpose of education "'is to preserve the good and to repudiate the evil which now exists.'" Mann, the Beards concluded, intended to "bring wisdom, knowledge, and virtue to bear upon the improvements of the conditions of the people."[37]

The *Bethel* Court's emphasis on civility and values contrasted sharply with the *Tinker–Healy* insistence that we must tolerate pugnacious, offensive, and even indecent expression within the constant give-and-take of the pluralist democratic arena. Instead, the *Bethel* Court stressed that the "fundamental values of 'habits and manners of civility' essential to a democratic society must . . . take into account consideration of the sensibilities of others." Given this more republican democratic depiction of American government, the *Bethel* Court reasoned that "[t]he inculcation of these values is truly the 'work of the schools.'" Consequently, the Court concluded, "The First Amendment does not prevent the school officials from determining that to permit a vulgar and lewd speech such as respondent's would undermine the school's basic educational mission."[38]

In *Hazelwood School District v. Kuhlmeier*, decided in 1988, the Court upheld a high school principal's decision to delete articles discussing divorce and teen pregnancy from a school-sponsored newspaper. Although Justice Byron White began the majority opinion by acknowledging *Tinker*, he then stressed the *Bethel* retreat. "[T]he First Amendment rights of students in the public schools 'are not automatically coextensive with the rights of adults in other settings.'" Thus, under *Bethel*, "[a] school need not tolerate student speech that is inconsistent with its 'basic educational mission.'" Even so, the *Hazelwood* Court further chipped away at students' free-expression rights by creating an explicit exception to the *Tinker* (and thus, presumably, the *Bethel*) doctrine. The *Tinker* (*Bethel*) doctrine applies when school officials seek to restrict "a student's personal expression that happens to occur on the school premises," but it does not apply to school-sponsored activities that "may fairly be characterized as part of the school curriculum."[39]

In the latter instance, free-expression rights turn on whether the school created a designated (or limited) public forum. Throughout the pluralist democratic era, the Court had distinguished two types of governmental property. Property such as the streets and parks that had been open for public speaking from time immemorial was deemed a public forum. In the public forum, the First Amendment prohibited the government from restricting speech based on its content unless the government satisfied strict scrutiny, showing that the restriction was narrowly tailored to achieve a compelling governmental purpose. On other governmental property, however, the government could impose any reasonable restrictions on expression, except if the government had specially designated the property for public speaking. In such cases, the government would have in effect transformed the property into a limited public forum, thus triggering the speech-protective public forum rules.[40]

"[S]chool facilities may be deemed to be [limited] public forums," the *Hazelwood* Court explained, "only if school authorities have 'by policy or by practice' opened those facilities 'for indiscriminate use by the general public,' or by some segment of the public, such as student organizations." The Court concluded that the school-sponsored newspaper was not a public forum and that school officials were, therefore, empowered "to regulate the contents of [the paper] in any reasonable manner." Thus, while *Hazelwood* created a large exception to *Tinker–Bethel*, the *Hazelwood* doctrinal approach harmonized closely with *Bethel* by showing great deference to school officials. At least when a school has not created a designated public forum, "educators do not offend the First Amendment by exercising editorial control over the style and content of student speech in school-sponsored expressive activities so long as their actions are reasonably related to legitimate pedagogical concerns." Unsurprisingly, then, the *Hazelwood*

Court emphasized that school officials could censor student publications to promote the values of civility and even to avoid political controversy. "A school must . . . retain the authority to refuse to sponsor student speech that might reasonably be perceived to advocate drug or alcohol use, irresponsible sex, or conduct otherwise inconsistent with 'the shared values of a civilized social order,' or to associate the school with any position other than neutrality on matters of political controversy."[41]

In these cases adjudicating students' free-expression rights, the Court has undoubtedly shifted in the neoconservative direction—showing enhanced deference to school officials seeking to teach certain moral values and inculcate virtue—yet even the neocon justices have hesitated, refusing to adopt an unequivocally republican democratic approach. The justices displayed their ambivalent attitudes in the most recent case in this area, *Morse v. Frederick*, decided in 2007. A high school principal, Deborah Morse, decided to allow students to watch the Olympic Torch Relay as it passed by her school in Juneau, Alaska. As the torchbearers and accompanying camera crews passed the school, a student, Joseph Frederick, "unfurled a 14-foot banner bearing the phrase: 'BONG HiTS 4 JESUS.'" Morse confiscated the banner and suspended Frederick. A five-justice majority, with an opinion written by Roberts, held that this punishment did not violate Frederick's free-expression rights.[42]

The justices disagreed strongly about the meaning of "BONG HiTS 4 JESUS." While the dissenting Stevens deemed it "a nonsense message," Roberts wrote, "The message on Frederick's banner is cryptic. It is no doubt offensive to some, perhaps amusing to others. To still others, it probably means nothing at all. Frederick himself claimed 'that the words were just nonsense meant to attract television cameras.' But Principal Morse thought the banner would be interpreted by those viewing it as promoting illegal drug use, and that interpretation is plainly a reasonable one." More important, the justices' various opinions in the case implicitly disagreed about whether students' free-expression rights should be conceptualized in accord with republican or pluralist democracy. Despite Roberts's strong neoconservative credentials, his opinion surprisingly waffled between republican democratic and pluralist democratic concepts of free expression in the public schools, though Roberts ultimately leaned toward a more conservative and republican democratic interpretation of the First Amendment. More predictably, Thomas's concurrence strongly favored a republican democratic approach, while Stevens's dissent resonated with pluralist democracy. Most unexpectedly, Alito's concurrence also favored pluralist democracy.[43]

Roberts reviewed the precedents running from *Tinker* through *Hazelwood*. Even while Roberts recognized that the Court has modified the *Tinker* doctrine, he suggested that *Tinker* is still a vital decision. Roberts characterized the black armbands in *Tinker*, worn to protest the Vietnam War, as "political speech," which is "'at the core of what the First Amendment is designed to protect.'" Roberts thus alluded to the self-governance theory, which justifies a strong reading of the First Amendment. Significantly, the judicial and scholarly emphasis on self-governance arose only after the rise of pluralist democracy in the 1930s. Free expression became a constitutional lodestar because, in part, political participation cannot be fair and open for all citizens—a prerequisite for pluralist democracy—unless each individual can freely express his or her interests in the democratic arena. Free expression, in other words, became an integral component of the pluralist democratic processes. Unsurprisingly, then, given his allusion to self-governance theory, Roberts refused to adopt a rule, more consonant with republican democracy, that would allow school officials to restrict expression because it was offensive or unpleasant.[44]

Yet Roberts did not merely follow *Tinker*. To the contrary, he discerned two principles embodied in its progeny—two principles that reflect a serious weakening of the *Tinker* precedent. First, students' free-expression rights are less than the full rights enjoyed by individuals outside a school context; second, *Tinker* no longer provided the doctrinal rule for determining the scope of students' free-expression rights. Given these principles, Roberts wrote approvingly of parts of *Bethel* and *Hazelwood* that resonated strongly with republican democracy. Roberts quoted from the *Bethel* Court's judgment that a school district could punish a student's "'offensively lewd and indecent speech,'" and from the *Hazelwood* Court's ruling that school officials can control the "'content of student speech in school-sponsored expressive activities so long as their actions are reasonably related to legitimate pedagogical concerns.'" And, ultimately, Roberts reached the conservative conclusion—Frederick's expression was constitutionally unprotected—by deferring to the principal's interpretation of the banner as "promoting illegal drug use." Following this interpretation, Roberts reasoned that the danger in *Morse* "is far more serious and palpable" than in *Tinker*. "The particular concern to prevent student drug abuse at issue here, embodied in established school policy, extends well beyond an abstract desire to avoid controversy."[45]

Thomas's concurrence was less equivocal in its preference for a republican democratic concept of free expression in the public schools. Thomas argued to overrule *Tinker* because it was not grounded "in the history of education." According to Thomas, "[T]he history of public education suggests that the First Amendment, as originally understood, does not protect student speech in public schools." The purpose of the mid-nineteenth-century common schools, Thomas emphasized, was to inculcate children with the values necessary to become virtuous citizens who would pursue the republican democratic common good. "[E]arly public schools were not places for freewheeling debates or exploration of competing ideas," Thomas wrote; "[r]ather, teachers instilled 'a core of common values' in students and taught them self-control." Parents bore the duty to train their children to become "virtuous members of society," and with that duty, parents necessarily had the power to discipline, "to command obedience." Acting *in loco parentis*, schools shared the same duty and power, a power that would therefore allow schools "to regulate student speech." Thomas concluded by quoting from an 1859 state court opinion: A teacher's power to punish student expression was "'essential to the preservation of order, decency, decorum and good government in schools.'" From Thomas's republican democratic perspective, then, the principal, Morse, could punish the student, Frederick, for any expression that Morse deemed unvirtuous, including the banner proclaiming, "BONG HiTS 4 JESUS."[46]

Like Thomas, Alito concurrred, but despite his neoconservative leanings, his opinion harmonized with pluralist democracy. Alito began by strongly endorsing the *Tinker* doctrine, which protects student expression unless it "threatens a concrete and 'substantial disruption.'" Because *Tinker* resonates strongly with pluralist democracy, Alito was understandably wary of allowing school officials "to censor any student speech that interferes with a school's 'educational mission,'" a doctrinal approach that seemingly would be more consonant with *Bethel* than with *Tinker*. The "educational mission" approach, resonating with republican democracy, would afford school officials broad discretion to inculcate their preferred values or "political and social views." This position, Alito declared, "strikes at the very heart of the First Amendment." Why, then, did Alito concur instead of dissent? While the *Healy* Court had interpreted *Tinker* to harmonize with the *Brandenburg* doctrine, protecting expression unless it creates an imminent risk of proscribed conduct, Alito argued that in "the school environment, school officials must have greater authority to intervene before speech leads to violence." From Alito's vantage, the *Tinker* "'substantial disruption' standard permits school officials to step in before actual violence erupts." Alito agreed with Roberts that Frederick's banner should be interpreted as "advocating illegal drug use," which poses "a grave and in many ways unique threat to the physical safety of students." Thus, Alito concluded, Morse could punish Frederick pursuant to the *Tinker* doctrine.[47]

Stevens's dissent, joined by Souter and Ginsburg, also emphasized the *Tinker* doctrine, but Stevens interpreted *Tinker* more consistently with *Brandenburg*. "[U]nder *Tinker*, 'regulation of student speech is generally permissible only when the speech would substantially disrupt or interfere with the work of the school or the rights of other students. . . . *Tinker* requires a specific and significant fear of disruption, not just some remote apprehension of disturbance.'" The majority's approach, Stevens protested, allowed Morse to discipline Frederick "because she disagreed with the pro-drug viewpoint she ascribed to the message on the banner." But Stevens argued that students, in accord with pluralist democracy, ought to be able to express their diverse political views without fear of punishment. The Court's holding "strikes at 'the heart of the First Amendment' because it upholds a punishment meted out on the basis of a listener's disagreement with her understanding (or, more likely, misunderstanding) of the speaker's viewpoint." Specifically, "the Court's ham-handed, categorical approach is deaf to the constitutional imperative to permit unfettered debate, even among high-school students, about the wisdom of the war on drugs or of legalizing marijuana for medicinal use." Not only must school officials allow students to voice their sundry political positions, Stevens asserted, but officials should be precluded from enforcing values previously associated with republican democratic virtue and civility. "'If there is a bedrock principle underlying the First Amendment, it is that the Government may not prohibit the expression of an idea simply because society finds the idea itself offensive or disagreeable.'" Thus, like the *Tinker* Court, Stevens concluded that we must "'risk'" the "'hazardous freedom'" of the First Amendment because it is crucial in our "'relatively permissive, often disputatious, society.'"[48]

Coming from the progressive side, Stevens's support for a pluralist democratic approach was predictable, but why did the neocon justices display such ambivalence in *Morse*? Roberts, to be sure, might have been vote counting. His opinion was joined by only four other justices: Thomas, Scalia, Kennedy, and Alito (Breyer, concurring in the judgment in part and dissenting in part, reasoned that qualified immunity shielded the school principal and thus did not reach the First Amendment issue). Most likely, Thomas and Scalia would have signed on to Roberts's opinion even if it had been more unequivocally republican democratic, yet Alito and Kennedy might have resisted. Kennedy joined not only Roberts's majority opinion but also Alito's concurrence, following a pluralist democratic approach. And for Roberts and Alito (as well as Kennedy), the precedential weight of *Tinker* apparently played a strong role. Despite *Bethel* and *Hazelwood*, *Tinker* remains the seminal case in this area, so any dispute raising issues involving students' free-expression rights will come within its gravitational pull. Just as one could not possibly write an opinion resolving an abortion dispute without accounting for *Roe v. Wade*, one cannot disregard *Tinker*. And as much as any free-expression case, *Tinker* accepts the pluralist democratic substantiation of free expression as a constitutional lodestar.

Free Expression and Religion

Free-speech issues have arisen repeatedly when private (nongovernmental) actors have sought to express certain religious views or values on government-owned property. *Widmar v. Vincent*, decided in 1981, was the first case to raise such an issue squarely. A state university opened its facilities for meetings held by registered student organizations but refused to allow its buildings and grounds to be used "for purposes of religious worship or religious teaching." In this particular instance, the university refused access to Cornerstone, a student "organization of evangelical Christian students from various denominational backgrounds." Cornerstone members challenged the university policy by arguing that it violated both their free-expression and free-exercise rights. The university, meanwhile, maintained that allowing religious organizations to use its facilities would violate the Establishment Clause. This swirl of free-expression and religious freedom claims generated an odd political alignment of justices. The conservative Powell wrote a majority opinion joined by conservatives (Burger, Rehnquist, and O'Connor) and liberals (Brennan, Marshall, and Blackmun) which concluded that the university policy violated free expression. The liberal Stevens concurred in the judgment only, while the conservative White dissented.[49]

University property ordinarily would not constitute a public forum, but in *Widmar*, the Court explicitly held that "[t]hrough its policy of accommodating their meetings, the University has created a forum generally open for use by student groups." In other words, the university had transformed its property into a designated (or limited) public forum. Having done so, the university could restrict speech based on its content—here, the religious content—only if it could satisfy the strict scrutiny standard. The Court then concluded that the university failed to offer a compelling purpose for proscribing the religious speech. Contrary to the university's argument, the university would not have violated the Establishment Clause if it had allowed such speech; the university's avoidance of a specious constitutional (Establishment Clause) violation could not amount to a compelling purpose.[50]

White, dissenting, questioned the sagacity of the Court's decision to focus on free expression rather than on the free-exercise claim. And to be sure, the majority's emphasis on free expression and disregard for free exercise was significant in and of itself. White's analysis of the free-exercise claim led him to conclude that the university had not violated the First Amendment—the university was strongly positioned vis-à-vis the Free Exercise Clause—but once the majority turned instead toward free expression, the university's chances seemingly diminished. After all, ever since the Court had turned to pluralist democracy in 1937, it had treated free expression as a constitutional lodestar. In his opinion concurring in the judgment, Stevens, too, criticized the majority's free-expression approach; he wondered whether the application of public forum doctrine was appropriate. Stevens maintained that universities must constantly decide what ideas to teach and communicate to students, and such decisions are necessarily content-based. Applying public forum doctrine and its strict scrutiny standard would hamstring university officials and professors as they attempted to structure a curriculum and shape educational life.[51]

Over the next twenty years, three more of these hybrid free-expression–free-exercise cases arose. Given that the Court did not decide the next one, *Lamb's Chapel v. Center Moriches Union Free School District*, until 1993, after the Court had shifted toward neoconservatism, the justices unsurprisingly continued to emphasize free expression (rather than free exercise), to apply public forum doctrine, and to conclude that the government must allow Christian organizations to spread their messages on school properties. In *Lamb's Chapel*, a public school district opened its buildings during non-school hours for various community uses other than religion. Pursuant to this policy, the school district refused to allow a Christian evangelical church "to show a six-part film series containing lectures by Doctor James Dobson." A promotional brochure explained that "the film series would discuss Dr. Dobson's views on the undermining influences of the media that could only be counterbalanced by returning to traditional, Christian family values instilled at an early stage." The Court again applied public forum doctrine, but unlike in *Widmar*, the *Lamb's Chapel* Court assumed *arguendo* that the school district had not created a designated public forum. Even so, the Court explained that a restriction on religious expression in a nonpublic forum must be both "reasonable and viewpoint neutral." And in this case, the Court found viewpoint discrimination: The school district permitted "school property to be used for the presentation of all views about family issues and child rearing except those dealing with the subject matter from a religious standpoint." Thus, despite assuming that the school property had not been designated a public forum, the Court still held the restriction on religious speech to be unconstitutional.[52]

If one looks at *Lamb's Chapel* in conjunction with the subsequent cases, *Rosenberger v. Rectors and Visitors of the University of Virginia*, decided in 1995, and *Good News Club v. Milford Central School*, decided in 2001, two key points become evident. First, the conservative justices coalesced into a bloc supporting the promotion of overtly Christian messages in school settings. While in *Lamb's Chapel* the liberal and conservative justices still mixed together, the justices in *Rosenberger* fell into their more typical five-to-four conservative–liberal split. Kennedy wrote a majority opinion (joined by Rehnquist, Scalia, Thomas, and O'Connor) holding that the First Amendment required the University of Virginia to fund a student newspaper, *Wide Awake*, dedicated to evangelical "proselytizing." *Wide Awake* explicitly challenged "'Christians to live, in word and deed, according to the faith they proclaim and to encourage students to consider what a personal relationship with Jesus Christ means.'" In *Good News Club*, the five conservative justices, joined by Breyer, held that a public school violated free expression by denying access to "a private Christian organization for children ages 6 to 12" that sought to hold club meetings on school property. Writing for the majority, Thomas chastised the lower court for its seeming hostility toward Christianity. *Lamb's Chapel* and *Rosenberger* already had established the constitutional protection of Christian education and proselytizing on public property, including schools, and the *Good News Club* case was indistinguishable. Thus, Thomas wrote, "The only apparent difference between the activity of Lamb's Chapel and the activities of the Good News Club is that the Club chooses to teach moral lessons from a Christian perspective through live storytelling and prayer, whereas Lamb's Chapel taught lessons through films."[53]

Second, in these cases the conservative justices consistently reached the pro-Christian result despite the vagaries of a convoluted public forum doctrine. In *Widmar*, the Court held that the state university had created a designated public forum and thus applied the strict scrutiny test ordinarily used to determine the scope of free expression in a traditional public forum, like the streets and parks. In *Lamb's Chapel*, the Court assumed that the school district had not created a designated public forum and therefore claimed to apply a less rigorous standard of judicial scrutiny. Yet the *Lamb's Chapel* Court imbued its scrutiny with such a surprising degree of bite that it reached the same result as in *Widmar*: invalidating the government's restriction on the use of its school properties. Then, in *Rosenberger*, the Court again held, as in *Widmar*, that a state university had created a designated public forum, but unlike in *Widmar*, the Court now did not apply strict scrutiny. Instead, the *Rosenberger* Court applied the ostensibly less rigorous degree of scrutiny that it had articulated in *Lamb's Chapel*. Suddenly, the Court's initial finding of whether the government had created a designated public forum no longer appeared to determine the Court's level of scrutiny. Even so, just as in *Lamb's Chapel*, the *Rosenberger* Court imbued its scrutiny with bite and invalidated the government's restriction on Christian expression. Finally, in *Good News Club*, the Court followed *Rosenberger* by finding the government's creation of a designated public forum, by articulating a less rigorous degree of scrutiny, by imbuing that scrutiny with bite, and by invalidating the governmental policy. In sum, the Court in these cases might or might not conclude that the government had created a designated public forum, and the Court might or might not apply strict scrutiny. But ultimately, regardless of the doctrinal conclusion, the Court always reaches the same result: protecting the promotion of Christian messages and values.[54]

What happens, though, if the government seeks to restrict the dissemination or display on its property of a non-Christian (or nontraditional) message? Would not *Widmar* and its progeny suggest that the Court should uphold the free-expression rights of the non-Christian speakers in such cases? The neoconservative justices have avoided this result by implementing "the recently minted government speech doctrine." Basically, in these cases, the Court has structured the legal doctrine so that the justices can toggle between two approaches: first, treat the case as a public forum issue and concentrate on whether the government has justified its restriction of private expression; or, second, treat the case as raising a government speech issue, which allows the government to escape First Amendment (free-expression) limitations. In *Widmar*, in reply to White's dissenting and Stevens's concurring opinions that doubted the propriety of a free-expression public forum approach, the majority stated, "Nor do we question the right of the University to make academic judgments as to how best to allocate scarce resources or 'to determine for itself on academic grounds who may teach, what may be taught, how it shall be taught, and who may be admitted to study.'" Regardless, the *Widmar* Court bypassed the university (or government) right (or power) to make content-based distinctions because, according to the majority, the university had created a designated public forum. Yet, in *Rosenberger*, the University of Virginia relied on the *Widmar* Court's acknowledgment of a governmental right (or power) and argued that it must be allowed to make "content-based funding decisions," even if doing so entailed restricting Christian speech. And, in fact, the *Rosenberger* Court responded by articulating a government speech doctrine: When the government speaks or sponsors or funds private speech, then the government can "regulate the content of what is or is not expressed." Thus, in such situations, the government "is entitled to say what it wishes," without concern for normal First Amendment (free-expression) constraints.[55]

In the end, the *Rosenberger* Court concluded that this government speech doctrine was beside the point. The Court explained that, in the factual circumstances of the case, "the University does not itself speak or subsidize transmittal of a message it favors but instead expends funds to encourage a diversity of views from private speakers." But, then, how might one identify these two types of legally opposed yet factually similar cases? That is, how might one distinguish cases where the government spoke or subsidized private speech—and thus the government speech doctrine toggled on (while the public forum doctrine toggled off)—from cases where the government instead encouraged "a diversity of views from private speakers"—and the government speech doctrine toggled off (while the public forum doctrine toggled on)? Unfortunately, the Court did not adequately elaborate.[56]

In a more recent case, *Pleasant Grove City v. Summum*, decided in 2009, the Court confronted this ambiguity lingering between government speech and public forum cases. Pleasant Grove displayed in its city park several privately donated monuments, including one showing the Ten Commandments, contributed years earlier by the Fraternal Order of Eagles. Summum, a religious group, offered to donate a monument for the park showing its Seven Aphorisms (also called the Seven Principles of Creation). The city refused to accept the monument. Was this a public forum case, where the government violated Summum's free-expression rights, or was it a government speech case, where the government could choose its own message without regard for First Amendment limits? In response to a petition for a preliminary injunction, the Court of Appeals held that a public park was a traditional public forum, that strict scrutiny should therefore be applied, and that the city was unlikely to satisfy this rigorous standard.[57]

The Supreme Court reversed. "[T]he display of a permanent monument in a public park is not a form of expression to which forum analysis applies," Alito concluded in his opinion for an eight-justice majority. "Instead, the placement of a permanent monument in a public park is best viewed as a form of government speech and is therefore not subject to scrutiny under the Free Speech Clause." As Alito explained, under the government speech doctrine, "[t]he Free Speech Clause restricts government regulation of private speech; it does not regulate government speech." Why, though, was this a government speech case rather than a public forum case? Why switch on the government speech doctrine and switch off the public forum doctrine? The Court's primary reason was that a monument is permanent. "Speakers, no matter how long-winded, eventually come to the end of their remarks; persons distributing leaflets and carrying signs at some point tire and go home." But unlike a speaker who climbs on a soapbox and begins orating, a monument will "endure." Monuments "monopolize the use of the land on which they stand and interfere permanently with other uses of public space." For this very reason, cities and other local governments tend to be "selective": They "take some care in accepting donated monuments" because, with the limited available space, each accepted and displayed monument defines and communicates "the identity that a city projects to its own residents and to the outside world."[58]

To be sure, Alito's distinction between permanent and temporary expression seemed a reasonable mechanism for identifying government speech (and thus the applicability of the government speech doctrine). The ephemerality of a spoken speech (or a distributed leaflet) given in a public park suggests that many listeners would not associate such a message with the government, but those same listeners might infer that a monument represents an accepted governmental viewpoint. Yet one should recognize that the Court, parading its neoconservative epaulets, proclaimed in effect that the government can openly choose to adopt and display the values, symbols, and viewpoints of some of its citizens while rejecting those of other citizens—even when those values, symbols, and viewpoints are specific to certain religions. Indeed, given the Court's imprimatur of the government's selective approval of certain values, one must wonder how the Court would decide a case with the facts reversed. That is, if (in some science fiction world) a city had already long displayed a Seven Aphorisms monument (or a monument from some other minority religion), and then the Fraternal Order of Eagles offered to donate a Ten Commandments monument, would the Court allow the city to reject the Ten Commandments monument because of the government speech doctrine? Or would the Court conclude that a park was a public forum and that rejecting the Ten Commandments monument amounted to unconstitutional content or viewpoint discrimination? Indeed, partly because of such concerns, the four progressive justices all expressed wariness in *Summum* about the appropriateness and application of the government speech doctrine (Stevens, Ginsburg, and Breyer concurred, while Souter concurred in the judgment only), though they all also ultimately agreed with the (conservative) majority's conclusion concerning the constitutionality of the governmental action.[59]

Establishment Clause

Widmar and its progeny, involving religious speech on public property, all raised Establishment Clause issues. The government (universities and public schools) feared that it would violate the Establishment Clause by allowing religious organizations to use public property for the teaching and inculcation of religious values and views. And in all of the cases, the Court concluded that a religious organization's beneficial use of public property would not violate the Establishment Clause.

As is well known, the Court's doctrinal approach to Establishment Clause issues has been unsettled for many years. The Court first incorporated or applied the Establishment Clause against state and local governments only after 1937, in *Everson v. Board of Education*, decided in 1947. In *Everson*, the Court adopted Thomas Jefferson's metaphorical "wall of separation between Church and State" and stated that the wall "must be kept high and impregnable." Yet, apparently, the wall was not insurmountable, as *Everson* upheld the public reimbursement of transportation costs for children attending religious (or public) schools. Even so, conservatives have long criticized the wall metaphor as being too hostile toward religion. Instead, they often advocate for the so-called nonpreferentialist position: The government cannot prefer one religion over another, but it can accommodate and even favor religion over irreligion. And of course, some conservatives, especially traditionalists, go even further, arguing that the government ought to be able to promote Christianity as the traditional religion of the United States.[60]

Regardless, the post–World War II Court continually invoked and applied the wall metaphor. For instance, in *Engel v. Vitale*, decided in 1962, the Court invalidated the recitation of a supposedly nondenominational prayer in the public schools. Any such prayer, the Court reasoned, favored religion over irreligion, impermissible under the Establishment Clause, which rests "on the belief that a union of government and religion tends to destroy government and to degrade religion." By 1971, in *Lemon v. Kurtzman*, the Court had synthesized its prior Establishment Clause decisions into a three-pronged standard embodying the wall metaphor: "First, the statute must have a secular legislative purpose; second, its principal or primary effect must be one that neither advances nor inhibits religion; finally, the statute must not foster 'an excessive government entanglement with religion.'" In subsequent cases, however, the Court applied the *Lemon* test unevenly. For example, in one case, *Stone v. Graham*, the Court invalidated a statute that required the posting of the Ten Commandments on public classroom walls, but in another case, *Lynch v. Donnelly*, the Court upheld a governmental display of a crèche.[61]

Despite the obvious flexibility of the *Lemon* test, which facilitated outcomes like that of *Lynch*, decided in 1984, the conservative justices became increasingly disgruntled with *Lemon* and its instantiation of the wall metaphor. Burger's majority opinion in *Lynch* emphasized that, *Lemon* notwithstanding, the Court had been unwilling "to be confined to any single test or criterion in this sensitive area." Meanwhile, O'Connor wrote a concurrence in *Lynch* that proposed an alternative to *Lemon*. O'Connor's endorsement test contained two prongs: First, does the state action create excessive governmental entanglement with religion, and second, does the state action amount to governmental endorsement or disapproval of religion? Before long, another moderate conservative, Kennedy, introduced one more alternative test. Kennedy's coercion test also consisted of two parts: First, the "government may not coerce anyone to support or participate in any religion or its exercise," and second, the government "may not, in the guise of avoiding hostility or callous indifference, give direct benefits to religion in such a degree that it in fact 'establishes a [state] religion or religious faith, or tends to do so.'"[62]

The coercion test became the favorite of neoconservatives because, compared with the *Lemon* and endorsement tests, it allowed the government the widest latitude in promoting religious values and displaying religious symbols. Indeed, depending on the definition of *coercion*, Kennedy's test seemed to prohibit little governmental conduct beyond that already proscribed by the Free Exercise Clause (which prohibited the government from forcing individuals either to follow or not to follow any particular religion). Moreover, Kennedy appeared to design the coercion test to harmonize with nonpreferentialism. When he first articulated the test, he criticized judicial attempts to enforce "an absolute 'wall of separation'" and then wrote, "Government policies of accommodation, acknowledgment, and support for religion are an accepted part of our political and cultural heritage." Thus, the coercion test would seem to allow the government to favor religion over irreligion so long as, in doing so, the government did not coerce support for or participation in religion. Indeed, the second prong seemed to underscore the possibility of giving benefits to religion so long as those benefits fell short of establishing a specific governmental religion or faith.[63]

Through the 1990s and after, the justices sometimes applied the endorsement and coercion tests, but they also continued to apply the *Lemon* test. When applying *Lemon*, however, the justices whittled away at its rigor, to the point that the reconstituted *Lemon* test no longer embodied the wall metaphor. Start with the third prong: entanglements. *Lemon* specified two types of impermissible governmental entanglements with religion. First, administrative entanglement might arise when the government monitors religious institutions to ensure that they do not use any supplied public funds for religious activities. Second, if governmental action, such as a public funding program, politically divides the people in accord with their religious differences, then the governmental action and the concomitant political divisiveness might constitute excessive (and therefore unconstitutional) entanglement.[64]

The entanglements prong, though, has not fared well over the years, as the transition from *Aguilar v. Felton* to *Agostini v. Felton* demonstrates. Pursuant to statute, the federal government funded New York City teachers who provided remedial instruction for religious school students at the (religious) school premises. In 1985, *Aguilar v. Felton* held this program unconstitutional because of excessive entanglements. The moderate conservative Powell joined the four liberals then on the Court—Brennan, Marshall, Blackmun, and Stevens—to constitute a five-justice majority, with Brennan writing the opinion. The Court emphasized administrative entanglement because city personnel needed to "visit and inspect the religious school regularly, alert for the subtle or overt presence of religious matter in [the remedial] classes." Powell's concurrring opinion, meanwhile, stressed political divisiveness. Whenever the government provides any type of funding for religious schools, Powell explained, then different religious groups will be motivated to lobby the legislature to provide additional funding most useful for their respective religions.[65]

By 1997, when the Court reconsidered the same funding program, the Court had moved rightward with predictable results. *Agostini v. Felton* overruled *Aguilar* by a five-to-four vote, with O'Connor writing a majority opinion joined by Rehnquist, Scalia, Thomas, and Kennedy. O'Connor, for the most part, eliminated the entanglements prong from the *Lemon* test. She reasoned that, because of overlaps between the second and third prongs, "it is simplest to . . . treat [entanglement] as an aspect of the inquiry into a statute's effect." When O'Connor therefore analyzed whether entanglement concerns might now lead the Court to conclude that the funding program violated the effects prong, she obviated consideration of political divisiveness, which she deemed "insufficient" by itself to render the program unconstitutional. Equally important, O'Connor diminished the relevance of administrative entanglements. The Court would no longer require the government to monitor the use of public funds in religious schools, and when monitoring did take place, the Court would allow governmental officials and school personnel to work cooperatively. Thus, regardless of the *Aguilar* Court's worries about entanglements, the *Agostini* Court held the funding program to be consonant with the Establishment Clause.[66]

Well, what about the effects prong, given that the Court, in Thomas's words, has "modified" *Lemon* by recasting entanglements "as simply one criterion relevant to determining a statute's effect," and an inconsequential criterion, at that? Has the Court imbued the effects prong with greater prominence, despite the results in *Agostini*? No. If anything, while the Court has all but eliminated the entanglements prong, it has simultaneously rendered the effects prong toothless. *Zelman v. Simmons-Harris*, decided in 2002, upheld a school voucher program that allowed parents to use public money to pay for religious school education. Rehnquist's majority opinion, joined by O'Connor, Scalia, Thomas, and Kennedy, ostensibly focused on the effects prong. Of apparent significance, then, while the voucher program appeared neutral on its face, statistical evidence showed that 96 percent of the beneficiaries sent their children to religious schools. But the Court dismissed such evidence as irrelevant to determining effects, even though statistics would seem to be an ideal means for demonstrating the actual societal effects or consequences of a facially neutral governmental program—at least if the effects prong were to have any bite. Nevertheless, Rehnquist explained that "the number of program beneficiaries attending religious schools" was beside the point: "The constitutionality of a neutral educational aid program simply does not turn on whether and why, in a particular area, at a particular time, most private schools are run by religious organizations, or most recipients choose to use the aid at a religious school."[67]

In practice, it seems, the Court has reduced the *Lemon* test to a single prong: the purpose prong. So long as the government constructs a program that appears to have a secular purpose—and just about any facially neutral law will do so—the government will not violate the Establishment Clause. As thus transformed, the *Lemon* test now corresponds more closely with the nonpreferentialist position than with the wall metaphor. Assuming that the government does not specify that funds should flow to particular religions—and such a program would not be facially neutral—then the government remains free to channel benefits to religious institutions, as was the case in *Zelman*. Moreover, in reality, any such facially neutral governmental program, aiding religious institutions, will likely funnel most of its benefits to mainstream (Christian) religions. After all, the overwhelming majority of Americans belong to those religions. In the end, the religious mainstream can direct benefits to itself under the guise of governmental neutrality without impinging on Establishment Clause proscriptions. In fact, the Court in some cases simply disregards all of the purported Establishment Clause tests, *Lemon* included. For example, in *Van Orden v. Perry*, a five-to-four decision, the Court upheld a display of the Ten Commandments etched on a monument that sat in a monument park surrounding the Texas state capitol. Rehnquist's plurality opinion, joined by Thomas, Scalia, and Kennedy, declared the *Lemon* test to be "not useful in dealing" with this type of case. Instead, Rehnquist emphasized tradition: The government, throughout history, had similarly displayed religious symbols and communicated religious messages and thus could continue to do so.[68]

The influence of the neoconservative justices on Establishment Clause doctrine is unmistakable. In the early 1970s, the Court articulated and applied the *Lemon* test as a manifestation of the wall metaphor. But as neocons advocated for greater moral clarity in a number of social realms, the justices themselves began to assail *Lemon*. Before long, the justices could draw on a mishmash of doctrinal approaches to Establishment Clause issues. They could apply a coercion test, an endorsement test, a reconstituted *Lemon* test, or no test at all, simply declaring that the government ought to be able to follow American traditions. And whatever test or tests the justices applied, the result was often the same: The Court sustained the promotion of traditional American (and Christian) values. In these cases, the government itself might be promoting the values—for instance, by providing funding to private religious groups—or the government, forced by the Court, might be granting religious groups access to a public realm where they could spread their religious messages. Either way, the justices shifted the case outcomes toward the neoconservative and nonpreferentialist positions.[69]

This transition in Establishment Clause doctrine was significant in the hybrid free-expression–free-exercise cases. In the first of those cases,

Widmar, the university argued that, regardless of public forum doctrine, it would violate the Establishment Clause if it allowed religious organizations to use its facilities. Given the year of the decision, 1981, the Court unsurprisingly applied the *Lemon* test in a straightforward fashion, articulating and applying each of the three original prongs—purpose, effects, and entanglement. Focusing on the effects prong, the Court reasoned that opening the university facilities to all student groups, including religious organizations, would provide "merely 'incidental' benefits" to religion. That is, the "primary effect" of creating the public forum would not be "to advance religion." Therefore, the Court concluded that the university could satisfy the *Lemon* test and would not violate the Establishment Clause. By the time the Court decided *Lamb's Chapel*, in 1993, the justices had already undermined the pristine *Lemon* test. In that case, the public school district also argued that the Establishment Clause prevented it from opening its buildings for religious uses. The *Lamb's Chapel* Court reasoned that *Widmar* controlled on this issue and then briefly mentioned that the school district could satisfy both the *Lemon* and the endorsement tests. But now, some of the conservative justices were dissatisfied. In a concurring opinion, Kennedy criticized the majority's invocation of the *Lemon* and endorsement tests. Scalia, concurring in the judgment and joined by Thomas, not only denounced the *Lemon* and endorsement tests at length but also asserted the nonpreferentialist position: "I would hold, simply and clearly, that giving Lamb's Chapel nondiscriminatory access to school facilities cannot violate [the Establishment Clause] because it does not signify state or local embrace of a particular religious sect."[70]

Two years later, in *Rosenberger*, the neoconservative influence was even more pronounced. While Kennedy's majority opinion recognized *Widmar* and *Lamb's Chapel* as controlling precedents, Kennedy also acknowledged that *Rosenberger* could be distinguished factually because, unlike in the earlier cases, the university was funding religious activities rather than merely opening its facilities. Regardless, Kennedy concluded that the university would not violate the First Amendment, though in reaching that conclusion Kennedy refused to articulate and apply any specific Establishment Clause test. Instead, Kennedy emphasized that the university's funding program would be religiously neutral so long as it extended "benefits to recipients whose ideologies and viewpoints, including religious ones, are broad and diverse." Thomas, while agreeing with Kennedy's reasoning and conclusion, nonetheless wrote a concurrence that pressed the neoconservative vantage. He started with originalism, arguing that the "right path [of analysis lay] in consulting the original meaning of the Establishment Clause." Because James Madison played a prominent role in the drafting of the First Amendment, many constitutional historians and Supreme Court justices, Thomas included, have assumed that Madison's *Memorial and Remonstrance* provides a window into the meaning of the Establishment Clause. Madison wrote the *Memorial and Remonstrance* in 1785 to oppose a Virginia state legislative bill proposing a general assessment tax for the support of Christianity. Thomas maintained, quite reasonably, that Madison's argument against the tax assessment bill was based (at least in part) on a republican democratic concept of equality. Because, as Thomas phrased it, "the bill singled out religious entities [that is, Christian religions] for special benefits," the bill proposed impermissible class legislation that would have furthered partial or private (or factional) interests rather than the common good. Madison himself wrote (and Thomas quoted): "As the Bill violates equality by subjecting some to peculiar burdens, so it violates the same principle, by granting to others peculiar exemptions." Finally, in Thomas's view, the best interpretation of the *Memorial and Remonstrance* supports nonpreferentialism: "the view that the Framers saw the Establishment Clause simply as a prohibition on governmental preferences for some religious faiths over others."[71]

In subsequent cases that raised but were not ultimately decided on Establishment Clause issues, the justices have continued to press the neoconservative outlook. In *Summum*, the Court relied on the government speech doctrine in upholding a city's refusal to allow the Summum to display a Seven Aphorisms monument in a public park. Alito's majority opinion acknowledged that, even in such situations, the "government speech must comport with the Establishment Clause." Unsurprisingly, then, the concurring justices jockeyed for position vis-à-vis any potential future Establishment Clause claims. While Souter, concurring in the judgment only, stressed that the Court would need to wrestle with these issues in the future, Scalia's concurrence, joined by Thomas, confidently declared that the city's decision to display the Ten Commandments but not the Seven Aphorisms did not violate the Establishment Clause. Meanwhile, in *Elk*

Grove Unified School District v. Newdow, a student's father challenged the public school recitation of the phrase "under God" in the Pledge of Allegiance. The four progressive justices, joined by Kennedy, skirted the Establishment Clause issue by holding that the father, Michael Newdow, lacked standing to bring the suit. Rehnquist, concurring in the judgment and joined by Thomas and O'Connor, reasoned that Newdow had standing but that the school had not violated the Establishment Clause. Rather than apply a specific Establishment Clause test, Rehnquist emphasized a deep national tradition "of patriotic invocations of God and official acknowledgments of religion's role in our Nation's history." The Court, Rehnquist explained, should hesitate before interfering with the attempts of other governmental institutions to promote and sustain such traditional values. "Here, Congress prescribed a Pledge of Allegiance, the State of California required patriotic observances in its schools, and the School District chose to comply by requiring teacher-led recital of the Pledge of Allegiance by willing students." The First Amendment required no more than that schools permit students "to abstain from the ceremony if they chose to do so."[72]

But it was Thomas who pushed the neoconservative envelope to its limits in *Newdow*. He agreed with Rehnquist that Newdow had standing to bring his First Amendment challenge, but unlike Rehnquist, Thomas then launched into an originalist analysis of the Establishment Clause. Referring to the text, contemporaneous interpretations from the time of the framing, and "prevailing" nineteenth-century views of the clause, Thomas concluded that the Establishment Clause should not apply against state and local governments: "The text and history of the Establishment Clause strongly suggest that it is a federalism provision intended to prevent Congress from interfering with state establishments." What did Thomas mean when he called the Establishment Clause a federalism provision? The clause, from this perspective, draws a jurisdictional boundary between national and state sovereignty: The clause "made clear that Congress could not interfere with state establishments, notwithstanding any argument that could be made based on Congress' power under the Necessary and Proper Clause." As Thomas phrased it, "States and only States were the direct beneficiaries" of the Establishment Clause. "Thus," Thomas concluded, "unlike the Free Exercise Clause, which does protect an individual right, it makes little sense to incorporate the Establishment Clause." In other words, if Thomas had his way, with the Court following his originalist analysis, state and local governments not only would be able to promote traditional values but also would be able to establish religions overtly and explicitly without violating the First Amendment. Given this conclusion, incorporation of the Establishment Clause would create a "peculiar" conundrum: "It would prohibit precisely what the Establishment Clause was intended to protect—*state* establishments of religion."[73]

Thomas realized that the other justices (and other Americans, for that matter) might resist undoing more than sixty years of jurisprudence based on the incorporation and application of the Establishment Clause against state and local governments. Therefore, Thomas asked: If one were to stretch to interpret the Establishment Clause as originally protecting an individual right against the national government—an individual right that could at least feasibly be incorporated to apply against state and local governments—what would be the content of that individual right? The "best argument," according to Thomas, "would be that, by disabling Congress from establishing a national religion, the [Establishment] Clause protected an individual right, enforceable against the Federal Government, to be free from *coercive* federal establishments." Translating Thomas's argument into the language of the competing Establishment Clause doctrines—the *Lemon* test, the endorsement test, and the coercion test—if any individual right is to be incorporated, its contours should be determined pursuant to the coercion test. Moreover, Thomas conceptualized coercion in its narrowest sense: Only legal "compulsion" would amount to coercion. While some other justices had reasoned that coercion could arise indirectly from psychological pressure (to conform to certain religious practices), Thomas agreed with Scalia: To be constitutionally cognizable, coercion must be "by force of law and threat of penalty." When conceptualized in this manner, Thomas added, the coercion test corresponds with nonpreferentialism. True, government cannot *prefer* "particular religious faiths," but constitutionally cognizable governmental preference does not exist unless the government coerces citizens (by force of law and threat of penalty) to follow or support (financially) a specific religion or religions. Finally, and perhaps needless to say, given this minimalist interpretation of the Establishment Clause, Thomas concluded that the First Amendment does not preclude schools from leading students in the recitation of the phrase "under God" in the Pledge of Allegiance.[74]

Counterfactual Cases

This section examines cases (or series of cases) where the Court appears to decide contrary to what the previous discussion might suggest. In other words, these are the decisions where the reader might declare, "Wait a second! You claim that neoconservatism influences the Court, or at least four of the justices, but what about such-and-such a case?" I will approach these counterfactuals in order of increasing complexity, starting with substantive due process, moving to foreign policy, and ending with campaign finance.

Substantive Due Process

Does the substantive due process right of privacy preclude the government from criminally punishing acts of homosexual sodomy? The neoconservative answer to this question would seem clear: The drive for moral clarity demands that society be empowered to differentiate homosexuality from heterosexuality. If a particular community would prefer to discourage and punish homosexuality (because of moral and religious values), then the Court should not stand in the way.

The Court first addressed this issue in 1986 in the case of *Bowers v. Hardwick*. In a five-to-four decision, the Court held that the state of Georgia's criminal conviction of Hardwick for engaging in homosexual sodomy in his own home did not violate his constitutional right of privacy. The majority opinion emphasized that a state can legislate morality—that it was constitutional for Georgia to declare homosexual sodomy "immoral and unacceptable." As Chief Justice Burger declared in the Court's post–oral argument conference, "Our society has values that should be protected."[75]

The issue returned to the Court in 2003, in *Lawrence v. Texas*. Given the *Lawrence* Court's conservative bona fides and the precedent of *Bowers*, one might have reasonably expected the justices to hold, once again, that the government can punish homosexual conduct without contravening the right of privacy. Yet *Lawrence* went in the opposite direction. In a six-to-three decision, the Court overruled *Bowers* and held that a law criminalizing homosexual sodomy violated substantive due process. The three neoconservative justices then sitting on the Court (Scalia, Thomas, and Rehnquist) all dissented. Who conspicuously refused to join this dissenting group? The country-club Republicans: Kennedy and O'Connor. In other words, Kennedy and

O'Connor, economically conservative but indifferent or moderate on many social issues, prevented the neocons from imposing their desired moral clarity.[76]

Thus, in terms of understanding neoconservatism and its influence on the Court, *Lawrence* is unsurprising. If the neocons—Scalia, Thomas, and Rehnquist—had voted to invalidate the restriction on homosexuality, then the case would have been shocking. But the fact that Kennedy and O'Connor voted with the liberals in this context is not unexpected. In fact, Kennedy wrote the majority opinion, joined by the four liberals: Stevens, Ginsburg, Breyer, and Souter (O'Connor concurred in the judgment only and wrote her own opinion focusing on equal protection rather than on due process). Kennedy emphasized that substantive due process protects, as a matter of dignity, the right of individuals to make choices regarding intimate conduct and relationships. But what about moral clarity? Kennedy acknowledged that *Bowers* was based on the broad point "that for centuries there have been powerful voices to condemn homosexual conduct as immoral. The condemnation has been shaped by religious beliefs, conceptions of right and acceptable behavior, and respect for the traditional family." Yet, Kennedy reasoned, these moral considerations were not determinative: "'Our obligation is to define the liberty of all, not to mandate our own moral code.'"[77]

Scalia was furious. In his dissent, he wrote, "State laws against bigamy, same-sex marriage, adult incest, prostitution, masturbation, adultery, fornication, bestiality, and obscenity are likewise sustainable only in light of *Bowers'* validation of laws based on moral choices." Of course, in most constitutional realms, Kennedy agrees with his neoconservative colleagues, but in cases involving individual dignity, he often goes his own way (though when O'Connor was on the Court, she and Kennedy sometimes agreed). Thus, whereas Kennedy reasoned in *Lawrence* that "[h]istory and tradition are the starting point but not in all cases the ending point of the substantive due process inquiry," Scalia instead insisted that substantive due process protects only rights "which are 'deeply rooted in this Nation's history and tradition.'" Indeed, Kennedy's desire to protect individual dignity and liberty in the face of claims to moral clarity also explains his controversial votes and opinions in substantive due process cases involving a woman's right to choose abortion, such as *Planned Parenthood v. Casey*, in which he co-wrote the joint opinion reaffirming *Roe v. Wade*.[78]

Foreign Policy

Neoconservative foreign policy can be reduced to three fundamental principles: first, an emphasis on moral clarity, including the universal superiority of democracy and freedom; second, the necessity of pressing regime change so as to promote democracy and freedom; and third, the willingness of the United States to take unilateral action, if necessary, to generate regime change and otherwise fulfill the nation's moral mission. Given this, the Court has *not* adjudicated any foreign policy cases that allowed the justices to articulate positions either harmonious or incompatible with these principles.

The Court, however, has decided in recent years important cases involving the war on terrorism, several of which concerned the scope of executive authority. Specifically, would the justices subscribe to the theory of a unitary executive? In general, according to this theory, the president holds "unitary authority over the execution of federal law." Consequently, the president must have the "power to remove subordinate policy-making officials at will, the . . . power to direct the manner in which subordinate officials exercise discretionary executive power, and the power to veto or nullify such officials' exercises of discretionary executive power." While even a weak manifestation of this theory can prove controversial, President George W. Bush pushed for the implementation of a "super-strong" unitary executive.[79]

In the aftermath of the attacks of September 11, 2001, Bush insisted that he had seemingly unfettered power in the battle against terrorists. The administration argued that the president's status as commander-in-chief of the armed forces combined with his power under the "take care" clause to invest him with an inherent power to take whatever actions were necessary to press the war on terror, even if such actions otherwise violated congressional and constitutional directives. Thus, for example, in the infamous "torture memorandum" of August 1, 2002, Jay S. Bybee and John Yoo of the Office of Legal Counsel concluded that the Constitution shielded executive officials from potential prosecutions: "[B]oth courts and prosecutors should reject prosecutions that apply federal criminal laws to activity that is authorized pursuant to one of the President's constitutional powers." In effect, the administration insisted that the president could infringe civil liberties and disregard statutory and constitutional law without being subject to judicial control. Pursuant to this position, the administration argued that it could hold a citizen indefinitely, without according him or her due process, if it designated the citizen an "enemy combatant." Likewise, the administration maintained that it could hold prisoners at Guantánamo, Cuba, without giving them an opportunity to challenge the legality of their detentions. In short, Bush II acted pursuant to such an extreme version of the unitary executive theory that the administration inevitably found itself challenged in court.[80]

To be clear, Bush II's super-strong theory of the unitary executive was not (and is not) a fundamental neoconservative principle. Rather, the Bush administration developed the super-strong theory as a political expedient. When Bush eventually encountered political opposition against his efforts to fight the war on terror and the Iraq War, his administration articulated the super-strong theory to justify persistence, despite ongoing controversy. In other words, some members of the administration advocated for the super-strong theory of the unitary executive as a tool that could help the president achieve certain goals, such as the indefinite detainment of enemy combatants and the continued fighting of the Iraq War. Of course, this designation of the super-strong theory as merely instrumental and therefore distinct from neoconservatism proper can be contested. For instance, one might argue that the nation needs a super-strong unitary executive to implement unilateralism: that the dispersal or diminishment of executive power would render unilateral national action difficult or even impossible. Moreover, as already discussed, the extensive cross-pollination among the various forms of conservatism renders any precise categorization of specific policies problematic, whether we are focusing on the unitary executive and neoconservatism or otherwise. Nevertheless, the fact remains: Leading foreign policy neocons like Norman Podhoretz and William Kristol never advocated for unfettered executive power. Bush administration officials were the first to articulate the super-strong theory of the unitary executive, and they did so only when necessary to justify certain controversial political positions and actions. Unsurprisingly, then, some neocons eventually accepted the super-strong theory; the political scientist Harvey Mansfield is the most conspicuous example.[81]

Even if the super-strong theory was grounded on neoconservative principles, one might expect the justices to resist any such challenge to their own judicial power. Thus, given the actual disjunction between the super-strong theory and neoconservatism, the Court's repudiations of the

Bush administration's positions when adjudicating aspects of the unitary executive were entirely predictable. For example, in *Hamdi v. Rumsfeld*, the administration clearly asserted powers commensurate with the super-strong theory. "The Government contends that Hamdi [who is a U.S. citizen] is an 'enemy combatant,'" O'Connor's plurality opinion explained, "and that this status justifies holding him in the United States indefinitely—without formal charges or proceedings—unless and until it makes the determination that access to counsel or further process is warranted." Eight of the justices rebuked the administration's position. According to O'Connor (joined by Rehnquist, Kennedy, and Breyer), even though Hamdi was an enemy combatant, due process required that he "be given a meaningful opportunity to contest the factual basis for that detention before a neutral decisionmaker." Meanwhile, Scalia wrote an opinion—joined by Stevens!—reasoning that the government's detention of Hamdi was illegal in the first place and that the Court therefore did not need to prescribe due process requirements. In sum, the justices would not succumb to the administration's demands for largely unfettered power, free of judicial oversight. As a Court majority declared in another case, quite simply, "the Executive is bound to comply with the rule of law."[82]

Campaign Finance

Are campaign finance regulations constitutional? More specifically, can Congress restrict the amount of money that corporations can spend on political campaign advertisements without violating the First Amendment protection of free speech? In *Citizens United v. Federal Election Commission*, decided in 2010, Kennedy joined the four neoconservative justices to outvote the four liberal justices and to invalidate just such a restriction.[83]

The analysis of the constitutionality of campaign finance regulations might seem to turn in part on whether the expenditure of money on political campaigns constitutes expression: Either spending money is deemed to be expression, or it is not. Yet under republican democracy the result would be the same, either way. If, on the one hand, spending money is not expression, then campaign finance regulations literally do not raise any First Amendment issues. Such regulations would unquestionably be constitutional, at least vis-à-vis free expression. If, on the other hand, spending money on political campaigns constitutes a form of expression—as the

Citizens United majority concluded it does—then the regulations should still be deemed constitutional. Why so? Because during the republican democratic era, the Court upheld restrictions on free expression so long as the restrictions promoted a virtuous citizenry and the common good. Under republican democracy, the right to free expression—even for political speech and writing—always remained subordinate to the common good. And, in fact, the Court found every judicially challenged restriction on free expression to be constitutional until 1931.[84]

How do restrictions on corporate political spending promote the common good? From an empirical standpoint, evidence suggests that corporate expenditures on political campaigns corrupt citizens and elected officials and thus ultimately skew democracy. If corporate spending is speech, in other words, then it is speech with bad tendencies, to use republican democratic parlance. As Justice Stevens, joined by the other liberal justices—Ginsburg, Breyer, and Sotomayor—stressed in his *Citizens United* dissent, Congress had relied on "evidence of corruption" when legislating the campaign restrictions. Moreover, extensive social science research shows that wealth—especially massive corporate wealth—affects democracy in two ways. First, it can shape the outcomes of elections. For instance, because running for office requires massive funding, wealthy contributors can "determine the pools of potential officeholders." More broadly, social and cognitive psychology research demonstrates that wealth can be used to fund campaign strategies that purposefully manipulate the electorate and "induce sub-optimal vote decisions." Second, after the elections, wealth can influence the behavior of elected officials. Money buys "privileged access for contributors [including] the special attention of [congressional committee] members who reward them with vigorous help in minding their business in the committee process."[85]

The *Citizens United* majority acknowledged that prior cases had recognized that the government has an interest in thwarting "corruption or its appearance"—an interest that sometimes justifies campaign finance restrictions. For two interrelated reasons, though, the majority concluded that this governmental interest could not justify the restrictions on expenditures at issue in *Citizens United*. First, the majority used such a cramped concept of corruption that much of the empirical evidence (of corruption) was rendered irrelevant. Second, because the Court emphasized that free expression is a constitutional lodestar, the Court required the government to satisfy strict scrutiny by showing that the disputed restrictions were narrowly tailored to achieve a compelling purpose. And from the majority's perspective, the government failed to present any purposes—preventing corruption or otherwise—that could be found compelling. As the Court concluded, "The anticorruption interest is not sufficient to displace the speech here in question."[86]

But isn't this all backward? The dissenting liberal justices were worried about "moral decay" in the polity, while the conservative majority, including the neocons, categorized free speech as a constitutional lodestar and invoked the self-governance rationale, which became predominant only during the pluralist democratic era. "Speech is an essential mechanism of democracy," Kennedy wrote. "The right of citizens to inquire, to hear, to speak, and to use information to reach consensus is a precondition to enlightened self-government and a necessary means to protect it." How did the conservative justices ever end up here?[87]

There is an explanation, and it's rooted in pluralist democracy itself or, more precisely, in the transformation of pluralist democracy into a consumers' and then corporate-dominated democracy, discussed in chapter 3. During the first decades of the post–World War II (pluralist democratic) era, conservatives rarely supported assertions of civil liberties and generally agreed that governmental interests—for instance, in national security—could overcome the First Amendment protection of free expression. To put it in different words, during the early pluralist democratic epoch, conservatives resisted the claim that free expression was a constitutional lodestar.[88] Yet as pluralist democracy evolved, entwining with the mass-consumer culture, conservatives became increasingly protective of free expression, at least in certain contexts.

In 1942, soon after pluralist democracy supplanted republican democracy, the Supreme Court held that the First Amendment did not protect commercial expression. The regulation of commercial advertising, at the time, seemed no different from other permissible governmental regulations of the economic marketplace. But after World War II, as the mass-consumer culture became increasingly entangled with democratic processes, the Court modified its treatment of commercial expression. *Bigelow v. Virginia*, decided in 1975, arose when a newspaper editor ran an advertisement for the Women's Pavilion, which provided abortion services in another state. The state of Virginia convicted the editor for violating a statute that proscribed any "advertisement" that would "encourage or prompt the procuring of abortion." Justice Harry Blackmun wrote an opinion for a seven-justice majority holding the conviction unconstitutional. He began by acknowledging the Court's prior recognition of several low-value "categories of speech—such as fighting words, or obscenity, or libel, or incitement—[which] have been held unprotected." Nonetheless, Blackmun insisted that "commercial advertising enjoys a degree of First Amendment protection." Advertising was no longer "unprotected per se," though the Court allowed that it could "be subject to reasonable regulation." Then, by applying a balancing test, weighing the governmental interest in regulation against the First Amendment interest in free expression, the Court held this particular statutory proscription unconstitutional.[89]

In subsequent cases, the Court continued to resolve commercial-expression issues pursuant to a balancing test, though the justices would repeatedly tinker with the details of the test. Equally important, the Court explained that the First Amendment protected advertising because commercial expression and pluralist democracy were inseparable. By the mid-1970s, practically all constitutional law scholars and justices agreed that free expression was a prerequisite for pluralist democracy. If citizens could not freely express their political interests and values, then they could not fully participate in democracy. And if this self-governance rationale held true for political speech and writing, then commercial expression required at least some degree of constitutional protection, too—or at least so reasoned the Court in *Virginia State Board of Pharmacy v. Virginia Citizens Consumer Council*, which held unconstitutional a state law prohibiting licensed pharmacists from advertising prescription drug prices. Democracy involves the allocation of resources in society, the Court explained, but most resource-allocation decisions are made through the economic marketplace. Capitalism and democracy, to the Court, are correlative. "Advertising, however tasteless and excessive it sometimes may seem, is . . . dissemination of information as to who is producing and selling what product, for what reason, and at what price," Blackmun wrote for an eight-justice majority. "So long as we preserve a predominantly free enterprise economy, the allocation of our resources in large measure will be made through numerous private economic decisions. It is a matter of public interest that those decisions, in the aggregate, be intelligent and well informed. To this end, the free flow of commercial information is indispensable." In other words, the

Court concluded that advertising is essential for "the proper allocation of resources in a free enterprise system." Furthermore, advertising contributes to intelligent decision making about how the economic marketplace "ought to be regulated or altered." Finally, regardless of the overarching importance of broad political debates and democratic decision making—whether about economic regulations, candidates for high office, or otherwise—Blackmun stressed that most people care more about their personal consumer-oriented decisions. "As to the particular consumer's interest in the free flow of commercial information, that interest may be as keen, if not keener by far, than his interest in the day's most urgent political debate."[90]

In short, the development of the consumers' democracy changed how the justices, particularly the conservative ones, viewed free expression. Free expression no longer was merely a civil liberty to be asserted by minorities and dissidents. Because of the fusion of democracy and the mass-consumer culture, the expenditure of wealth had become integral to politics. Spending money, it now seemed, became a form of political expression. In this context, the Court first examined the constitutionality of campaign finance regulations. The seminal *Buckley v. Valeo*, decided in 1976, invalidated a statutory restriction on campaign expenditures made by candidates, individuals, or groups (read: political action committees). The Court stressed the political importance of spending money in our consumers' democracy. "A restriction on the amount of money a person or group can spend on political communication during a campaign necessarily reduces the quantity of expression by restricting the number of issues discussed, the depth of their exploration, and the size of the audience reached." Money had now become speech "because virtually every means of communicating ideas in today's mass society requires the expenditure of money." Emphasizing the confrontational political battles characteristic of pluralist democracy (rather than the supposedly virtuous civil exchanges that might generate the republican democratic common good), the Court evoked the self-governance rationale in concluding that limits on expenditures were unconstitutional. "[T]he concept that government may restrict the speech of some elements of our society in order to enhance the relative voice of others is wholly foreign to the First Amendment, which was designed 'to secure "the widest possible dissemination of information from diverse and antagonistic sources,"' and 'to assure unfettered interchange of ideas for the bringing about of political and social changes desired by the people.'"[91]

The *Buckley* Court did not explicitly discuss restrictions on corporate campaign expenditures, but the justices addressed that issue two years later in *First National Bank of Boston v. Bellotti*. The Court invalidated a state law that prohibited business corporations from spending money to influence voters in referendum elections. The crux of the Court's reasoning was, again, the self-governance rationale: "[T]here is practically universal agreement that a major purpose of [the First] Amendment was to protect the free discussion of governmental affairs." If the speakers here were not corporations, no one would suggest that the state could silence their proposed speech. It is the type of speech indispensable to decision making in a democracy, and this is no less true because the speech comes from a corporation rather than an individual. The inherent worth of the speech in terms of its capacity for informing the public does not depend upon the identity of its source, whether corporation, association, union, or individual.[92]

Cases subsequent to *Buckley* and *Bellotti* revealed the justices to be waffling somewhat about the degree to which the government could regulate corporate political expression. But the emergence of corporate-controlled democracy—Democracy, Inc.—augured a definitive end to the waffling, and it arrived in *Citizens United*. The conservative justices forming the *Citizens United* majority stressed that the self-governance rationale mandates free expression to be a constitutional lodestar, that spending money on campaigns is political speech, and that most restrictions on corporate political expenditures must, therefore, be held unconstitutional. What about originalism, though? Conservatives—and especially neocons—typically advocate for an originalist reading of the Constitution, and indeed, the *Citizens United* majority claimed to follow an originalist interpretation of the Free Speech Clause. "There is simply no support for the view that the First Amendment, as originally understood, would permit the suppression of political speech by media corporations," the Court stated. Yet surely this conclusion is inconsistent with the republican democratic history of the Constitution. Indeed, Justice Stevens's *Citizens United* dissent highlighted the hollowness of the majority's originalist argument. "[T]he Framers and their contemporaries conceived of speech more narrowly than we now think of it," Stevens wrote. "[T]hey held very different views about the nature of the First Amendment right and the role of corporations in society." Nevertheless, given the development of Democracy, Inc., the stance of the conservative justices is unsurprising. While the neocons generally seek to implement republican democratic principles, such as moral clarity, the justices still must decide cases within the current context of pluralist democracy. And within that context, within Democracy, Inc., the conservatives could readily define corporate wealth to be a proxy for speech and deem the First Amendment a shield for corporate expenditures, thus assuring even greater corporate control over democracy and government.[93]

6

The Supreme Court in the Future

Most commentators would agree that five of the current Supreme Court justices are conservatives, but many of those same commentators would quarrel with my characterization of four of those justices—Scalia, Thomas, Roberts, and Alito—as neoconservatives. Yet, if neoconservatism, as I define it, is compared with the other leading contemporary forms of conservatism, traditionalism and libertarianism, one discovers that neoconservatism best fits the corpus of the Court's decisions and opinions over approximately the previous two decades. Confusion arises partly because neoconservatism overlaps with traditionalism and libertarianism. The predominant neoconservative themes, derived from the critique of pluralist democracy and concomitant advocacy for republican democracy, are twofold: first, an insistence on and drive for moral clarity; and second, a skepticism toward governmental social engineering programs (particularly of the liberal variety). Traditionalists, though, also tend to emphasize moral clarity: They revere tradition and religion as sources of values. Meanwhile, libertarians also stress skepticism toward governmental programs; they emphasize individual liberty and minimal government above all else.

Consequently, many Supreme Court decisions and opinions that I categorize as neoconservative could also be deemed either traditionalist or libertarian. But—and here's the crucial point—many cases could not be reasonably categorized as both traditionalist *and* libertarian (or could be categorized as such but only with great difficulty). In other words, cases promoting moral clarity, such as *Morse v. Frederick* (upholding a principal's punishment of a student who displayed a "BONG HiTS 4 JESUS" banner) or *Pleasant Grove City v. Summum* (upholding the government's decision to ban a minority religious display in a public park), can be fairly characterized as both neoconservative and traditionalist but cannot be characterized as libertarian. If anything, in these cases the Court upheld governmental actions that diminish individual liberty. Simultaneously, cases repudiating governmental power to create and implement social programs, such as *United States v. Lopez* (invalidating a statute prohibiting guns on school property) and *Boerne v. Flores* (invalidating a statute protecting religious minorities), can be fairly characterized as both neoconservative and libertarian but cannot be characterized as traditionalist. In these cases, the Court refused to allow the government to promote certain values (nonviolence and religiosity, respectively). In short, some cases are traditionalist and some are libertarian, but the largest number fit under the umbrella of neoconservatism.

But isn't there still a catch? Namely, I argue that the corpus of the Court's work over the past twenty years corresponds closely with neoconservatism, *as I define it*. But some commentators would insist that my characterization of neoconservatism is wrong. And to be sure, at this point in time, any definition or depiction of neoconservatism will inevitably be controversial. In a sense, neoconservatism lost a degree of coherence when it cross-pollinated with other conservative movements and sacrificed its precision for political power. Remember, it was none other than the neoconservative impresario Irving Kristol who admitted, "The task, as I saw it, was to create . . . a Republican majority—so political effectiveness was the priority."[1] On top of that, as neoconservatives became politically prominent, some critics would too readily label almost any objectionable conservative policy as neoconservative. Indeed, this ambiguity—the loose use of the term *neoconservatism*—prompted the first goal of this book: to present a narrative history of neoconservatism that would illuminate its purposes and policies. To do so, I primarily went to the origins. I sought to uncover the themes that early neocons—Kristol, Daniel Bell, Norman Podhoretz, and their ilk—developed. With regard to foreign policy, I followed developments from Cold War neoconservatives to the next generation, such as William Kristol. Most important, by closely attending to the neoconservative texts, I was able to depict a coherent intellectual and political movement. It is that coherent movement—neoconservatism—that I then used to achieve the second goal of the book: to explain how neoconservatism influenced or was manifested in Supreme Court constitutional adjudication. Undoubtedly, some readers will react, "But what about so-and-so? Isn't he or she a neocon?" Or, "What about such-and-such Bush II policy? Isn't that neoconservative?" I have two reactions to such criticisms. First, I do not claim that my definition of *neoconservatism* is the only reasonable one. Rather, I claim that my definition is valid—based on the neoconservative texts themselves—and illuminating, especially when used to analyze Supreme Court cases. Second, I caution against defining *neoconservatism* too capaciously. If too many people and too many principles and policies are brought within the circle of neoconservatism, then the term loses its significance. *Neoconservatism* becomes synonymous with *conservatism*.

In any event, despite the movement's many successes, the neoconservative agenda has not been completely fulfilled in any constitutional realm. Establishment Clause jurisprudence is typical. Neoconservative justices have strongly influenced case outcomes: Over the past twenty-five years, the Court's decisions have consistently bolstered governmental and private efforts to promote traditional American (and Christian) values. While the Court has not explicitly repudiated the wall metaphor—the idea that a high wall separates church and state—case outcomes have corresponded increasingly with the nonpreferentialist position—the idea that government can support religion so long as it does not prefer one religion over another. Yet the Court has never expressly adopted nonpreferentialism. Moreover, as advocated by neocons, the justices will discuss originalist interpretations of the Establishment Clause, but a majority has never committed to following the original meaning and nothing else. Ultimately, those judicial opinions in which the most enthusiastic neoconservative justices proffer their strongest neoconservative arguments turn out to be concurring or dissenting rather than majority.

Taken together, the two opposed Ten Commandments cases decided in 2005 exemplify the only-partial realization of the neoconservative agenda. In *Van Orden v. Perry*, the Court decided five to four that a Ten Commandments monument standing in a monument park near the Texas state capitol did not violate the Establishment Clause. Rehnquist announced the Court's judgment, but he could not carry a majority on his opinion. Scalia, Thomas, and Kennedy joined Rehnquist, but Breyer wrote separately to concur in the judgment only. Rehnquist's plurality opinion emphasized that religion has played a "strong role . . . throughout our Nation's history" and that "[o]ur institutions presuppose a Supreme Being." Rehnquist refused to apply the *Lemon* test and instead concluded that the Establishment Clause allowed the government to display a monument promoting traditional and religious values because such displays were, well, traditional. Quoting from *Lynch v. Donnelly*, which had upheld the public display of a crèche, Rehnquist wrote, "'There is an unbroken history of official acknowledgment by all three branches of government of the role of religion in American life from at least 1789.'" Basically, the government can continue to promote religious values and symbols because it has always done so. "Simply having religious content or promoting a message consistent with a religious doctrine does not run afoul of the Establishment Clause."[2]

But in *McCreary County v. ACLU*, Breyer joined the *Van Orden* dissenters—the other three progressive justices (Stevens, Ginsburg, and Souter)—and O'Connor to form a five-justice majority holding that displays of the Ten Commandments in county courthouses violate the Establishment Clause. Souter's opinion, molded perhaps to retain O'Connor in the majority, avoided explicit reliance on *Lemon*. Souter explained that *Lemon* had "summarized . . . three familiar considerations for evaluating establishment clause claims," yet he never expressly articulated the three prongs. Indeed, when he emphasized that the postings of the Ten Commandments revealed a purpose "to favor religion," Souter quoted from O'Connor's *Lynch* concurrence explicating the endorsement test. Meanwhile, Scalia's *McCreary* dissent, joined by Rehnquist, Thomas, and Kennedy (in part), asserted the neoconservative viewpoint. Scalia used an originalist analysis to underscore the importance of moral clarity: "Those who wrote the Constitution believed that morality was essential to the well-being of society and that encouragement of religion was the best way to foster morality." The Establishment Clause thus should not prevent the government from continuing to acknowledge "the contribution that religion has made to our Nation's legal and governmental heritage." Consequently, Scalia repudiated the *Lemon* test and the wall metaphor, which required "neutrality between religion and irreligion," and advocated instead for nonpreferentialism. But it bears emphasis that Scalia wrote only a dissenting opinion in *McCreary*, though the conservatives managed to carry the day in *Van Orden*. Plus, Scalia could not hold Kennedy for all of his dissent. Kennedy refused to join the part that most strongly asserted a neoconservative vantage: that because the Establishment Clause allows the government to recognize and support religion in general, the clause inevitably allows government, in the United States, to recognize and support specifically monotheistic religions, particularly those that follow the Ten Commandments.[3]

Neocons Empowered

Neoconservativism has strongly influenced Supreme Court decision making in Establishment Clause cases: Many case outcomes correspond with neoconservative views, and many opinions reveal neoconservative influences. Even so, the neocons have neither won every case nor carried majorities when most aggressively pronouncing their positions. And the same is true in other constitutional areas, whether congressional power, affirmative action, free expression, or elsewhere. But what about the future? Recent political developments have set the stage for a long-running play ridden with tension between the Court and the other federal branches. The Democrats captured the presidency and retained Congress in the 2008 elections, yet the Court had already become more strongly neoconservative than ever before, given the recent additions of Roberts and Alito—especially with Alito replacing the more moderate O'Connor in 2006. Thus, it bears repeating, despite the appointments of Sotomayor and Kagan and the possibility that President Obama might eventually appoint another justice, the Court will likely retain its current alignment, with five conservatives and four liberals (or progressives), for several years. Most Court observers identify Kennedy's as the swing vote on the Roberts Court, and he scored a solidly conservative .365 on the Segal–Cover political ideology rankings. Moreover, even though Republicans will occasionally control Congress and the presidency over the next few years, the aggressive and confident neoconservative justices will push ahead, seeking to implement their interpretation of the Constitution. Regardless of whether Republicans or Democrats control the coordinate branches, the neoconservative judicial approach will inevitably clash with congressional and executive actions—more so, certainly, when Democrats hold the levers of power. Assuming, then, as is most probable, that the current conservative–progressive alignment of the Court remains intact, how will the neoconservative justices shape the likely constitutional disputes?[4]

Of course, sustained political tension between the Supreme Court and other governmental institutions is not historically unprecedented. The earliest conflict arose soon after the adoption of the Constitution. In the first decades of nationhood, political parties as we know them did not exist (a party was considered to be a faction bent on corrupting republican democratic government). Nonetheless, during the 1790s, the people's loyalties divided between two "proto-parties": the Federalists, led by Alexander Hamilton and John Adams, and the Republicans, led by Thomas Jefferson and James Madison. When the Republicans swept the elections of 1800, capturing the presidency and Congress, the lame-duck Adams administration and Federalist Senate sought to stock the federal judiciary with as many Federalist judges as possible within the brief time remaining before the Republicans took control. These events led directly to the Supreme Court's 1803 decision in *Marbury v. Madison*. William Marbury was one of the last Federalist judicial appointees, and in fact, despite having already been appointed and confirmed, he had not officially received his commission when the Adams presidency expired. The new president, Jefferson, and his Secretary of State, Madison, refused to deliver the commission, so Marbury sued in the Federalist-controlled Supreme Court for a writ of *mandamus* that would order Madison to deliver the commission. Although wary of the political hostilities, the Federalist Chief Justice, John Marshall, writing for a unanimous Court, held that the Court possessed the power to review the constitutionality of executive and congressional actions. But after articulating the Court's power of judicial review, Marshall avoided issuing a direct challenge to the Republicans—and the likely refusal of President Jefferson to enforce a Supreme Court order—by ultimately holding that the Court lacked jurisdiction to decide the case. Thus, the Republicans were not especially perturbed with the outcome: Marbury lost because the Court would not issue his requested *mandamus*. Still, the

Republicans remained disgruntled with the Federalist-controlled judiciary, especially with Justice Samuel Chase. Openly flaunting his Federalist politics while riding circuit, Chase charged the Republicans with leading the nation toward "mobocracy." Seeking retribution, Republicans in the House of Representatives impeached Chase in early 1804 on eight counts alleging various partisan actions related to his judicial duties. At the time, Republicans held twenty-one of the thirty-four Senate seats, but they could not muster the two-thirds supermajority needed to convict on any count (a slight majority supported conviction on two of the counts). If the Senate had removed Chase, some Republicans purportedly were ready to attempt next to remove Marshall from office.[5]

Another famous dispute between the Court, on the one hand, and the president and Congress, on the other hand, erupted in the 1930s. With the nation struggling through the Great Depression, a conservative and mostly Republican Court clashed repeatedly with President Franklin Roosevelt and a Democratic Congress that sought to implement the New Deal. During the early 1930s, the Court sometimes upheld and sometimes invalidated New Deal statutes, often condemning them as promoting a partial or private interest rather than the common good. But in a spate of cases decided in 1935 and 1936, the Court seemed to become determined to thwart New Deal legislation. Roosevelt, after being reelected in a landslide in 1936, responded by proposing what became known as the Court-packing plan: For every justice over the age of seventy, the president could appoint an additional justice, up to a maximum of fifteen. Of course, if implemented, this plan would have allowed Roosevelt to fill the Court with New Deal supporters. Such a bald political attempt to manipulate the Court generated concern even among New Dealers, but before Congress could vote, the Court took its 1937 turn toward pluralist democracy. From that point forward, the Court's implementation of its power of judicial review changed, and the justices consistently upheld New Deal legislation. Then, in May 1937, during congressional debates over the Court-packing plan, a conservative justice retired, giving Roosevelt his first opportunity to appoint a New Dealer to the Court. Thus, when Congress finally voted on and defeated the plan, its importance had been rendered moot and a constitutional crisis averted.[6]

To be sure, if either of these two disputes—the *Marbury*–Chase affair or the Court-packing plan—had ended differently, the role of the Supreme

Court in American government and politics might have been profoundly transformed. As it is, the two confrontations reveal key aspects of Supreme Court relations with the more partisan political branches. On the one side, the justices are likely to realize that if they depart too far from the partisan political mainstream, other governmental institutions can bring to bear extraordinary political pressure. Thus, political scientists have long observed that, as a general matter, the Court rarely drifts too far left or right from the contemporary political middle. On the other side, political actors in the executive branch and Congress are likely to recognize that overt political measures intended to pressure the justices can be difficult to implement. Even when dissatisfaction with the Court is widespread, the perception that such measures might undermine judicial independence can diminish public support. Yet in many instances, the mere threat to implement such political measures might suffice to influence the justices; actual implementation might be unnecessary.[7]

These two aspects of Supreme Court relations with Congress and the presidency—which bespeak moderation—are likely to shape the evolving positions of the current neoconservative Court whenever it confronts the legislative and executive branches. Yet neocons are renowned for their confident and aggressive assertions of power. Might the neoconservative justices thus repudiate temperance and push hard to the right? Probably not. Surrounding circumstances might demand a degree of moderation, whether the neoconservative justices embrace it happily or not. For years now, neocons in general and neoconservative constitutional theorists in particular have advocated for the resurrection of republican democracy, but the successful fulfillment of this overarching neoconservative goal has always been problematic if not impossible, as I have argued. The social and cultural foundations for republican democracy no longer exist in the United States, and consequently, over time, pluralist democracy has become deeply ensconced. Given this situation, one should not expect the neoconservative justices to usher in a new republican democratic regime. So long as American society remains committed to a pluralist democratic form of government—likely to be true for the foreseeable future—one should expect the Court to incorporate only bits and pieces of republican democracy into the larger pluralist democratic framework. That is, our neoconservative Court is likely to cut and paste: cutting elements of pluralist democracy and pasting in swatches of republican democratic judicial review, when possible, but recognizing that the system remains pluralist democratic. To be sure, the neoconservative justices might contemplate pushing further, disregarding the main parameters of our pluralist democratic system. They might, after all, think they have nothing to lose—enjoying, of course, lifetime appointments—yet more likely, they would fear that pushing too hard, especially against a Democratic Congress, Democratic president, or both, could generate a constitutional crisis. Ultimately, the justices are likely to heed the forces of moderation and not depart too radically from the political mainstream.[8]

In fact, "cutting and pasting" usefully describes much of the Court's jurisprudence over the past two decades, during the Rehnquist Court and early Roberts Court years. In the realm of Congress's commerce power, for instance, the *Lopez* Court injected certain formalist elements characteristic of republican democratic judicial review into its review of the Gun-Free School Zones Act, which proscribed the possession of firearms at school. Yet the *Lopez* Court claimed only to reformulate the rational basis test—Congress would still be empowered to regulate activities substantially affecting interstate commerce—even though such a doctrinal approach resonated with pluralist democracy. In the Establishment Clause realm, the neoconservative justices have severely weakened the *Lemon* test and its implementation of the wall metaphor, yet the neocons have been unable to persuade a majority to adopt nonpreferentialism unequivocally. This "cutting and pasting" leads the justices, in effect, to joust with other governmental officials and institutions in a type of dialogue: The justices will attempt to influence or force others to accept or incorporate elements of republican democracy into our governmental system, while other governmental actors and institutions compel the justices to acquiesce in the operation of pluralist democracy. When the *Lopez* Court invalidated the GFSZA, it questioned Congress's failure to make sufficiently detailed findings in support of the statute. So, when Congress enacted the Violence Against Women Act, it deliberated extensively and reported detailed findings connecting interstate commerce with violence against women. The *Morrison* Court nonetheless dismissed these findings as inadequate and held part of VAWA unconstitutional, but Congress continued, of course, to implement its commerce power, twice reauthorizing other parts of VAWA. The Court and the Congress—the Congress and the Court—each will continue to speak and to react to the other as they proclaim their respective positions.[9]

Where, then, will the neoconservative justices seek to paste in pieces of republican democracy in the future? One might expect the Court to continue stressing the limits of congressional power pursuant to the *Lopez* reformulated rational basis test for the Commerce Clause and the *Boerne* doctrine for the Fourteenth Amendment, section five. The specific statutes targeted by the Court likely will depend on the new legislation enacted by Congress. For instance, the Court might invalidate sections of the recently passed Patient Protection and Affordable Care Act (PPACA). While this book was in production, the Court agreed to review a challenge to the PPACA and set March 26–28, 2012, for oral argument. Health care reform is so central to the Democratic agenda that the justices might hesitate before completely chopping down the PPACA, for fear of provoking sustained political backlash, but hopes for upcoming Republican electoral victories (in November 2012) might temper any such fear. Certainly, though, some older extant statutes are candidates for judicial assault: A prominent example is the Endangered Species Act. The Court could conclude that, under the *Lopez* rational basis test, Congress exceeded its power in passing the Act because its environmental goals are not substantially related to interstate commerce—at least from the perspective of the neoconservative justices. Federal antidiscrimination statutes might also be at risk. The justices could apply the *Lopez* and *Boerne* doctrines to hold that Congress exceeded its commerce and section five powers in passing statutes that protect the elderly, the disabled, and others. In a similar fashion, the justices are likely to push forward their neoconservative precedents in the affirmative action field. Expect the justices to continue emphasizing traditional (strict-in-theory-but-fatal-in-fact) strict scrutiny rather than strict scrutiny lite while narrowing the precedential value of *Grutter*, which upheld Michigan Law School's affirmative action admissions program. The key to such cases, of course, will be Kennedy. While he shies away from joining the most aggressive neoconservative opinions, he nonetheless has joined the majorities in *Lopez*, on the commerce power, and *Adarand* and *Parents Involved*, on affirmative action. Would the neoconservative justices be able to convince Kennedy to take an extra step—for instance, in affirmative action cases—by holding that the Constitution demands the government to be colorblind? *Parents Involved*, in which Kennedy refused to join that part of Roberts's opinion emphasizing colorblindness, suggests otherwise. Kennedy, thus, might dampen any neoconservative impulses to turn hard to the right, thus avoiding a tense confrontation between the Court and other governmental institutions.[10]

What about free expression? Many neoconservative constitutional theorists have argued that the Court should return to a republican democratic approach in free-expression cases so as to facilitate the promotion of "traditional" American values. And certainly, the hybrid free-expression–free-exercise cases demonstrate that the Court is willing to interpret free-expression doctrines to reach republican democratic results in at least some contexts. But will the Court push further? Will the Court, for example, follow Walter Berns's argument that would allow the government to cultivate greater civility by punishing profane or offensive speech? Most recently, the Court upheld a Federal Communications Commission policy that punished television broadcasts of "fleeting expletives," regardless of context. Scalia's majority opinion (joined by Roberts, Alito, Thomas, and Kennedy) explicitly focused on administrative law rather than First Amendment issues, but the decision nonetheless suggested the possibility of a growing judicial acceptance of suppression. Despite skirting potential free-expression issues as improperly raised before the Supreme Court, Scalia added that "any chilled references to excretory and sexual material 'surely lie at the periphery of First Amendment concern.'"[11]

For some neocons, the ultimate goal in the free-expression realm would be to resurrect the bad tendency test that predominated during the republican democratic regime. The return of the bad tendency test would allow the government to punish not only profane and offensive expression but any speech or writing that had bad tendencies or likely harmful consequences. Under the bad tendency test, in other words, the government could punish expression that might be deemed antithetical to a virtuous citizenry or to the common good. Yet the Court seems unlikely to move so dramatically to the right in free-expression cases. *Morse v. Frederick* demonstrates the justices' likely hesitancy in this field. The Court reached the neoconservative result—holding that the school principal could restrict what she deemed to be offensive student expression—but, except for Thomas, the neocon justices wrote opinions retaining pluralist democratic sentiments. And moving beyond the realm of student expression, one can readily discern why the neocon justices might temper their pursuit of republican democracy in free-expression cases. As the discussion of campaign finance in the previous chapter shows, the politics of free expression in general has been rendered ambiguous because of the evolution of pluralist democracy into, first, a consumers' democracy and, then, Democracy, Inc. Conservatives might wish to diminish free-expression rights so as to allow governmental restrictions of offensive or profane expression—hence, the result in *Morse*—but they simultaneously might wish to expand free-expression rights in other areas, particularly to facilitate the protection of monetary expenditures as forms of expression—hence, the result in *Citizens United*, holding that congressionally imposed limits on corporate (and union) spending for political campaign advertisements violate the First Amendment. In short, for many conservatives, an across-the-board return to the bad tendency test might be unacceptable. When the Court can construe the spending of wealth, including corporate wealth, as a form of expression—as it has done in numerous cases besides *Citizens United*—then the justices might be just as comfortable rhapsodizing about free speech being a constitutional lodestar as discerning whether legislatures can designate particular types of speech (or spending) to be harmful (or bad). In the end, if the Court were to institute any major changes in the free-expression realm in the near future, such changes would probably be due to odd coalitions of conservatives and liberals rather than to strong neoconservative influences. For instance, while unlikely, a strange voting alignment could possibly lead the Court to uphold proscriptions on pornography or hate speech. Conservatives might favor such restrictions as a means of promoting civility and virtue, while liberals might favor them as a means of promoting sexual or racial equality.[12]

Finally, where does Kennedy stand in the free-expression area? His votes and opinions manifest his usual moderate conservatism: He seems inclined to reach the neoconservative result, but he does so by applying doctrine that remains at least partly consonant with pluralist democracy rather than suggesting a return to republican democratic doctrine. His votes in *Morse* exemplify his moderation: He joined Roberts's majority opinion, which articulated both republican and pluralist democratic viewpoints while reaching the neoconservative conclusion, and he also joined Alito's concurrence, which reached the same result while relying solely on pluralist democratic principles. Moreover, Kennedy's concern for individual dignity and liberty might sometimes separate him from the neocons in free-speech cases. Only five months after the Court decided *Citizens United*, in which Kennedy joined the neocons—Thomas, Scalia, Alito, and Roberts—the

Court decided another free-expression case, *Christian Legal Society v. Martinez*, but this time, Kennedy joined the liberals—Ginsburg, Stevens, Breyer, and Sotomayor. The CLS chapter at the University of California, Hastings College of the Law, argued that the school's "all comers" policy, prohibiting student-funded organizations from discriminating against gays and lesbians (and others), violated the First Amendment. Kennedy and the four liberal justices upheld the policy. Alito wrote a dissent, joined by the three other neocons, that repeatedly emphasized the importance of protecting CLS, a religious organization dedicated to encouraging a Christian outlook and "moral clarity." According to Alito, the only way to explain the school's policy and the Court's decision was that the school and the Court reacted against the Christian identity of the student organization and the content of its message. Over and over again, Alito emphasized that the school had applied its antidiscrimination ("all comers") policy in a manner that discriminated against religion: "[R]eligious groups were not permitted to express a religious viewpoint by limiting membership to students who shared their religious viewpoints. Under established precedent, this was [unconstitutional] viewpoint discrimination." From a neoconservative standpoint, the government (that is, the law school) should have supported efforts by religious organizations to promote morality, but the school's policy and the Court's decision would instead lead to the "marginalization" of religion. Kennedy, in this instance, was unpersuaded. He wrote a concurrence emphasizing that the "all comers" policy would allow all students, including homosexuals, "to interact with their colleagues across a broad, seemingly unlimited range of ideas, views, and activities." He was more concerned with the dignity of gays and lesbians than the "moral clarity" professed by CLS.[13]

Neoconservative inroads in the First Amendment field are most likely to be made in Establishment Clause cases, again exactly because of Kennedy. Quite simply, Kennedy looks most like a neoconservative in the Establishment Clause context. He was, in 1988, the first justice to articulate the coercion test, and he has continued to champion its advantages over the competing (*Lemon* and endorsement) tests. Kennedy tailored the coercion test to harmonize with the neocons' favored nonpreferentialism and to provide "a minimum" of constitutional protection against government–religion connections. Now that Alito has replaced O'Connor—who always continued to press for her endorsement test—he is likely to join Kennedy,

Thomas, Scalia, and Roberts in explicitly repudiating *Lemon* and adopting the coercion test instead. Most recently, in *Salazar v. Buono*, involving the display of a large Latin (Christian) cross in honor of American soldiers who died in World War I, Kennedy wrote a plurality opinion that focused on the law related to injunctions rather than the Establishment Clause. Yet Kennedy managed to display his neoconservative bona fides by insisting that the cross could serve as a universal symbol honoring all deceased soldiers regardless of their religious orientations. Tellingly, Alito's concurrence echoed this ecumenical view of the Latin cross. Even so, Kennedy has diverged from the neocons in several Establishment Clause contexts. Whereas the neoconservative justices have insisted on a narrow concept of coercion—coercion must be "by force of law and threat of penalty"—Kennedy has joined the liberal justices in defining *coercion* to include, in some contexts, psychological or social pressure, such as that imposed on teenagers by their peers. Moreover, Kennedy has refused to join a Scalia dissent that advocated going beyond the nonpreferentialist position to allow government, in some situations, to favor certain religions over others (rather than favoring religion in general over irreligion).[14]

In conclusion, the neoconservative outlook is most likely to be pressed forward in constitutional realms where it has already gained a foothold, such as in congressional power cases. The neocons are unlikely to achieve major breakthroughs in other areas, with the possible exception of the Establishment Clause. Of course, neocons might dream: For instance, they might fantasize about promoting moral values by eliminating the right of privacy, which encompasses a woman's right to choose abortion. But such dreams will almost certainly remain chimerical because Kennedy would have to supply a fifth vote, an improbable scenario given his focus on individual dignity in the substantive due process realm. Of course, if Sotomayor, Kagan, or another Democratic appointee were to surprise by siding with the conservatives on the abortion issue, neoconservative dreams could become reality.

What's a Progressive to Do?

How should political progressives (or liberals) confront the challenge of a neoconservative Supreme Court? They can argue at the most general level that the overarching neoconservative goal of resurrecting republican democracy is wrongheaded as well as futile. Progressives can make the case that, as a theory, pluralist democracy is preferable to republican democracy because, for instance, a pluralist democratic system encourages more widespread political participation. Of course, neocons are neocons partly because they have already decided that republican democracy holds significant appeal, so broad theoretical arguments might be unavailing from the outset. Progressives could therefore emphasize a more practical though still general argument: Because of the current state of American culture and society and the entrenchment of pluralist democracy, a complete return to republican democracy is impossible. Needless to say, though, this obstacle has not yet prevented the neoconservative justices from attempting to "cut and paste" elements of republican democracy into the pluralist democratic system.

Progressives might next consider attacking more specific neoconservative arguments and methods. They can, for instance, criticize originalism, which neoconservatives claim to be an apolitical interpretive approach justifying many of their constitutional conclusions. Progressives can emphasize that the choice to follow originalism is just that: a choice, and a political one, at that. Numerous interpretive methods exist, with originalism merely being one of them. Indeed, conservatives themselves have demonstrated that the very definition of *originalism* can be controversial, as they have shifted from a definition focused on the framers' intentions to one focused on original public meaning. Progressives also can argue that other interpretive approaches are preferable to originalism. Justice Breyer has written a book sketching an "active liberty" interpretive approach that emphasizes citizen participation in government. Finally, progressives can argue that even if all the justices were to follow an originalist approach, uncontroversial and apolitical case outcomes would not be the result. In numerous cases, the majority and dissenting justices largely explore the same historical sources yet reach different conclusions, disagreeing about the original meaning of the Constitution. Even Meese's 1988 Justice Department *Guidelines on Constitutional Litigation*, after claiming that originalism is apolitical, admitted that "there is no mechanistic formula for discovering underlying [constitutional] values and principles and applying them to particular issues."[15]

Unsurprisingly, conservative originalists often seem to skew their historical conclusions to fit their political goals. Libertarians such as Richard Epstein and Randy Barnett argue that the Court took a wrong turn in 1937 when it accepted pluralist democracy: The Court therefore should resurrect a form of republican democratic judicial review. One problem is that they then interpret the history of the republican democratic regime as supporting a *return* to libertarianism: Supposedly based on the original meaning of the Constitution, courts should presume that governmental actions are illegitimate whenever they infringe on individual liberty. But from the nation's inception through, at least, most of the nineteenth century, republican democracy did not equate with libertarianism. The government could and did regulate (and restrict individual liberty) whenever such regulation would promote the common good. True, *Congress* did not extensively regulate the economy until the early twentieth century, but that fact reflected economic structures rather than governmental philosophy. During the nineteenth century, economic activity was limited largely to local markets—no substantial national marketplace existed until after the post–Civil War growth of the railroads—so state and local governments, rather than Congress, imposed most regulations. But there was no shortage of regulations: State and local governments regularly used the so-called police power to impose restrictions that were deemed for the common good. If such a restriction were challenged, a court would determine its legality by discerning whether the disputed governmental action was either for the common good (and therefore permissible) or for private or partial interests (and therefore impermissible). Some regulations were upheld and some were not, but, if anything, through much of the nineteenth century, courts were more apt to uphold than to invalidate governmental actions.[16]

Thus, because of the extensive reach of state and local police powers, governmental limitations on individual liberty were commonplace and legal. As Chancellor James Kent of New York proclaimed, "[P]rivate interest must be made subservient to the general interest of the community." For example, in an 1845 case, a Boston entrepreneur sought to sell poultry that he had acquired in New Hampshire, but he ran afoul of strict regulations on the marketplace. Specifically, the city required a seller to show "that all the said articles are the produce of his own farm, or of some farm not more than three miles distant from his own dwelling-house." The seller objected, contending that "the by-law is contrary to common right, in restraint of trade, against public policy, unreasonable and void." The court disagreed. In an opinion by Lemuel Shaw, the court reasoned that the city had provided "accommodations" for sales by "actual producers." Consequently, the city had "a right so to control them, as best to promote the welfare of all the citizens. And we think [the regulations] are well calculated to promote the public and general benefit," notwithstanding the restrictions on the economic marketplace.[17]

In 1851, Shaw explained that "the nature of well ordered civil society" required that public purposes take priority over individual liberties, including property ownership. "All property in this commonwealth [is] held subject to those general regulations, which are necessary to the common good and general welfare." Shaw elaborated with a partial yet lengthy list of legitimate governmental exercises of the police power.

> It is much easier to perceive and realize the existence and sources of this [police] power, than to mark its boundaries, or prescribe limits to its exercise. There are many cases in which such a power is exercised by all well ordered governments, and where its fitness is so obvious, that all well regulated minds will regard it as reasonable. Such are the laws to prohibit the use of warehouses for the storage of gunpowder near habitations or highways; to restrain the height to which wooden buildings may be erected in populous neighborhoods, and require them to be covered with slate or other incombustible material; to prohibit buildings from being used for hospitals for contagious diseases, or for the carrying on of noxious or offensive trades; to prohibit the raising of a dam, and causing stagnant water to spread over meadows, near inhabited villages, thereby raising noxious exhalations, injurious to health and dangerous to life.[18]

In the late-nineteenth century, courts responded to a variety of factors, including economic developments, by generally narrowing the concept of the common good. In doing so, they expanded the scope of individual liberty, at least in some contexts (such as liberty of contract). But even so, courts never pushed this transformation of the common good to the point where they enforced a laissez-faire capitalism with an unregulated marketplace. Regulations always persisted. Even Thomas Cooley's famed constitutional law text, tellingly called *A Treatise on the Constitutional Limitations Which Rest Upon the Legislative Power of the States of the American Union*, acknowledged the importance and breadth of state police powers. Thus, on the one hand, Cooley emphasized the significance of individual liberties: "The fundamental maxims of a free government seem to require that the rights of personal liberty and private property should be held sacred." Yet, on the other hand,

Cooley unequivocally recognized that, under the state police power, "persons and property are subjected to all kinds of restraints and burdens, in order to secure the general comfort, health, and prosperity of the State." Cooley, moreover, cautioned against judicial aggressiveness: The exercise of judicial review is a "delicate" task, and legislation should be held unconstitutional "only . . . with reluctance and hesitation." In short, according to Cooley, judges were not to invalidate legislation merely because they believed it inconsistent with some natural right to liberty or property.[19]

While progressives can present such historical arguments countering broad neoconservative positions, they also can specifically target narrower neoconservative propositions and assumptions. For instance, neocons typically assume that affirmative action programs generate white resentment and stigmatize participating minorities, but empirical research undermines the validity of this assumption. Of course, rather than criticize neoconservative views, progressives might instead offer their own alternative approaches. In this vein, some progressives have articulated a theory of "judicial minimalism." Cass Sunstein explains: Minimalist judges "seek to avoid broad rules and abstract theories, and attempt to focus their attention only on what is necessary to resolve particular disputes." That is, minimalist decisions (and opinions) are narrow and shallow, as illustrated in the case of *Romer v. Evans*, decided in 1996. Several Colorado municipalities had enacted ordinances prohibiting sexual-orientation discrimination in housing, employment, education, and other public services and accommodations. These ordinances prompted a statewide referendum that resulted in the adoption of a state constitutional amendment (Amendment 2). Amendment 2 prohibited "all legislative, executive or judicial action at any level of state or local government designed to protect . . . homosexual persons or gays and lesbians." Thus, Amendment 2 repealed the previously enacted municipal ordinances to the extent that they prohibited discrimination on the basis of "'homosexual, lesbian or bisexual orientation, conduct, practices or relationships.'" The Court held that Amendment 2 violated the Equal Protection Clause of the Fourteenth Amendment.[20]

As interpreted by Sunstein, the *Romer* Court's majority opinion, written by Kennedy (joined by Stevens, O'Connor, Souter, Ginsburg, and Breyer) left much undecided. The opinion was narrow because it invalidated Amendment 2 without holding that all or indeed any other laws discriminating on the basis of sexual orientation are unconstitutional. Subsequent cases could arise in which the Court might uphold such discrimination. Likewise, the opinion was shallow because the Court did not apparently base its decision on any deeply theorized principles of equality. Indeed, the case presented the Court with a perfect opportunity to decide whether gays and lesbians should be deemed either a suspect or quasi–suspect class, which would trigger heightened judicial scrutiny (such as strict scrutiny) under the Court's equal protection methodology. The Court, though, refused to decide this fundamental question regarding the nature of equality under the Fourteenth Amendment. Instead, the Court concluded that Amendment 2 failed the rational basis test, the lowest level of judicial scrutiny under equal protection, and thus was unconstitutional. Because Amendment 2 could not satisfy even rational basis review, the Court did not need to contemplate applying any level of heightened scrutiny and therefore left undecided whether gays and lesbians constituted a suspect or quasi–suspect class.[21]

According to Sunstein, minimalist judges and justices leave things undecided, as in *Romer*, because they accept "humility in the face of limited judicial capacities and competence." Even if this account of minimalism is accurate, the strategic appeal of minimalism is obvious from a progressive political perspective, given the current makeup of the Supreme Court. When progressives argue for a minimalist decision, they attempt to persuade the justices to temper their political and legal goals, to leave more and deeper decisions to other institutions. If progressives cannot trust the Supreme Court to reach acceptable (progressive) outcomes, then they will naturally prefer that the justices leave more decisions to other governmental institutions, especially when Democrats control those other institutions. Mark Tushnet pushed this position to the extreme by arguing to strip the power of judicial review from the federal judiciary; he literally wants to take the Constitution away from the courts. In truth, progressives here are engaged in damage control: The neocons control the Court, so the progressives hope to mitigate potential political and legal disaster. Conservatives, like Robert Bork, championed judicial restraint in the 1960s and 1970s in response to Warren and early–Burger Court decisions, and now progressives in effect advocate for restraint because of the Rehnquist and Roberts Courts.[22]

Whatever progressives argue to the Court—whether it's for minimalism, or against originalism, or for a particular originalist or historical understanding of the Constitution, or otherwise—they will inevitably confront a titanic obstacle: the neoconservative presence. The neoconservative justices are not likely to find progressive arguments persuasive—not in this era of sclerotic pluralist democracy. For example, if progressives advocate for judicial minimalism, nobody is going to be fooled. Regardless of the theoretical arguments for minimalism, the neoconservative justices will not find the progressive political strategy too opaque to discern. Even if progressives sincerely believe in the merits of minimalism as a judicial methodology—and most likely, many of them are sincere—the political implications of leaving more decisions to other governmental institutions will be obvious, especially when those other institutions are controlled by Democrats. Given this fact, progressives might be reduced to three tacks. First, avoid the Court whenever possible. Bring progressive arguments, for example, to state legislatures or Congress. If litigation is expedient, go to state courts and invoke state constitutional provisions (thus sidestepping the Court's conservative interpretations of the federal Constitution). Second, use an interest-convergence strategy if it fits. In rare instances, the political interests of progressives and neocons might overlap or coincide, and if so, progressives might as well emphasize this happenstance, regardless of the forum, whether they are in state court, federal court, or elsewhere. In this way, progressives might be able to forge a temporary alliance with neocons and advance their agenda. Third, when forced to advocate before the Court, progressives would be wise to narrow their arguments, in most cases, to one target: Justice Kennedy.[23]

In most politically charged cases—those that are most salient in separating conservatives and progressives—progressives will win only if they can convince Kennedy to vote with the four progressive-liberals rather than with the four neoconservatives. Because Kennedy is a moderate conservative, progressives will always face a difficult task; Kennedy's legal and political inclinations will be to follow the neocons in most cases. Progressives will probably fare best, then, if they accentuate those points that separate Kennedy from the neocons. For instance, whereas the neoconservative justices—like neocons in general—tend to assert their views confidently and aggressively, Kennedy tends to be more prudential, more cautious. Thus, in *Newdow*, Kennedy joined the four progressive justices in sidestepping the merits of the Establishment Clause challenge to the "under God" provision in the Pledge of Allegiance. Tellingly, while Kennedy and the progressives relied on Newdow's lack of standing to resolve the case, all of the other conservative justices argued that the Court should have reached the merits and should have held that the "under God" provision did not violate the Establishment Clause. In a case such as *Newdow*, one senses that Kennedy abandoned the neocons more than he accepted the progressive view. Yet in some instances Kennedy might go further and actually accept the progressive position on the merits, especially in cases revolving around human dignity, such as *Lawrence v. Texas* (right of privacy and homosexuality) and *Christian Legal Society* (free speech and discrimination against gays and lesbians).[24]

Finally, progressives should realize that, in many instances, Kennedy will vote with the neocons, but he might nonetheless be influenced to temper the (conservative) majority's line of reasoning. Consider the Establishment Clause context. As already discussed, Alito's replacement of O'Connor increases the likelihood that a (conservative) majority of justices will settle upon Kennedy's coercion test as the prevailing standard, replacing the *Lemon* test. Even so, progressives could ameliorate the coercion test by persuading Kennedy to continue defining *coercion* expansively. If the Court characterizes *coercion* as including psychological and social pressure—rather than being limited to threatened legal penalties, as the neocons desire—then the Establishment Clause is more likely to be deemed a barrier to the public expression or adoption of mainstream religious values and views. If, instead, Kennedy merely signs onto a neoconservative opinion adopting the coercion test—say, one written by Scalia or Thomas—then the Establishment Clause is likely to become little more than precatory, a plea to the predominant religions to consider minorities before displaying mainstream symbols and attempting to inculcate religious values.[25]

Of course, just as neocons have dreamed about completely fulfilling their goals at the Supreme Court, so can progressives dream. The kernel of the progressive dream lies buried in the plans, in the futures, of the conservative justices themselves. If, in the next few years, one conservative justice were to resign—however surprising and premature it would be—then President Obama (or perhaps another Democratic president) could appoint a replacement who would (probably) swing the Court toward a five-to-four progressive majority. Suddenly, the politics of Supreme Court adjudication would change dramatically. Instead of arguing to Kennedy, if he remained on the Court, progressives would assert their positions with more assurance, seeking to hold together the progressive majority. The remaining neocons, whether Thomas, Scalia, Roberts, or Alito, would end their careers confronting a profound frustration. Ironically, these justices could become the new Thurgood Marshall and William Brennan, lonely voices persistently dissenting against powerful political and legal opponents. For progressives, though, this romantic future remains no more than a dream—and a remote one, at that. The neoconservative justices might at times be politically isolated, depending on the results of the most recent elections, but they will almost certainly continue to exercise substantial control over legal and political developments.

NOTES

On the Format of the Notes: Whenever feasible, I append one note for an entire paragraph, rather than use multiple notes within individual paragraphs. If a paragraph contains multiple quotations (but only one note), I cite the source of the first quotation first, the source of the second quotation next, and so on. If, however, a subsequent quotation in the paragraph is derived from a source previously cited in the same note, then I add the page number to the earlier citation of that source (without repeating the entire citation). After citing the sources for all quotations, I sometimes cite additional materials, whether primary or secondary, that provide supplemental support and information. If I have already cited one of those additional primary or secondary sources in that particular note—because it was the source of a quotation—then I include the additional page numbers in the original citation (to obviate the need to cite the same source more than once in any note).

CHAPTER 1

1. Jacob Heilbrunn, They Knew They Were Right 164–66 (2008); *see* Stephen M. Feldman, Free Expression and Democracy in America: A History 291–348 (2008) (explaining pluralist democracy). Sources on neoconservatism cited in this chapter include: Murray Friedman, The Neoconservative Revolution (2005); Douglas Murray, Neoconservatism: Why We Need It (2006); George H. Nash, The Conservative Intellectual Movement in America Since 1945 (2008 ed.); Justin Vaïsse, Neoconservatism: The Biography of a Movement (Arthur Goldhammer trans., 2010); The Neocon Reader (Irwin Stelzer ed., 2004) [hereinafter Reader]; Jacob Heilbrunn, *Neoconservatism*, *in* Varieties of Conservatism in America 105 (Peter Berkowitz ed., 2004) [hereinafter Neoconservatism].
2. Pleasantville (New Line Cinema, 1998).
3. *Citizens United*, 130 S.Ct. 876 (2010); U.S. Census Bureau, Statistical Abstract of the United States: 2002 (122d ed.) at 245 (Table No. 379: Composition of Congress by Political Party: 1973 to 2002).

4. Friedrich A. Hayek, The Road to Serfdom (1944); Nash, *supra* note 1, at 104–15; Steven H. Shiffrin, Dissent, Injustice, and the Meanings of America 123–24 (1999); Peter Berkowitz, *Introduction*, *in* Varieties of Conservatism in America xiii, xiv–xxii (2004); Neoconservatism, *supra* note 1, at 105, 107, 123–26; Adam Wolfson, *Conservatives and Neoconservatives* (2004), *reprinted in* Reader, *supra* note 1, at 213, 216–24. I use *progressivism* and *liberalism* interchangeably in this book. To be clear, to describe current-day politics, I use the term *progressivism* (with a lowercase *p*) rather than *Progressivism*, which was a political movement of the early twentieth century. Although progressivism and Progressivism have commonalities, there are also differences. Most important, Progressivism tended to be conservative in the realm of cultural values. Feldman, *supra* note 1, at 190–97.
5. Wolfson, *supra* note 4, at 219; Murray, *supra* note 1, at xiv; Nash, *supra* note 1, at 567–69; Neoconservatism, *supra* note 1, at 107; Friedman, *supra* note 1, at 80.
6. Friedman, *supra* note 1, at 183 (quoting Kristol); Francis Fukuyama, America at the Crossroads 38 (2006); Murray, *supra* note 1, at 61; Nash, *supra* note 1, at 559; Vaïsse, *supra* note 1, at 3–4; The Future of Conservatism ii–viii (Charles W. Dunn ed., 2007). I explain the categorization of justices as neocons in chapter 6.
7. David Brooks, *The Neocon Cabal and Other Fantasies* (2004), *reprinted in* Reader, *supra* note 1, at 39, 42; Irving Kristol, Neoconservatism: The Autobiography of an Idea (1995); Norman Podhoretz, The Norman Podhoretz Reader (Thomas L. Jeffers ed., 2004).
8. Mark Tushnet, *Foreword: The New Constitutional Order and the Chastening of Constitutional Aspiration*, 113 Harv. L. Rev. 29, 86–87 (1999) (discussing Scalia's reliance on tradition); *e.g.*, Kiryas Joel Village School District v. Grumet, 512 U.S. 687, 751 (1994) (Scalia, J., dissenting) (advocates relying on tradition in Establishment Clause case).

CHAPTER 2

1. Virginia Bill of Rights (1776), *reprinted in* 2 The Federal and State Constitutions, Colonial Charters, and other Organic Laws of the United States 1908, 1908–09 (Ben Perley Poore ed., 2d ed. 1878); Gordon S. Wood, The Creation of the American Republic 59 (1969); Stephen M. Feldman, Free Expression and Democracy in America: A History (2008).
2. Wood, *supra* note 1, at 100 (quoting Josiah Quincy); Letter from Thomas Jefferson to James Madison (Dec. 20, 1787), *reprinted in* 2 Great Issues in American History 112, 115 (Richard Hofstadter ed., 1982) [hereinafter Great]; The Federalist No. 2, at 38 (John Jay) (Clinton Rossiter

ed., 1961); Thomas J. Curry, The First Freedoms: Church and State in America to the Passage of the First Amendment 219 (1986); Stephen M. Feldman, Please Don't Wish Me a Merry Christmas: A Critical History of the Separation of Church and State 161–68 (1997); Edmund S. Morgan, The Birth of the Republic 7 (rev. ed. 1977).

3. The Federalist No. 10, at 78 (James Madison) (Clinton Rossiter ed., 1961); David M. Potter, *Social Cohesion and the Crisis of Law*, *in* History and American Society 389, 401–04 (Don E. Fehrenbacher ed., 1973).
4. Stanley Elkins & Eric McKitrick, The Age of Federalism 596–617 (1993); Edward Pessen, Jacksonian America 197–232 (rev. ed. 1985); Harry L. Watson, Liberty and Power 171–74 (1990); Erik W. Austin, Political Facts of the United States Since 1789, at 378–79 (1986) (Table 3.12: National Voter Turnout, 1824–1984).
5. The Statistical History of the United States from Colonial Times to the Present 409 (1965) (Table: Manufactures Summary) [hereinafter Statistical]; *id.* at 74 (Table: Industrial Distribution of Gainful Workers); The Statistics of the Wealth and Industry of the United States; Compiled from the Original Returns of the Ninth Census 392 (1872); Compiled from 1900 Census; Richard F. Bensel, The Political Economy of American Industrialization 19–100 (2000); Feldman, *supra* note 1, at 166–97.
6. Statistical, *supra* note 5, at 14 (Table: Population in Urban and Rural Territory); Frederick Jackson Turner, *The Significance of the Frontier in American History* (July 12, 1893).
7. Statistical, *supra* note 5 at 7 (Table: Estimated Population); *id.* at 44–47 (Table: Estimated Net Intercensal Migration); Austin, *supra* note 4, at 470 (Table 7.4, Total Number of Immigrants Arriving Annually).
8. Laurence R. Veysey, The Emergence of the American University 2, 9, 12, 58 (1965); George M. Marsden, The Soul of the American University 155 (1994); Herbert Hovenkamp, *The Political Economy of Substantive Due Process*, 40 Stan. L. Rev. 379, 381 (1988); Richard T. Ely, Studies in the Evolution of Industrial Society 90–91 (1903; 1971 reprint ed.); Andrew Abbott, The System of Professions 206 (1988); Magali Sarfatti Larson, The Rise of Professionalism (1977); Bensel, *supra* note 5 at 207–08; Stephen Steinberg, The Ethnic Myth 36–38 (1989 ed.); Edward S. Corwin, *The Impact of the Idea of Evolution on the American Political and Constitutional Tradition*, *in* Evolutionary Thought in America 182, 185 (Stow Persons ed., 1956); Robert Scoon, *The Rise and Impact of Evolutionary Ideas*, *in* Evolutionary Thought in America 4, 19 (Stow Persons ed., 1956).
9. Ely, *supra* note 8 at 15; Marsden, *supra* note 8, at 155; Maxwell Bloomfield, Peaceful Revolution 39 (2000); Larson, *supra* note 8, at 167; Richard Hofstadter, The Age of Reform 155 (1955); William M. Wiecek, The Lost World of Classical Legal Thought 188 (1998); Abbott, *supra* note 8, at 2.

10. Robert Stevens, Law School: Legal Education in America from the 1850s to the 1980s, at 40 (1983) (quoting Harvard Law Professor James Barr Ames); Joseph Beale, I A Treatise on the Conflict of Laws 143 (1916); John W. Burgess, 1 Political Science and Comparative Constitutional Law 88, 175–76 (1890); Thomas M. Cooley, A Treatise on the Constitutional Limitations Which Rest Upon the Legislative Power of the States of the American Union 21–25, 35 (1868, Da Capo Press ed. 1972); Stephen M. Feldman, American Legal Thought from Premodernism to Postmodernism: An Intellectual Voyage 49–105 (2000) [hereinafter Voyage].
11. United States Immigration Commission (Chair: Senator William P. Dillingham), *Dictionary of Races or Peoples* 32–33, 54, 74, 82–83 (Dec. 5, 1910) (printed 1911); Austin, *supra* note 4, at 472 (Table 7.5, Number of Immigrants from Selected Countries); Melvyn Dubofsky, The State and Labor in Modern America (1994); Howard Gillman, The Constitution Besieged (1993); John Higham, Strangers in the Land 59–61 (1992 ed.); Desmond King, Making Americans (2000); Karen Orren, Belated Feudalism (1991).
12. Feldman, *supra* note 1, at 314–35; William E. Leuchtenburg, Franklin D. Roosevelt and the New Deal 332 (1963); Edward A. Purcell Jr., The Crisis of Democratic Theory 197–266 (1973).
13. Statistical, *supra* note 5, at 73 (Table: Unemployment); *id.* at 92 (Table: Hours and Earnings for Production Workers in Manufacturing); *id.* at 278 (Table: Farms, Land in Farms, and Value of Farm Property and Real Estate); *id.* at 139 (Table: Gross National Product); Anthony J. Badger, The New Deal 12 (1989); Lizabeth Cohen, Making a New Deal 240–43 (1990); David M. Kennedy, Freedom from Fear 86–87 (1999).
14. Cohen, *supra* note 13, at 100-58, 249; Feldman, *supra* note 1, at 296-303.
15. Leuchtenburg, *supra* note 12, at 339; Franklin D. Roosevelt, *First Inaugural Address* (March 4, 1933), *reprinted in* III Great, *supra* note 2, at 343, 346.
16. Louis L. Jaffe, *Law Making by Private Groups*, 51 Harv. L. Rev. 201, 201–03 (1937); Franklin D. Roosevelt, *Commonwealth Club Speech* (Sept. 23, 1932), *reprinted in* III Great, *supra* note 2, at 335, 341–42; The National Labor Relations Act (July 5, 1935), 49 Stat. 449; National Labor Relations Board, Legislative History of the National Labor Relations Act, 1935, at 1620–21 (1985 Commemorative ed.); Cohen, *supra* note 13, at 254–57, 362–66. Roosevelt was far more solicitous of African American interests than any previous president, yet he often sacrificed black interests so as to keep white Southerners aligned with the Democratic Party. Also, Roosevelt eventually broke with and became antagonistic toward big business. Feldman, *supra* note 1, at 318–28.

17. William O. Douglas, *Wage Earner Bankruptcies—State v. Federal Control*, 42 Yale L.J. 591, 593 (1933); Walter Lippmann, A Preface to Morals 283 (1929); Charles E. Merriam, New Aspects of Politics (1925); Charles E. Merriam, Non-Voting (1924); George E.G. Catlin, The Science and Method of Politics 4 (1927; 1964 reprint) (explaining that one should study history "to gather an omen of future progress"); Voyage, *supra* note 10, at 19, 84–85; G. Edward White, *The Arrival of History in Constitutional Scholarship*, 88 Va. L. Rev. 485, 506 (2002).
18. The Social Security Act (Aug. 14, 1935), 49 Stat. 620; Austin, *supra* note 4, at 378–79 (Table 3.12, National Voter Turnout); Feldman, *supra* note 1, at 183–208.
19. Lippmann, *supra* note 17, at 3–4, 8; George H. Sabine, A History of Political Theory viii (1937).
20. Joseph A. Schumpeter, Capitalism, Socialism, and Democracy 250–51 (1942, 3d ed. 1950); Purcell, *supra* note 12, 197–217.
21. John Dewey, Freedom and Culture 176 (1939); John Dewey & James H. Tufts, Ethics 400 (1936 ed.).
22. Wilfred E. Binkley & Malcolm C. Moos, A Grammar of American Politics 8–11 (1949) (quoting H. L. Childs, *Pressure Groups and Propaganda*, *in* The American Political Scene 225 (E. B. Logan ed., 1936); R. M. MacIver, The Web of Government 298 (1946)).
23. Robert A. Dahl, Democracy and Its Critics 30, 83, 106, 109–11 (1989); Robert A. Dahl, A Preface to Democratic Theory 6, 67–71 (1956). Several intellectual developments undermined republican democracy, with ethical relativism being but one. As discussed, the jurisprudential repudiation of natural law and the embrace of positivism was another. An early-twentieth-century critique of the monistic theory of the state also weakened republican democracy. According to the monistic theory, which predominated in nineteenth-century American political theory, all individuals and groups join to concentrate sovereign power within a unitary state. The state was an absolute. Harold J. Laski, Studies in the Problem of Sovereignty 4–6 (1917). During the World War I era, however, this concentration of power seemed especially menacing. *Id.* at 20–21. At this time, then, Laski and a few other theorists criticized the monistic theory and articulated instead a pluralistic theory of the state. Laski argued that numerous entities or associations, such as churches and unions, retained independence from the state and played ongoing political roles. *Id.* at 9–11; *see* Kung Chuan Hsiao, Political Pluralism: A Study in Contemporary Political Thought 7–8, 126 (1927); Raymond G. Gettell, *Pluralistic Theories of Sovereignty*, *in* History of Political Thought 458, 458–69 (1924). Not all sovereign power was sacrificed to one centralized "collective unity." John G. Gunnell, The Descent of Political

Theory 105 (1993). To be clear, the pluralistic theory of the state was not equivalent to pluralist democratic theory, which would emerge only subsequently. For instance, while pluralist democratic theorists would eventually argue that individuals and groups legitimately pursue their own interests, Laski maintained that "men should give their allegiance to that which is possessed of superior moral purpose." Laski, *supra*, at 24. The pluralistic theory of the state, though, was one of a series of intellectual developments that combined with concrete political developments, such as the Great Depression, to prompt many political theorists to doubt the coherence and functionality of republican democracy. *E.g.*, Pendleton Herring, *A Prescription for Modern Democracy*, 180 Annals of the Am. Academy of Pol. & Social Sci. 138 (1935); John Dickinson, *Democratic Realities and Democratic Dogma*, 24 Am. Pol. Sci. Rev. 283 (1930); *see* Feldman, *supra* note 1, at 305–14.

CHAPTER 3

1. Strauss's writings include: Leo Strauss, Liberalism Ancient and Modern (1968) [hereinafter Liberalism]; Leo Strauss, The City and Man (1964) [hereinafter City]; Leo Strauss, What Is Political Philosophy (1959) [hereinafter Political]; Leo Strauss, Natural Right and History (1953) [hereinafter Natural]; Leo Strauss, The Political Philosophy of Hobbes (Elsa M. Sinclair trans., 1952) [hereinafter Hobbes]. Arendt's writings include: Hannah Arendt, On Revolution (1963); Hannah Arendt, The Human Condition (1958); Hannah Arendt, The Origins of Totalitarianism (1973 ed., 1951). Voegelin's writings include: Eric Voegelin, Order and History: Israel and Revelation (1956); Eric Voegelin, The New Science of Politics (1952). Books and essays discussing Strauss include: Shadia B. Drury, Leo Strauss and the American Right (1997); Ted V. McAllister, Revolt Against Modernity (1996); George H. Nash, The Conservative Intellectual Movement in America Since 1945 (2008 ed.); Thomas L. Pangle, Leo Strauss (2006); Steven B. Smith, Reading Leo Strauss (2006); Daniel Tanguay, Leo Strauss (Christopher Nadon trans., 2007); Nathan Tarcov & Thomas L. Pangle, *Leo Strauss and the History of Political Philosophy, in* History of Political Philosophy 907 (Leo Strauss & Joseph Cropsey eds., 3d ed. 1987).
2. Natural, *supra* note 1, at 19; City, *supra* note 1, at 4; Political, *supra* note 1, at 59, 67.
3. Natural, *supra* note 1, at 26–27, 97; Political, *supra* note 1, at 26–27, 63; Thomas S. Kuhn, The Structure of Scientific Revolutions (2d ed. 1970).
4. Natural, *supra* note 1, at 16–17, 39–41; Political, *supra* note 1, at 19–25; Max Weber, The Methodology of the Social Sciences (Edward A. Shils & Henry A. Finch trans., 1949).

5. Natural, *supra* note 1, at 4–5, 40–42; Political, *supra* note 1, at 18–19.
6. Political, *supra* note 1, at 37–38; Liberalism, *supra* note 1, at 3–25; Pangle, *supra* note 1, at 77–78; Smith, *supra* note 1, at ix; Tarcov & Pangle, *supra* note 1, at 909; Drury, *supra* note 1, at 133–35.
7. City, *supra* note 1, at 11–12; Political, *supra* note 1, at 11–12, 66; Tarcov & Pangle, *supra* note 1, at 910–19. Straussians might claim that Strauss himself engaged in esoteric writing. He distinguished the exoteric (political writings or teachings that were useful and palatable in the philosopher's particular context) from the esoteric (political writings or teachings that were aimed for universal truths but that were left more obscure). Political, *supra* note 1, at 226–29; Pangle, *supra* note 1, at 56–65.
8. Natural, *supra* note 1, at 7, 144, 182; Hobbes, *supra* note 1, at xi–xii; McAllister, *supra* note 1, at 30; Tanguay, *supra* note 1, at 118; Stephen M. Feldman, American Legal Thought from Premodernism to Postmodernism: An Intellectual Voyage 85–89 (2000); *see* Natural, *supra* note 1, at 144 ("natural right or, rather, natural law becomes independent of the best regime and takes precedence over it").
9. Natural, *supra* note 1, at 177–81; Hobbes, *supra* note 1, at xii; Niccolo Machiavelli, The Prince and the Discourses (Christian E. Detmold trans., Modern Library ed. 1950); Thomas Hobbes, Leviathan (C. B. Macpherson ed., 1968); McAllister, *supra* note 1, at 154–56; Tanguay, *supra* note 1, at 102–03, 118. While Aristotelian virtue strove for human excellence, Machiavellian *virtù* strove for political usefulness, for the preservation of the political community (or republic) in a treacherous world. Feldman, *supra* note 8, at 12, 14–15; Tarcov & Pangle, *supra* note 1, at 916–17.
10. Jeremy Bentham, *Anarchical Fallacies*, *reprinted in* 2 The Works of Jeremy Bentham 501, ¶ 6905 (John Bowring ed., 1843); John Austin, The Province of Jurisprudence Determined 19, 158 (Wilfrid E. Rumble ed., 1995; 1st ed. 1832); Oliver Wendell Holmes Jr., *Natural Law*, 32 Harv. L. Rev. 40 (1918), *reprinted in* The Essential Holmes 180, 181 (Richard A. Posner ed., 1992); Calder v. Bull, 3 U.S. (3 Dall.) 386, 399 (1798) (Iredell, J., concurring); Natural, *supra* note 1, at 7–8, 298–99; Feldman, *supra* note 8, at 93–94.
11. Natural, *supra* note 1, at 9–34, 97, 102–08, 133–34; Political, *supra* note 1, at 40, 94.
12. Dana R. Villa, Arendt and Heidegger: The Fate of the Political 8 (1996).
13. McAllister, *supra* note 1, at 221–23, 271; Nash, *supra* note 1, at 74, 536.
14. Natural, *supra* note1, at 130–33; City, *supra* note 1, at 5; Dana R. Villa, Politics, Philosophy, Terror 156 (1999); Tarcov & Pangle, *supra* note 1, at 933; Pangle, *supra* note 1, at 83–85.

15. Stephen M. Feldman, Free Expression and Democracy in America: A History 322–33 (2008).
16. Lynn Dumenil, The Modern Temper 89 (1995); The Statistical History of the United States from Colonial Times to the Present 178 (1965) (Table: Personal Consumption Expenditures) [hereinafter Statistical]; *id.* at 139 (Table: Gross National Product); Lizabeth Cohen, A Consumers' Republic 113 (2003); Gary Cross, An All-Consuming Century (2000); Ronald K.L. Collins & David M. Skover, *Commerce and Communication*, 71 Tex. L. Rev. 697, 700–02 (1993).
17. Statistical, *supra* note 16, at 526 (Table: Volume of Advertising); U.S. Census Bureau, Statistical Abstract of the United States: 2002 (122d ed.) 772 (Table No. 1253: Advertising—Estimated Expenditures by Medium) [hereinafter Abstract]; Cohen, *supra* note 16, at 336–38; Cross, *supra* note 16, at 34, 77, 100; Dumenil, *supra* note 16, at 90; Paul Starr, The Creation of the Media 327–84 (2004); Collins & Skover, *supra* note 16, at 703.
18. Collins & Skover, *supra* note 16, at 724–25; Cohen, *supra* note 16, at 9, 113–342.
19. Jack L. Walker Jr., Mobilizing Interest Groups in America 85 (1991); Mancur Olson, The Logic of Collective Action 60–62, 130–33 (2d ed. 1971; 1st ed. 1965); Robert A. Jackson & Thomas M. Carsey, *Group Effects on Party Identification and Party Coalitions Across the United States*, 30 Am. Pol. Research 66, 70 (2002); Anthony J. Nownes & Grant Neeley, *Toward an Explanation for Public Interest Group Formation and Proliferation*, 24 Policy Studies J. 74 (1996).
20. William Haltom & Michael McCann, Distorting the Law 24, 39, 47, 54–56, 181 (2004); Lawrence M. Friedman, Total Justice 15–23 (1985).
21. Sheldon S. Wolin, Democracy Incorporated 131, 149 (2008); Jacob S. Hacker & Paul Pierson, Winner-Take-All Politics 118–19 (2010).
22. Dara Z. Strolovitch, *A More Level Playing Field or a New Mobilization of Bias?*, *in* Interest Group Politics 86, 86 (Allen J. Cigler & Burdett A. Loomis eds., 7th ed. 2007) [hereinafter Interest7th]; David B. Truman, The Governmental Process 33, 39, 53–57, 106–08 (2d ed. 1971; 1st ed. 1951) (quoting V. O. Key Jr., Politics, Parties, and Pressure Groups 16–17 (3d ed. 1953; 1st ed. 1942)).
23. Key, *supra* note 22, at 25; Earl Latham, The Group Basis of Politics 35, 37 (1952); Robert A. Dahl, A Preface to Democratic Theory 137 (1956) [hereinafter Preface]; Robert A. Dahl, Who Governs? Democracy and Power in an American City 86 (1961).
24. Truman, *supra* note 22, at 129, 138, 512–13; Daniel J. Boorstin, The Genius of American Politics 1, 162 (1953); Louis Hartz, The Liberal Tradition in America 11 (1955); Robert A. Dahl, Democracy and Its Critics 162 (1989) [hereinafter Democracy]; Preface, *supra* note 23, at

4, 143; John Dewey, Freedom and Culture 162, 175 (1939); Will Herberg, Protestant-Catholic-Jew 88 (1955); A Report of the Committee on Political Parties, American Political Science Association, *Toward a More Responsible Two-Party System*, 44 Am. Pol. Sci. Rev. i, 1–2 (1950).

25. Olson, *supra* note 19, at 2, 21, 44, 76; Nownes & Neeley, *supra* note 19; Paul E. Johnson, *Interest Group Recruiting, in* Interest Group Politics 35, 60 (Allen J. Cigler & Burdett A. Loomis eds., 5th ed. 1998) [hereinafter Interest5th]; Charles L. Black Jr., Structure and Relationship in Constitutional Law 54 (1969); Theodore J. Lowi, The End of Liberalism 38, 86 (1969); C. Wright Mills, The Power Elite (1956); E. E. Schattschneider, The Semi-Sovereign People 35 (1960); Burdett A. Loomis & Allen J. Cigler, *Introduction: The Changing Nature of Interest Group Politics, in* Interest7th, *supra* note 22, at 1, 5; Mark P. Petracca, *The Rediscovery of Interest Group Politics, in* The Politics of Interests 3, 17 (1992).
26. Voting Rights Act of 1965, 79 Stat. 437 (Aug. 6, 1965); Civil Rights Act of 1964, 78 Stat. 241 (July 2, 1964); Preface, *supra* note 23, at 137–38; Walker, *supra* note 19, at 35–36; Mark V. Tushnet, The NAACP's Legal Strategy Against Segregated Education (1987); Derrick Bell, *Racial Realism*, 24 Conn. L. Rev. 363 (1992).
27. Abstract, *supra* note 17, at 776 (Table No. 1261: National Nonprofit Associations); Associations Unlimited (compiled from *Encyclopedia of Associations*); Gene M. Grossman & Elhanan Helpman, Special Interest Politics 2 (2001); Petracca, *supra* note 25, at 11–14.
28. Grossman & Helpman, *supra* note 27, at 3; Abstract, *supra* note 17, at 776 (Table No. 1261: National Nonprofit Associations). A peak association is a large interest group that seeks to speak for an "entire economic sector" or a number of related small groups. Robert H. Salisbury et al., *Who Works with Whom?*, 81 Am. Pol. Sci. Rev. 1217, 1229 (1987) [hereinafter Who]. Many individuals belong to multiple associations, yet, even so, the rate of participation is high: A 1981 Gallup poll revealed that 20 million Americans belonged to interest groups and another 20 million contributed money. Petracca, *supra* note 25, at 7.
29. Anthony J. Nownes & Allan J. Cigler, *Public Interest Groups and the Road to Survival*, 27 Polity 379, 397 (1995); Ronald J. Hrebenar, Interest Group Politics in America 17–18, 289 (3d ed. 1997); Truman, *supra* note 22, at 53, 56–57, 106–08; Loomis & Cigler, *supra* note 25, at 13, 21–22; Petracca, *supra* note 25, at 23–26.
30. Olson, *supra* note 19, at 2, 21, 44, 76; Friedman, *supra* note 20, at 5, 150; Robert A. Kagan, *How Much Do Conservative Tort Tales Matter?*, 31 Law & Soc. Inquiry 711, 728–30 (2006); David C. King & Jack L. Walker, *The Provision of Benefits by Interest Groups in the United States*, 54 J. of Pol. 394, 394, 397–98 (1992).

31. Morton Keller, America's Three Regimes 5, 228 (2007); Friedman, *supra* note 20, at 42–43, 51; Kagan, *supra* note 30, at 717–18.
32. Petracca, *supra* note 25, at 27; Steven M. Teles, The Rise of the Conservative Legal Movement 1–5 (2008); Walker, *supra* note 19, at 37–38; Jack L. Walker, *The Origins and Maintenance of Interest Groups in America*, 77 Am. Pol. Sci. Rev. 390, 397 (1983).
33. *E.g.*, Latham, *supra* note 23, at 35–37.
34. Mancur Olson, The Rise and Decline of Nations 37, 40–41 (1982) [hereinafter Rise].
35. Olson added that nations that had undergone serious disruptions or upheavals—a nation, for instance, that had been invaded or conquered—would likely be more efficient and enjoy a period of economic growth. *Id.* at 3–5, 47, 77–78, 210, 217.
36. To be sure, researchers have disputed some components of Olson's position. Robert L. Ross, *Relations Among National Interest Groups*, 32 J. of Pol. 96, 110–14 (1970); Ivo Bischoff, *Model Uncertainty, Political Learning, and Institutions*, 74 Southern Economic J. 34 (2007); Jac C. Heckelman, *Explaining the Rain*, 74 Southern Economic J. 18 (2007).
37. Allan Bloom, The Closing of the American Mind (1987); Isaac Kramnick & R. Laurence Moore, The Godless Constitution 204 (2005); James T. Patterson, Restless Giant 24–25, 86–88 (2005); Arthur M. Schlesinger Jr., The Disuniting of America (1992 ed.); Barbara Sinclair, Party Wars 46–52 (2006); David M. Potter, *Social Cohesion and the Crisis of Law*, *in* History and American Society 389, 412–18 (Don E. Fehrenbacher ed., 1973).
38. Truman, *supra* note 34, at 53, 56–57, 106–08; Rise, *supra* note 34, at 40–41.
39. Olson, *supra* note 19, at 133; Walker, *supra* note 25, at 85; Johnson, *supra* note 25, at 35, 38.
40. Letter from Wayne LaPierre, Executive Vice President of NRA (undated).
41. The NRA actually offered a folding knife in other promotional materials.
42. Diana Epstein & John D. Graham, *Polarized Politics and Policy Consequences*, Rand Occasional Paper, at 2–3 (2007); Sinclair, *supra* note 37, at 3–6; Karen M. Kaufmann et al., Unconventional Wisdom 48, 65 (2008); Geoffrey Layman, The Great Divide 15 (2001); Morris P. Fiorina et al., Culture War? The Myth of a Polarized America 5, 78 (2005); Potter, *supra* note 37, at 397–98; Richard Fleisher & Jon R. Bond, *Congress and the President in a Partisan Era*, *in* Polarized Politics 1, 2 (Jon R. Bond & Richard Fleisher eds., 2000) [hereinafter Polarized]; Gary Jacobson, *Party Polarization and National Politics*, *in* Polarized, *supra*, at 9, 10–11.

43. Democratic Party Platform; 1956 Democratic Party Platform; Epstein & Graham, *supra* note 42, at 10–13; Brown v. Board of Education, 347 U.S. 483 (1954); McCarty, *supra* note 44, at 1–3; Jacobson, *supra* note 42, at 26.
44. Epstein & Graham, *supra* note 42, at 9, 13 (quoting Geoffrey C. Layman et al., *Party Polarization in American Politics: Characteristics, Causes, and Consequences*, 8 Annual Rev. Pol. Sci. 83 (2006)); Nolan McCarty et al., Polarized America 193–94 (2006); Richard Fleisher & Jon R. Bond, *Polarized Politics: Does It Matter?*, *in* Polarized, *supra* note 42, at 186, 191–92; Roe v. Wade, 410 U.S. 113 (1973).
45. Marjorie Randon Hershey & Darrell M. West, *Single-Issue Politics*, *in* Interest Group Politics 31, 31–32 (Allen J. Cigler & Burdett A. Loomis eds., 1983) [hereinafter Interest1st]; Petracca, *supra* note 25, at 16 (quoting George F. Will, *Passionate Politics*, Newsweek, May 1, 1978, at 96); Andrew McFarland, Neopluralism (2004); Loomis & Cigler, *supra* note 25, at 2; John F. Manley, *Neo-Pluralism: A Class Analysis of Pluralism I and Pluralism II*, 77 Am. Pol. Sci. Rev. 368 (1983).
46. One should recognize that, despite such resolute obstinacy, single-issue interest groups can bend in some ways. An organization might desire the passage of a particular piece of legislation, but, falling short of such success, it might be satisfied with blocking other legislative action. "An organized single-cause minority that can marshal 3 to 5 percent of the vote can rarely provide the margin of victory," writes one commentator. "Its opposition though often ensures defeat." In other words, "[t]he single-cause pressure group paralyzes." Also, while a single-issue organization will rarely compromise on or moderate its goal, it might join into a "broader alliance." For example, when President Ronald Reagan disappointed pro-life (anti-abortion) groups by appointing Sandra Day O'Connor to the Supreme Court in 1981, the groups strengthened their political forcefulness by allying together. Not coincidentally, Reagan would subsequently nominate stauncher abortion opponents Antonin Scalia and Robert Bork. Hershey & West, *supra* note 45, at 32–34, 41, 54, 56; Peter F. Drucker, The New Realities 102–03 (1989); The Oxford Companion to the Supreme Court of the United States 965, 971 (Kermit L. Hall ed., 1992) (App. 2: Nominations and Succession of the Justices).

CHAPTER 4

1. Irving Kristol, Neoconservatism: The Autobiography of an Idea x, 4–5, 11–13 (1995); Howard M. Sachar, A History of the Jews in America 330 (1992); Leonard Dinnerstein, Antisemitism in America 84–87 (1994); Francis Fukuyama, America at the Crossroads 15–16 (2006); Jacob Heilbrunn, They Knew They Were Right 10–15 (2008) [hereinafter Right];

Norman Podhoretz, The Norman Podhoretz Reader (Thomas L. Jeffers ed., 2004); Justin Vaïsse, Neoconservatism: The Biography of a Movement (Arthur Goldhammer trans., 2010); Jacob Heilbrunn, *Neoconservatism, in* Varieties of Conservatism in America 105, 112–13 (Peter Berkowitz ed., 2004) [hereinafter Neoconservatism].

2. Neoconservatism, *supra* note 1, at 113–14; Kristol, *supra* note 1, at 19–21; Norman Podhoretz, *Neoconservatism: A Eulogy* (1996), *reprinted in* Podhoretz, *supra* note 1, at 269, 273–75 [hereinafter Eulogy]; Fukuyama, *supra* note 1, at 16–17.
3. Norman Podhoretz, *My Negro Problem—and Ours*, Commentary, Feb. 1963, at 93–100; Fukuyama, *supra* note 1, at 19; Kristol, *supra* note 1, at x, 29–31; Murray Friedman, The Neoconservative Revolution 118–19 (2005); George H. Nash, The Conservative Intellectual Movement in America Since 1945, at 513–18 (2008 ed.); Neoconservatism, *supra* note 1, at 108.
4. Norman Podhoretz, *Liberalism and the Culture: A Turning of the Tide?*, Commentary, Oct. 1996, at 25; Kristol, *supra* note 1, at x, 31–32; Jeane Kirkpatrick, *Neoconservatism as a Response to the Counter-Culture, in* The Neocon Reader 233, 235–40 (Irwin Stelzer ed., 2004) [hereinafter Reader].
5. Kirkpatrick, *supra* note 4, at 235–36, 239–40; Allan Bloom, The Closing of the American Mind 194 (1987).
6. John Kifner, *Cornell Negroes Seize a Building*, New York Times, April 20, 1969, at 1, 77; John Kifner, *Armed Negroes End Seizure; Cornell Yields*, New York Times, April 21, 1969, at 1; Homer Bigart, *Cornell Faculty Votes Down Pact Ending Take-Over*, New York Times, April 22, 1969, at 1; Homer Bigart, *Cornell Faculty Reverses Itself on Negroes*, New York Times, April 24, 1969, at 1; Fukuyama, *supra* note 1, at 18; Douglas Murray, Neoconservatism 27 (2006); Neoconservatism, *supra* note 1, at 119.
7. Bloom, *supra* note 5, at 313–14, 317, 319; Kristol, *supra* note 1, at 31–32; Kirkpatrick, *supra* note 4, at 239–40.
8. Kristol, *supra* note 1, at 7; Leo Strauss, Natural Right and History 1–8 (1953) [hereinafter Natural]; Ted V. McAllister, Revolt Against Modernity 160–61 (1996); Thomas L. Pangle, Leo Strauss 15–16 (2006). In this chapter, I also will cite Leo Strauss, Liberalism Ancient and Modern (1968) [hereinafter Liberalism]; Leo Strauss, The City and Man (1964) [hereinafter City]; Leo Strauss, What Is Political Philosophy (1959) [hereinafter Political]. "Michael Harrington has been credited with having coined the term 'neoconservatives' in the late 1960s." Friedman, *supra* note 3, at 127. Podhoretz argued that Harrington was not the first to use the term, but that after Harrington used it, it became more common. Podhoretz, *supra* note 2, at 270.

9. Kristol, *supra* note 1, at 235–52.
10. Liberalism, *supra* note 8, at 24; City, *supra* note 8, at 11; Natural, *supra* note 8, at 313–16; Friedman, *supra* note 3, at 40–41; Fukuyama, *supra* note 1, at 23; Murray, *supra* note 6, at 10–21; Pangle, *supra* note 8, at 26–28, 83–84.
11. Neoconservatism, *supra* note 1, at 120–21; Kristol, *supra* note 1, at x–xi; Norman Podhoretz, *Kissinger Reconsidered* (1982), *reprinted in* Podhoretz, *supra* note 2, at 195, 205–08; Friedman, *supra* note 3, at 137–41; George H. Nash, *The Uneasy Future of American Conservatism, in* The Future of Conservatism 1, 7 (Charles W. Dunn ed., 2007) [hereinafter Dunn].
12. Friedman, *supra* note 3, at 151–52; Murray, *supra* note 6, at 55; Neoconservatism, *supra* note 1, at 122.
13. Barbara Sinclair, Party Wars 37–39, 46–52 (2006); Joel Olson, *Whiteness and the Polarization of American Politics*, 61 Pol. Res. Q. 1 (2008); Paul Krugman, *Republicans and Race*, New York Times, Nov. 19, 2007; Erik W. Austin, Political Facts of the United States Since 1789, at 94, 98 (Table 3.1, National Electoral and Popular Vote Cast for President, 1789–1984); Joseph E. Lowndes, From the New Deal to the New Right 2, 7 (2008); Steven M. Teles, The Rise of the Conservative Legal Movement 89 (2008); Vaïsse, *supra* note 1, at 20; Mary D. Edsall & Thomas B. Edsall, Chain Reaction 137–38 (1992). "Over a period of about five years, Reagan told the story of the 'Chicago welfare queen' who had 80 names, 30 addresses, 12 Social Security cards, and collected benefits for 'four nonexisting deceased husbands,' bilking the government out of 'over $150,000.' The real welfare recipient to whom Reagan referred was actually convicted for using two different aliases to collect $8,000. Reagan continued to use his version of the story even after the press pointed out the actual facts of the case to him." The Mendacity Index, Washington Monthly, Sept. 2003.
14. Friedman, *supra* note 3, at 129–33, 183, 191; Fukuyama, *supra* note 1, at 38–39; Kristol, *supra* note 1, at 33; Murray, *supra* note 6, at 61; Nash, *supra* note 3, at 9–11, 559; Dunn, *supra* note 11, at vi, viii.
15. Lowndes, *supra* note 13, at 155 (quoting Reagan); Gertrude Himmelfarb, Poverty and Compassion (1991) [hereinafter Poverty]; Friedman, *supra* note 3, at 153; Kristol, *supra* note 1, at 40; Murray, *supra* note 6, at 4, 87–89; Vaïsse, *supra* note 1, at 283–87 (dividing neoconservatism into three ages and identifying key figures in each); Eulogy, *supra* note 2, at 270, 277–78; Irwin Stelzer, *Neoconservatives and Their Critics: An Introduction, in* Reader, *supra* note 4, at 3, 19 [hereinafter Introduction].
16. Irving Kristol, *The Neoconservative Persuasion* (Aug. 25, 2003), *reprinted in* Reader, *supra* note 4, at 31, 33; Murray, *supra* note 6, at ix.

17. Daniel Bell, The Cultural Contradictions of Capitalism xxiv–xxv, xxx–xxxi, 10–16, 37, 54–65, 71–72 (1978; 1st ed. 1976); Max Weber, The Protestant Ethic and the Spirit of Capitalism (Talcott Parsons trans., 1958).
18. Bell, *supra* note 17, at xxx, 11–12, 23–25, 196–98, 233.
19. *Id.* at 73, 81; Norbert Wiley, *Review*, 6 Contemporary Sociology 416, 418 (1977); *see* Ruth R. Wisse, If I Am Not for Myself: The Liberal Betrayal of the Jews (1992) (arguing that liberalism cannot fulfill its promises of rationality and progress).
20. Murray, *supra* note 6, at 99–107; Bloom, *supra* note 5, at 26, 31–32, 143.
21. Bloom, *supra* note 5, at 25–26, 30, 39, 141–42, 202.
22. Francis Fukuyama, *The End of History?*, 16 The National Interest 3 (Summer 1989); Murray, *supra* note 6, at 158.
23. Bloom, *supra* note 5, at 39; Glazer, *supra* note 1, at 71–76.
24. William Kristol, *Postscript: Neoconservatism Remains the Bedrock of U.S. Foreign Policy* (2004), *reprinted in* Reader, *supra* note 1, at 75, 75 [hereinafter Postscript]; Murray, *supra* note 6, at 46; Bell, *supra* note 1, at xxiv, 30, 171; Bloom, *supra* note 5, at 19–20, 194; Wiley, *supra* note 19, at 419.
25. Bloom, *supra* note 5, at 39; Natural, *supra* note 8, at 144; Kenneth R. Weinstein, *Philosophic Roots, The Role of Leo Strauss, and the War in Iraq*, *in* Reader, *supra* note 4, at 201, 204, 210.
26. Irving Kristol, *The American Revolution as a Successful Revolution* (1976), *reprinted in* Kristol, *supra* note 1, at 235, 238, 247–48.
27. Weinstein, *supra* note 25, at 204; Irving Kristol, *Pornography, Obscenity, and the Case for Censorship* (March 28, 1971), *reprinted in* Reader, *supra* note 4, at 167, 175–76 [hereinafter Censorship]; American Booksellers Association v. Hudnut, 771 F.2d 323 (7th Cir. 1985).
28. Censorship, *supra* note 27, at 175–77; Stephen M. Feldman, Free Expression and Democracy in America: A History 101–52, 209–40 (2008).
29. Kristol, *supra* note 1, at 47–48; Irving Kristol, *A Conservative Welfare State* (June 14, 1993), *reprinted in* Reader, *supra* note 4, at 143, 146 [hereinafter Welfare].
30. Glazer, *supra* note 1, at ix, 67–76, 167–95, 202; Charles Krauthammer, *Lott Fiasco Exposes Conservative Split*, Jewish World Review, Dec. 19, 2002. Glazer failed to discuss that many white families had themselves benefited from governmental assistance (and attained middle-class status) through the post–World War II GI Bill benefits. Ira Katznelson, When Affirmative Action was White (2005).
31. William J. Bennett, Our Children and Our Country 10, 71 (1988); Introduction, *supra* note 15, at 4; Robert D. Kamenshine, *The First Amendment's Implied Political Establishment Clause*, 67 Cal. L. Rev. 1104, 1133–34 (1979); I Education Sourcebook 10 (Jeanne Gough ed., 1997).

32. Introduction, *supra* note 15, at 20; James Q. Wilson & George L. Kelling, *Broken Windows* (March 1982), *reprinted in* Reader, *supra* note 4, at 149, 153–54, 158–59; Irving Kristol, *The Neoconservative Persuasion* (Aug. 25, 2003), *reprinted in* Reader, *supra* note 4, at 31, 34–35 [hereinafter Persuasion]; Gertrude Himmelfarb, *Victorian Values/Jewish Values*, Commentary, Feb. 1989, at 31; Kristol, *supra* note 1, at 230–33, 256, 258–59, 294–98; Friedman, *supra* note 1, at 178–83.
33. Poverty, *supra* note 15, at 388–89; Introduction, *supra* note 15, at 20; Welfare, *supra* note 29, at 145–48; Gertrude Himmelfarb, The De-Moralization of Society 4–12 (1995).
34. Fukuyama, *supra* note 1, at 7, 9; David Sanders, *International Relations*, *in* A New Handbook of Political Science 428, 429 (Robert E. Goodin & Hans-Dieter Klingemann eds., 1996).
35. Persuasion, *supra* note 32, at 36; Neoconservatism, *supra* note 1, at 105; Murray, *supra* note 6, at 46–53.
36. Murray, *supra* note 6, at 48, 60; UN General Assembly Resolution 3379, Nov. 10, 1975; Daniel P. Moynihan, *Statement as United States Representative (Ambassador) to the United Nations, in Plenary, in Response to the United Nations Resolution Equating Zionism with Racism and Racial Discrimination*, Nov. 10, 1975, *reprinted in* The Essential Neoconservative Reader 93, 93–95, 98 (Mark Gerson ed., 1996); Norman Podhoretz, *Israel and the United States*, Commentary, May 1998, at 28, 29–30; Kirkpatrick, *supra* note 4, at 236–40.
37. Ronald Reagan, Remarks at the Annual Convention of the National Association of Evangelicals (Orlando, Florida), March 8, 1983; Fukuyama, *supra* note 1, at 4–5; Neoconservatism, *supra* note 1, at 108–09; Kirkpatrick, *supra* note 4, at 236–40.
38. Fukuyama, *supra* note 1; Raymond L. Garthoff, The Great Transition 7–53, 375–502 (1994); Murray, *supra* note 6, at 61–63; Neoconservatism, *supra* note 1, at 123; G.W.F. Hegel, The Phenomenology of Spirit 49–57 (A. V. Miller trans., 1977); G.W.F. Hegel, *The Philosophy of History*, *reprinted in* The Age of Ideology 82–97 (Henry D. Aiken ed., 1956).
39. William Kristol & Robert Kagan, *Toward a Neo-Reaganite Foreign Policy*, 75 Foreign Affairs 18, 20–28 (1996); Murray, *supra* note 6, at 73–74; Norman Podhoretz, *After the Cold War*, Commentary, July 1991, at 55.
40. Project for the New American Century (PNAC), *Statement of Principles*, June 3, 1997; William Kristol & Robert Kagan, *National Interest and Global Responsibility* (2000), *reprinted in* Reader, *supra* note 4, at 55, 68.
41. George W. Bush, Remarks by the President at 2002 Graduation Exercise of the United States Military Academy (West Point, New York), June 1, 2002; Friedman, *supra* note 3, at 2; Fukuyama, *supra* note 1, at 1–3; Neoconservatism, *supra* note 1, at 105, 126.

42. Fukuyama, *supra* note 1, at 19, 30–31, 114–18. Few neocons supported a strong theory of the unitary executive as a matter of neoconservative principles. *See* chapter 6, *infra* (discussing foreign policy Supreme Court cases); Vaïsse, *supra* note 1, at 221–23, 232–36 (lengthy description of neoconservative foreign policy positions does not include theory of the unitary executive).
43. Howard Gillman, The Constitution Besieged 12–13 (1993); 198 U.S. 45, 59, 64 (1905); Feldman, *supra* note 44, at 155, 199–208.
44. Cong. Rec. 877 (1937); Feldman, *supra* note 44, at 354–59.
45. Wickard v. Filburn, 317 U.S. 111, 120 (1942); Thomas v. Collins, 323 U.S. 516, 529–30 (1945); Schneider v. State, 308 U.S. 147, 161 (1939).
46. Henry M. Hart Jr. & Albert Sacks, The Legal Process (Tentative ed. 1958); John H. Ely, Democracy and Distrust 73–75, 106, 117, 136 (1980); Alexander M. Bickel, The Least Dangerous Branch 25–26, 49–59 (2d ed. 1986; 1st ed. 1962).
47. United States v. Bennett, 24 F.Cas. 1093, 1103–04 (C.C.S.D.N.Y. 1879); Feldman, *supra* note 44, at 101–52, 209–90.
48. G. Edward White, *The First Amendment Comes of Age*, 95 Mich. L. Rev. 299, 300–01 (1996); Bridges v. California, 314 U.S. 252, 263 (1941); Feldman, *supra* note 44, at 383–419.
49. Schenck v. United States, 249 U.S. 47, 52 (1919); Walter Berns, Freedom, Virtue, and the First Amendment 26, 70 (1957) [hereinafter Freedom]; Walter Berns, The First Amendment and the Future of American Democracy xi (1976) [hereinafter Future]; Walter Berns, Taking the Constitution Seriously (1987); Nash, *supra* note3, at 246 n.32; 341, 347.
50. Freedom, *supra* note 49, at 26, 47, 70–72, 126, 225, 238–42, 250–56 (quoting Terminiello v. Chicago, 337 U.S. 1, 37 (1949) (Jackson, J., dissenting)).
51. Future, *supra* note 50, at 184–85, 221, 226, 231–33.
52. *See* Alexander M. Bickel, The Morality of Consent vii, 23–25, 77 (1975) [hereinafter Morality]; Nash, *supra* note 3, at 527; Edward A. Purcell Jr., *Alexander M. Bickel and the Post-Realist Constitution*, 11 Harv. C.R.-C.L. L. Rev. 521, 553–60 (1976). Starting in 1956 and continuing until his death, Bickel published extensively in the liberal *New Republic*. He began publishing in the neoconservative *Commentary* in June 1963 and continued to do so consistently until his death. He also published once in *Public Interest* in 1971. Morality, *supra*, at 144–49.
53. Alexander M. Bickel, The Supreme Court and the Idea of Progress 13, 99, 148–51, 165, 173, 175 (1978; 1st ed. 1970); Morality, *supra* note 52, at 25–28; *Brown*, 347 U.S. 483 (1954); *Roe*, 410 U.S. 113 (1973); Purcell, *supra* note 52, at 551–53.

54. Ronald Dworkin, Taking Rights Seriously (1977); Lino A. Graglia, Disaster by Decree (1976); Cornell W. Clayton, *Law, Politics and the Rehnquist Court*, *in* The Supreme Court in American Politics: New Institutionalist Interpretations 151, 153–55 (Howard Gillman & Cornell Clayton eds., 1999); Frank I. Michelman, *Foreword: On Protecting the Poor Through the Fourteenth Amendment*, 83 Harv. L. Rev. 7 (1969); Herbert Wechsler, *Toward Neutral Principles of Constitutional Law*, 73 Harv. L. Rev. 1 (1959).
55. Robert H. Bork, *Neutral Principles and Some First Amendment Problems*, 47 Ind. L.J. 1, 2–3, 8, 10 (1971) [hereinafter Neutral]; Robert H. Bork, The Tempting of America 188 (1990) [hereinafter Tempting]; Robert H. Bork, Slouching Towards Gomorrah (1996) [hereinafter Slouching].
56. Neutral, *supra* note 55, at 6–11, 17; *see* Robert H. Bork, The Impossibility of Finding Welfare Rights in the Constitution, 1979 Wash. U.L.Q. 695; Raoul Berger, Government by Judiciary 45, 363–72 (1977) (emphasizing framers' original intentions); Steven M. Teles, *Transformative Bureaucracy: Reagan's Lawyers and the Dynamics of Political Investment*, 23 Studies in American Political Development 61, 76 (2009) [hereinafter Transformative] (emphasizing importance of Bork's advocacy of originalism).
57. Neutral, *supra* note 55, at 20–29.
58. Tempting, *supra* note 55, at 321; Slouching, *supra* note 55, at 59–60, 63, 70, 160, 268, 276; Right, *supra* note 1, at 158. For Bork essays in neoconservative journals, see Robert H. Bork, *Olympians on the March*, New Criterion, May 2004, at 5 [hereinafter Olympians]; Robert H. Bork, *Adversary Jurisprudence*, New Criterion, May 2002, at 4 [hereinafter Adversary].
59. Tempting, *supra* note 55, at 2-6, 139-44, 245-46; Slouching, *supra* note 55, at 5, 276; Transformative, *supra* note 56, at 80.
60. Slouching, *supra* note 55, at 8, 99; Tempting, *supra* note 55, at 242; Adversary, *supra* note 58; *Cohen*, 403 U.S. 15 (1971).
61. Slouching, *supra* note 55, at 141; Robert H. Bork, *'Thanks a Lot': Free Speech and High Schools*, National Review, April 16, 2007, at 24; Adversary, *supra* note 58.
62. Adversary, *supra* note 58; Randy E. Barnett, Restoring the Lost Constitution (2004) [hereinafter Restoring]; Randy Barnett, The Structure of Liberty (1998) [hereinafter Liberty]; Richard A. Epstein, Takings (1985) [hereinafter Takings]; Richard A. Epstein, Principles for a Free Society: Reconciling Individual Liberty with the Common Good (1998) [hereinafter Principles]; Richard A. Epstein, *The Proper Scope of the Commerce Power*, 73 Va. L. Rev. 1387 (1987) [hereinafter Commerce]; Lino

A. Graglia, *"Constitutional Theory": The Attempted Justification for the Supreme Court's Liberal Political Program*, 65 Tex. L. Rev. 789 (1987).

63. Tempting, *supra* note 55, at 6, 144; Restoring, *supra* note 62, at 89, 92; Keith E. Whittington, Constitutional Interpretation xi, 3, 35–36 (1999); Department of Justice Office of Legal Policy, *Guidelines on Constitutional Litigation* 3–13 (Feb. 19, 1988); *The Constitution in the Year 2000* 138 (Oct. 11, 1988).
64. Restoring, *supra* note 62, at 53–86, 260–61, 274–334; Liberty, *supra* note 62, at 1–28.
65. Tempting, *supra* note 55, at 6; Bork, Adversary, *supra* note 58; Slouching, *supra* note 55, at 11–12, 142; Olympians, *supra* note 58.
66. Restoring, *supra* note 62, at 80; Douglas H. Ginsburg, *Delegation Running Riot*, Regulation, No. 1, 1995, at 83, 84; Cass R. Sunstein, Radicals in Robes 1–19 (2005); William W. Van Alstyne, *The Constitution in Exile*, 51 Duke L.J. 1 (2001); Bruce Ackerman, *The Art of Stealth*, London Review of Books, Feb. 17, 2005; Jeffrey Rosen, *The Unregulated Offensive*, New York Times, April 17, 2005.
67. Takings, *supra* note 62, at ix–x, 5, 9–15, 20, 24, 280–81, 344–46; U.S. Const. amend. V; Principles, *supra* note 62, at 3–4. Not coincidentally, no constitutional provision is more of an atavistic throwback to the republican democratic era than the Takings Clause, with its express requirement that a taking be for a public use—or the common good. It should be noted, though, that Epstein defines the common good in such individualist terms that it seems to resonate more closely with pluralist than republican democracy. Principles, *supra* note 62, at 4 (conceiving of the common good "as the summation of interests of those individuals subject to state power").
68. Commerce, *supra* note 62, at 1387; Rosen, *supra* note 66.
69. Commerce, *supra* note 62, at 1388–89, 1395–1400, 1408–10, 1446, 1451–52.
70. *Id.* at 1454–55; Richard A. Epstein, *The Mistakes of 1937*, 11 Geo. Mason U. L. Rev. 5, 20 (1988–1989); Restoring, *supra* note 62, at 274–318; Richard A. Posner, Economic Analysis of Law (1973); Daniel A. Farber & Philip P. Frickey, Law and Public Choice (1991). With regard to other conservative constitutional theorists, Patrick M. Garry argued that the Court should return to its pre-1937 methods for enforcing federalism and separation of powers limits on national power. Patrick M. Garry, An Entrenched Legacy (2008). Likewise, Lynn A. Baker and Ernest A. Young argued that federalism restrictions on national power should be retrieved from the "Constitution-in-exile." Lynn A. Baker & Ernest A. Young, *Federalism and the Double Standard of Judicial Review*, 51 Duke

L.J. 75, 75 (2001). And Douglas H. Ginsburg argued that the Court should resurrect the nondelegation doctrine as a limit on congressional action. Ginsburg, *supra* note 66. David E. Bernstein argued that republican democratic judicial review limited state and local governmental power in ways that enhanced individual liberty. David E. Bernstein, Only One Place of Redress (2001); David E. Bernstein, *Lochner Era Revisionism, Revised*, 92 Geo. L.J. 1 (2003). Bernard H. Siegan argued that the Court should return to a pre-1937 protection of economic liberties. Bernard H. Siegan, Economic Liberties and the Constitution 318–26 (1980).

71. Future, *supra* note 49, at 233.
72. Right, *supra* note 1, at 264–80; Robert A. Kagan, *How Much Do Conservative Tort Tales Matter?*, 31 Law & Soc. Inquiry 711, 712, 723–26 (2006).
73. Nash, *supra* note 3, at 570; Introduction, *supra* note 15, at 3; Murray, *supra* note 6, at ix–x; Teles, *supra* note 13, at 6, 9, 58–264; Robert Post & Reva Siegel, *Originalism as a Political Practice*, 75 Fordham L. Rev. 545 (2006); Transformative, *supra* note 56, at 75–78.
74. Feldman, *supra* note 44, at 291–348.
75. Fukuyama, *supra* note 22.
76. Natural, *supra* note 8, at 133–34; Political, *supra* note 8, at 40, 94; Fukuyama, *supra* note 1, at 30–31, 114–18.
77. Poverty, *supra* note 15, at 388; Welfare, *supra* note 29, at 146; Austin, *supra* note 13, at 472 (Table 7.5, Number of Immigrants from Selected Countries); Feldman, *supra* note 44, at 23–26, 32–45; Irving Kristol, *Pornography, Obscenity, and the Case for Censorship* (March 28, 1971), *reprinted in* Reader, *supra* note4, at 167.
78. City, *supra* note 8, at 11.
79. Hannah Arendt, On Revolution (1963); Hannah Arendt, The Human Condition (1958); Hannah Arendt, The Origins of Totalitarianism (1973 ed., 1951); Eric Voegelin, Order and History: Israel and Revelation (1956); Eric Voegelin, The New Science of Politics (1952); John McGowan, Hannah Arendt 33–34 (1998); Pangle, *supra* note 8, at 56–65. *See* Barry Cooper, Eric Voegelin and the Foundations of Modern Political Science (1999); Michael P. Federici, Eric Voegelin (2002); George Kateb, Hannah Arendt (1983); Dana R. Villa, Arendt and Heidegger (1996); Richard J. Bernstein, *Judging—the Actor and the Spectator, in* Philosophical Profiles 221 (1986); Richard J. Bernstein, *Rethinking the Social and the Political, in* Philosophical Profiles 238 (1986); Stephen A. McKnight, *Voegelin's New Science of History, in* Eric Voegelin's Significance for the Modern Mind 46 (Ellis Sandoz ed., 1991).
80. Bloom, *supra* note 5, at 30 (accusing John Rawls of "folly").

CHAPTER 5

1. The Federalist No. 78, at 465 (Alexander Hamilton) (Clinton Rossiter ed., 1961); Marbury v. Madison, 5 U.S. (1 Cranch) 137 (1803).
2. Ronald Dworkin, Justice in Robes (2006); Ronald Dworkin, Freedom's Law (1996); Richard A. Posner, *Foreword: A Political Court*, 119 Harv. L. Rev. 31 (2005); Jeffrey A. Segal & Harold J. Spaeth, The Supreme Court and the Attitudinal Model 64–69 (1993); Stephen M. Feldman, *The Rule of Law or the Rule of Politics? Harmonizing the Internal and External Views of Supreme Court Decision Making*, 30 L. & Soc. Inquiry 89, 96–98 (2005) [hereinafter Harmonizing]; Stephen M. Feldman, *Do Supreme Court Nominees Lie? The Politics of Adjudication*, 18 S. Cal. Interdisc. L.J. 17 (2008) [hereinafter Adjudication]; Barry Friedman, *The Politics of Judicial Review*, 84 Tex. L. Rev. 257, 257–60 (2005).
3. District of Columbia v. Heller, 128 S. Ct. 2783 (2008) (applying originalist approach to Second Amendment to uphold individual right to possess a gun); Bruce Ackerman, *The Stealth Revolution, Continued*, London Review of Books, Feb. 9, 2006 [hereinafter Continued]; Bruce Ackerman, *The Art of Stealth*, London Review of Books, Feb. 17, 2005 [hereinafter Stealth]; Erwin Chemerinsky, *When It Matters Most, It Is Still the Kennedy Court*, 11 Green Bag 2d 427, 429–31 (2008); Robert Post & Reva Siegel, *Originalism as a Political Practice*, 75 Fordham L. Rev. 545, 562–65 (2006).
4. Department of Justice Office of Legal Policy, *The Constitution in the Year 2000* iii, 185 (Oct. 11, 1988); *Roe*, 410 U.S. 113 (1973); David M. O'Brien, Storm Center 1–32 (8th ed. 2008).
5. *Perceived Qualifications and Ideology of Supreme Court Nominees, 1937–2005* [hereinafter Scores] (data drawn from Jeffrey Segal & Albert Cover, *Ideological Values and the Votes of Supreme Court Justices*, 83 Am. Pol. Sci. Rev. 557–565 (1989); updated in Lee Epstein & Jeffrey A. Segal, Advice and Consent: The Politics of Judicial Appointments (2005); The Faculty Lounge http://www.thefacultylounge.org/2009/08/sotomayor.html; Thomas R. Hensley, The Rehnquist Court 19 (2006); The Oxford Companion to the Supreme Court of the United States 804 (Kermit L. Hall ed., 1992) (during his first term, Souter voted with Rehnquist in 86 percent of the cases); Charles Lane, *Kennedy Seen as the Next Justice in the Court's Middle*, Washington Post, Jan. 31, 2006, at A4. Additional information on the justices is drawn from the following web sites: http://www.supremecourtus.gov/index.html; http://www.oyez.org/. Of course, some commentators find the current Court insufficiently conservative. *E.g.*, Lino Graglia, *The Myth of a Conservative Supreme Court*, 26 Harv. J. L. & Public Policy 281 (2003).

6. Michael Avery, *Book Review: The Rise of the Conservative Legal Movement*, 42 Suffolk U. L. Rev. 89, 89–91 (2008); Bell Atlantic Corp. v. Twombly, 550 U.S. 544 (2007) (dismissing antitrust conspiracy action); Gonzales v. Carhart, 550 U.S. 124 (2007) (upholding restictions on partial-birth abortion).
7. Douglas H. Ginsburg, *Delegation Running Riot*, Regulation, No. 1, 1995, at 83; Shadia B. Drury, Leo Strauss and the American Right 3 (1997) (Thomas); Murray Friedman, The Neoconservative Revolution 131 (2005) (Scalia); Bruce Ackerman, *The Stealth Revolution, Continued*, London Review of Books, Feb. 9, 2006 (Roberts and Alito); Bruce Ackerman, *The Art of Stealth*, London Review of Books, Feb. 17, 2005 (Scalia and Thomas); Avery, *supra* note 6, at 95 & n.36; Josh Benson, *The Past Does Not Repeat Itself, but It Rhymes: The Second Coming of the Liberal Anti-Court Movement*, 33 Law & Soc. Inquiry 1071, 1103–05 (2008) (questioning the veracity of Roberts's confirmation-hearing claims). After the Senate rejected Bork for the Court, Reagan nominated Douglas Ginsburg, but Ginsburg soon withdrew because he had used marijuana. At that point, Reagan nominated Kennedy, a more moderate conservative. O'Brien, *supra* note 4, at 76–77. Given that Souter consistently voted with Rehnquist and Scalia during his first term, 1990–91, one might categorize him during that term as a neocon for voting purposes.
8. Mark Tushnet, Taking the Constitution Away from the Courts 148 (1999); Mark A. Graber, *Rethinking Equal Protection in Dark Times*, 4 U. Pa. J. Const. L. 314, 325 (2002); Posner, *supra* note 2, at 75.
9. Philip Bobbitt, Constitutional Interpretation 12–13 (1991) (specifying six acceptable modalities of constitutional argument); O'Brien, *supra* note 4, at 265–66.
10. Antonin Scalia, A Matter of Interpretation 40, 44 (1997); Antonin Scalia, *Originalism: The Lesser Evil*, 57 U. Cin. L. Rev. 849, 862 (1989); *Heller*, 128 S. Ct. 2783, 2788–2812 (2008); *id.* at 2824–36 (Stevens, J., dissenting); Harmonizing, *supra* note 2, at 96–98; Adjudication, *supra* note 2, at 32; Thomas M. Keck, *Party, Policy, or Duty*, 101 Am. Pol. Sci. Rev. 321, 337 (2007); Saul Cornell, *Heller, New Originalism, and Law Office History*, 56 UCLA L. Rev. 1095 (2009) (criticizing Scalia's new originalism).
11. *Alton*, 295 U.S. 330, 368, 374 (1935); *Carter*, 298 U.S. 238, 304 (1936); *Hammer*, 247 U.S. 251, 276 (1918); U.S. Const. art. I, § 8, cl. 3.
12. Wickard v. Filburn, 317 U.S. 111, 120 (1942); United States v. Darby, 312 U.S. 100, 124 (1941); John H. Ely, Democracy and Distrust (1980).
13. Hodel v. Indiana, 452 U.S. 314, 323–24 (1981); *Usery*, 426 U.S. 833, 852 (1976), overruled by Garcia v. San Antonio Metro. Transit Auth., 469 U.S. 528, 550–51 (1985).

14. *New York*, 505 U.S. 144, 157, 161, 175–77, 181, 188 (1992) (quoting United States v. Butler, 297 U.S. 1, 63 (1936)); Coleman v. Thompson, 501 U.S. 722, 759 (1991)).
15. *Lopez*, 514 U.S. 549, 558–59 (1995); *New York*, 505 U.S. at 160.
16. *Lopez*, 514 U.S. at 559–68; *id.* at 627–29 (Breyer, J., dissenting); *Hammer*, 247 U.S. 251, 274, 276 (1918).
17. *Lopez*, 514 U.S. at 562–63; *Hill*, 259 U.S. 44, 68–69 (1922); Board of Trade v. Olsen, 262 U.S. 1, 31–38 (1923) (upholding statute partly because Congress made sufficient findings); A. Christopher Bryant & Timothy J. Simeone, *Remanding to Congress: The Supreme Court's New "On the Record" Constitutional Review of Federal Statutes*, 86 Cornell L. Rev. 328, 356 (2001).
18. *Lopez*, 514 U.S. at 556; Lino A. Graglia, *The Myth of a Conservative Supreme Court*, 26 Harv. J.L. & Pub. Pol'y 281 (2003); Lino A. Graglia, *United States v. Lopez: Judicial Review Under the Commerce Clause*, 74 Tex. L. Rev. 719, 769–71 (1996).
19. *Lopez*, 514 U.S. at 585–90, 598–99 (Thomas, J., concurring); Carter v. Carter Coal Co., 298 U.S. 238 (1936); United States v. E. C. Knight Co., 156 U.S. 1 (1895); Richard A. Epstein, *The Proper Scope of the Commerce Power*, 73 Va. L. Rev. 1387, 1387–1455 (1987). Sanford Levinson has accused Thomas of plagiarizing from Epstein's article. Sanford Levinson, *Raoul Berger Pleads for Judicial Activism*, 74 Tex. L. Rev. 773, 775 & n.9 (1996).
20. 514 U.S. at 568 (Kennedy, J., concurring).
21. *Morrison*, 529 U.S. 598, 615 (2000); Barry Friedman, *The Cycles of Constitutional Theory*, 67 Law & Contemp. Probs. 149, 161 (2004); *Boerne*, 521 U.S. 527, 530 (1997); *Gonzales*, 545 U.S. 1 (2005); *id.* at 34-40 (Scalia, J., concurring in the judgment); Thomas M. Keck, The Most Activist Supreme Court in History 2 (2004); O'Brien, *supra* note 4, at 31; *e.g.*, Alden v. Maine, 527 U.S. 706 (1999) (Tenth Amendment prevents Congress from commandeering state courts); Printz v. United States, 521 U.S. 898 (1997) (Tenth Amendment prevents Congress from commandeering state executive officers). The Court also has expanded state sovereign immunity under the Eleventh Amendment. Kimel v. Fla. Bd. of Regents, 528 U.S. 62 (2000); Seminole Tribe v. Florida, 517 U.S. 44 (1996). This is not to say that the Court never upholds congressional acts. Pierce County, Washington v. Guillen, 537 U.S. 129 (2003) (holding federal statutes regulating state government efforts to improve road safety were within congressional power to regulate the channels and instrumentalities of interstate commerce); Reno v. Condon, 528 U.S. 141 (2000) (holding federal statute prohibiting state motor vehicle

departments from selling personal information did not violate Tenth Amendment).

22. United States v. Carolene Products Co., 304 U.S. 144, 152–53 n.4 (1938); Palmore v. Sidoti, 466 U.S. 429 (1984); Washington v. Davis, 426 U.S. 229 (1976); Korematsu v. United States, 323 U.S. 214 (1944); Gerald Gunther, *Foreword: In Search of Evolving Doctrine on a Changing Court*, 86 Harv. L. Rev. 1, 8 (1972).
23. 438 U.S. 265, 317 (1978) (Powell, J.); *id.* at 316–18 (discussing Harvard plan) (Powell, J.); *id.* at 361–64 (Brennan, J., concurring in the judgment in part and dissenting in part).
24. *Croson*, 488 U.S. 469 (1989); *id.* at 520–28 (Scalia, J., concurring in the judgment); Fullilove v. Klutznick, 448 U.S. 448 (1980).
25. *Adarand*, 515 U.S. 200, 239 (1995) (Scalia, J., concurring in part and concurring in the judgment); *id.* at 241 (Thomas, J., concurring in part and concurring in the judgment); *id.* at 227, 237–38; *Metro*, 497 U.S. 547, 564–65 (1990).
26. *Grutter*, 539 U.S. 306, 334 (2003); *Gratz*, 539 U.S. 244 (2003); Neal Devins, *Explaining* Grutter v. Bollinger, 152 U. Pa. L. Rev. 347, 348–49 (2003).
27. Harmonizing, *supra* note 2, at 121; 539 U.S. at 326, 328, 339; *id.* at 350, 394 (Thomas, J., concurring and dissenting); *id.* at 380 (Rehnquist, C.J., dissenting); *e.g.*, Adarand Constructors, Inc. v. Pena, 515 U.S. 200, 237 (1995) ("When race-based action is necessary to further a compelling interest, such action is within constitutional constraints if it satisfies the 'narrow tailoring' test this Court has set out in previous cases").
28. 539 U.S. at 276–77 (O'Connor, J., concurring).
29. 551 U.S. 701, 127 S. Ct. 2738, 2751–54 (2007); *id.* at 2767–68 (Roberts, C.J., plurality opinion); *id.* at 2811–20 (Breyer, J., dissenting).
30. *Id.* at 2797–98 (Stevens, J., dissenting); *id.* at 2768 (Thomas, J., concurring); *id.* at 2751–54, 2789–93 (Kennedy, J., concurring in part and concurring in the judgment); *id.* at 2817–20, 2836–37 (Breyer, J., dissenting).
31. *Id.* at 2789–93 (Kennedy, J., concurring in part and concurring in the judgment).
32. 393 U.S. 503, 505–06, 509–11 (1969); Ken I. Kersch, Constructing Civil Liberties 283–87 (2004) (emphasizing the role of education in building the pluralist democratic state).
33. *Tinker*, 393 U.S. at 508–09, 512 (quoting Shelton v. Tucker, 364 U.S. 479, 487 (1960)).
34. 408 U.S. 169, 170, 176, 188–94 (1972); *Brandenburg*, 395 U.S. 444 (1969).
35. *Healy*, 408 U.S. at 180–81, 194; *see* Papish v. Board of Curators of University of Missouri, 410 U.S. 667 (1973) (following *Healy*).

36. 478 U.S. 675, 680, 685 (1986).
37. *Id.* at 681; Charles A. Beard et al., A New Basic History of the United States 228 (1968 ed.).
38. 478 U.S. at 681, 683, 685.
39. 484 U.S. 260, 266, 271 (1988); J. Marc Abrams & S. Mark Goodman, *End of an Era*, 1988 Duke L.J. 706; Erwin Chemerinsky, *Students Do Leave Their First Amendment Rights at the Schoolhouse Gates*, 48 Drake L. Rev. 527 (2000).
40. Perry Education Assn. v. Perry Local Educators' Assn., 460 U.S. 37, 45–46 (1983); Adderley v. Florida, 385 U.S. 39 (1966).
41. 484 U.S. at 267, 270–73.
42. 127 S. Ct. 2618, 2622 (2007).
43. *Id.* at 2649 (Stevens, J., dissenting); *id.* at 2624.
44. *Id.* at 2626, 2629; Stephen M. Feldman, Free Expression and Democracy in America: A History 454–55 (2008).
45. 127 S. Ct. at 2626–29.
46. *Id.* at 2630–32, 2635 (Thomas, J., concurring).
47. *Id.* at 2637–38 (Alito, J., concurring).
48. *Id.* at 2645, 2649, 2651 (Stevens, J., dissenting).
49. 454 U.S. 263, 265 & n.2 (1981).
50. *Id.* at 267–77.
51. *Id.* at 288–89 (White, J., dissenting); *id.* at 278–80 (Stevens, J., concurring in the judgment); Stephen M. Feldman, *The Theory and Politics of First-Amendment Protections*, 8 U. Pa. J. Const. L. 431 (2006).
52. 508 U.S. 384, 386–88, 391–94 (1993).
53. *Rosenberger*, 515 U.S. 819, 826 (1995); *id.* at 874 (Souter, J., dissenting); *Good News*, 533 U.S. 98, 103, 108–12 (2001).
54. *Widmar*, 454 U.S. at 267–77; *Lamb's Chapel*, 508 U.S. at 391–94; *Rosenberger*, 515 U.S. at 830–33; *Good News*, 533 U.S. at 106–12.
55. Pleasant Grove City v. Summum, 129 S. Ct. 1125, 1139 (2009) (Stevens, J., concurring); *Widmar*, 454 U.S. at 276–77; *Rosenberger*, 515 U.S. at 833.
56. *Rosenberger*, 515 U.S. at 834.
57. 129 S. Ct. 1125, 1130 (2009).
58. *Id.* at 1129, 1131, 1133–34, 1137.
59. *Id.* at 1140 (Breyer, J., concurring). In *Capitol Square Review and Advisory Board v. Pinette*, 515 U.S. 753 (1995), the Court held that the government could allow a private actor, the Ku Klux Klan, to display a large Latin (Christian) cross on public property without violating the Establishment Clause. A majority of justices focused on the Establishment Clause, but public forum doctrine clearly influenced the analysis. *Id.* at 759–63 (Scalia, J., majority opinion). Scalia's plurality opinion, joined by Rehnquist, Thomas, and Kennedy, concluded: "Religious expression

cannot violate the Establishment Clause where it (1) is purely private and (2) occurs in a traditional or designated public forum, publicly announced and open to all on equal terms." *Id.* at 770 (Scalia, J., plurality opinion).

60. 330 U.S. 1, 16, 18 (1947); *see* McCreary County v. ACLU, 545 U.S. 844, 889–90 (2005) (Scalia, J., dissenting) (advocating for nonpreferentialism); Wallace v. Jaffree, 472 U.S. 38, 91–114 (1985) (Rehnquist, J., dissenting) (same).
61. *Engel*, 370 U.S. 421, 425, 430 (1962); *Lemon*, 403 U.S. 602, 612–13 (1971); *Stone*, 449 U.S. 39 (1980); *Lynch*, 465 U.S. 668 (1984).
62. 465 U.S. at 679; *id.* at 687–88 (O'Connor, J., concurring); County of Allegheny v. ACLU, 492 U.S. 573, 659 (1989) (Kennedy, J., concurring and dissenting).
63. *County of Allegheny*, 492 U.S. 573, 657, 659 (1989) (Kennedy, J., concurring and dissenting); Church of Lukumi Babalu Aye v. Hialeah, 508 U.S. 520 (1993) (ordinance targeting practices of Santería religion violated Free Exercise Clause); Elk Grove Unified School District v. Newdow, 542 U.S. 1, 53 n.4, 54 n.5 (2004) (Thomas, J., concurring in the judgment) (equating Establishment Clause coercion test with free-exercise proscriptions).
64. 403 U.S. at 614–24.
65. *Aguilar*, 473 U.S. 402, 412–13 (1985), overruled by *Agostini*, 521 U.S. 203 (1997); *Aguilar*, 473 U.S. at 416–18 (Powell, J., concurring). In a companion case, the Court invalidated under the effects prong a similar funding program that lacked the supervisory mandates of the New York City program. School District of Grand Rapids v. Ball, 473 U.S. 373 (1985).
66. 521 U.S. 203, 233–34 (1997).
67. Mitchell v. Helms, 530 U.S. 793, 807–08 (2000) (Thomas, J., plurality opinion); Zelman v. Simmons-Harris, 536 U.S. 639, 652, 658, 662 n.7 (2002); *id.* at 668 (O'Connor, J., concurring).
68. *Van Orden*, 545 U.S. 677, 686–90 (2005); Marsh v. Chambers, 463 U.S. 783 (1983) (upholding tradition of saying prayers in state legislatures); McCreary County v. ACLU, 545 U.S. 844, 860 (2005) (invalidating Ten Commandments display by focusing on governmental purposes). *But see id.* at 902 (Scalia, J., dissenting) ("I have urged that *Lemon*'s purpose prong be abandoned").
69. The Court, though, sometimes reached the opposite result. McCreary County v. ACLU, 545 U.S. 844 (2005) (Ten Commandments display in county courthouses violated Establishment Clause); Santa Fe Independent School Dist. v. Doe, 530 U.S. 290 (2000) (student-led prayers at school football games violated Establishment Clause); Lee v. Weisman, 505 U.S. 577 (1992) (recitation of prayer at a public school graduation violated Establishment Clause).

70. *Widmar*, 454 U.S. 263, 270–76 (1981); *Lamb's Chapel*, 508 U.S. 384 (1993); *id.* at 397 (Kennedy, J., concurring in part and concurring in the judgment); *id.* at 398–401 (Scalia, J., concurring in the judgment).
71. Rosenberger v. Rectors and Visitors of the University of Virginia, 515 U.S. 819, 839 (1995); *id.* at 852–55 (Thomas, J., concurring); James Madison, *Memorial and Remonstrance Against Religious Assessments* (1785), *reprinted in* The Complete Bill of Rights 46, 48 (Neil H. Cogan ed., 1997).
72. Pleasant Grove City v. Summum, 129 S. Ct. 1125, 1132 (2009); *id.* at 1141–42 (Souter, J., concurring in the judgment); *id.* at 1139 (Scalia, J., concurring); *Newdow*, 542 U.S. 1 (2004); *id.* at 26, 32–33 (Rehnquist, C.J., concurring in the judgment).
73. 542 U.S. at 49–51 (Thomas, J., concurring in the judgment).
74. *Id.* at 50–54 (Thomas, J., concurring in the judgment); Lee v. Weisman, 505 U.S. 577, 640 (1992) (Scalia, J., dissenting) (quoted in *Newdow*, 542 U.S. at 52 (Thomas, J., concurring in the judgment)). On psychological pressure, see Santa Fe Independent School District v. Doe, 530 U.S. 290, 311–12 (2000); Lee v. Weisman, 505 U.S. 577, 593–94 (1992).
75. *Bowers*, 478 U.S. 186, 196 (1986), *overruled by* Lawrence v. Texas, 539 U.S. 558 (2003); The Supreme Court in Conference (1940–1985): The Private Discussions Behind Nearly 300 Supreme Court Decisions 822 (Del Dickson ed., 2001).
76. 539 U.S. 558 (2003); Tushnet, *supra* note 8, at 148; Graber, *supra* note 8, at 325.
77. 539 U.S. at 567, 571 (quoting Planned Parenthood v. Casey, 505 U.S. 833, 850 (1992)).
78. *Id.* at 588, 590 (Scalia, J., dissenting); *id.* at 572; *Planned Parenthood*, 505 U.S. 833 (1992); Roe v. Wade, 410 U.S. 113 (1973). Kennedy's stance in substantive due process cases leads some commentators to characterize him as a libertarian. *E.g.*, Jeffrey Rosen, *Disorder in the Court*, The New Republic, July 14, 2011, at 7. Yet this characterization is difficult to square with some of his other votes and opinions, such as those in the Establishment Clause area (where Kennedy's coercion test, compared with other doctrines, allows the greatest degree of governmental regulation).
79. Steven Calabresi & Christopher Yoo, *The Unitary Executive During the Second Half-Century*, 26 Harv. J. of L. & Public Policy 667, 668 (2003); Mark Tushnet, *A Political Perspective on the Theory of the Unitary Executive*, 12 U. Pa. J. Const. L. 313 (2010).
80. Jay S. Bybee, Department of Justice Office of Legal Counsel, *Memorandum for Alberto R. Gonzales, Counsel to the President* (Aug. 1, 2002), at 36 (Yoo was an unsigned co-author); Harold Hongju Koh, *America and the World, 2020*, *in* The Constitution in 2020, at 313, 315–17 (Jack M. Balkin

& Reva B. Siegel eds., 2009); Neal Kumar Katyal, *Comment: Hamdan v. Rumsfeld: The Legal Academy Goes to Practice*, 120 Harv. L. Rev. 65, 69 n.16 (2006) (arguing that Bush II pushed beyond the limits of the unitary executive theory).

81. Harvey Mansfield, *The Law and the President: In a National Emergency, Who You Gonna Call?* in The Weekly Standard, Jan. 16, 2006, at vol. 11, no. 17; *see* Justin Vaïsse, Neoconservatism: The Biography of a Movement 221–23, 232–36 (Arthur Goldhammer trans., 2010) (lengthy description of neoconservative foreign policy positions that does not include theory of the unitary executive); Douglas H. Ginsburg & Steven Menashi, *Nondelegation and the Unitary Executive*, 12 U. Pa. J. Const. L. 251 (2010) (arguing for weak theory of unitary executive—focused on who can exercise executive powers rather than the breadth of those powers—as a corollary to the nondelegation doctrine).
82. Hamdi v. Rumsfeld, 542 U.S. 507, 509–11, 535–37 (2004) (O'Connor plurality opinion); *id.* at 554 (Scalia, J., dissenting); Hamdan v. Rumsfeld, 548 U.S. 557, 635 (2006); *see, e.g.*, Boumediene v. Bush, 553 U.S. 723 (2008) (holding five-to-four that even noncitizen prisoners held on foreign soil are entitled to petition for habeas corpus); Rasul v. Bush, 542 U.S. 466 (2004) (holding six-to-three that federal courts have habeas jurisdiction to consider legal challenges brought by Guantánamo prisoners).
83. 130 S. Ct. 876 (2010).
84. *Id.* at 898; Stromberg v. California, 283 U.S. 359 (1931) (upholding free-speech claim for first time); *see* Fiske v. Kansas, 274 U.S. 380 (1927) (upholding due process claim with free-speech connotations); Schenck v. United States, 249 U.S. 47 (1919) (rejecting free-speech claim).
85. *Citizens United*, 130 S. Ct. at 963 (Stevens, J., dissenting); Larry M. Bartels et al., *Inequality and American Governance*, *in* Inequality and American Democracy 88, 115–17 (Lawrence R. Jacobs & Theda Skocpol eds., 2005); Molly J. Walker Wilson, *Behavioral Decision Theory and Implications for the Supreme Court's Campaign Finance Jurisprudence*, 31 Cardozo L. Rev. 679, 684 (2010); *see* Jacob S. Hacker & Paul Pierson, Winner-Take-All Politics (2010) (emphasizing the influence of corporate wealth on government); Charles E. Lindblom, Politics and Markets (1977) (arguing that empirical evidence shows that corporate wealth dominates politics); Sheldon S. Wolin, Democracy Incorporated (2008) (discussing corporate influence on democracy); Jamin B. Raskin, *The Campaign-Finance Crucible: Is Laissez Fair?*, 101 Mich. L. Rev. 1532, 1550–51 (2003) (arguing that campaign expenditures are likely to lead to post-election rent seeking). The definition of *corruption* (or of what constitutes a defect) is normative. But once a definition is settled upon,

then, depending on the definition, the degree or amount of such corruption could feasibly be tested quantitatively. *See* Larry M. Bartels, Unequal Democracy (2008) (presenting empirical evidence of effects of income inequality on democracy and government); Lawrence R. Jacobs & Theda Skocpol, *American Democracy in an Era of Rising Inequality*, *in* Inequality and American Democracy 1 (Lawrence R. Jacobs & Theda Skocpol eds., 2005) (discussing social science research on the effects of wealth inequality on democracy). Daniel Bell's neoconservatism also supports the imposition of campaign finance regulations. Daniel Bell, The Cultural Contradictions of Capitalism (1978; 1st ed. 1976). From Bell's perspective, when economic rationality or logic invades the political realm, as it does in our consumers' (pluralist) democracy, then civic virtue is undermined. Citizens and officials become less likely to pursue the common good and more likely to seek to satisfy their own interests. To have even the semblance of a republican democratic regime, the nation needs to have a domain of political speech somewhat purified of external pressures, including especially the desire to maximize profits. This neoconservative position resonates with that of Jürgen Habermas. *See* Jürgen Habermas, Between Facts and Norms: Contributions to a Discourse Theory of Law and Democracy 322 (William Rehg trans., 1996) (discussing an ideal community); Jürgen Habermas, 1 The Theory of Communicative Action 340–43 (Thomas McCarthy trans., 1984) (discussing how economic and administrative rationality can skew symbolic interactions).

86. 130 S. Ct. at 898, 908; *see id.* at 904–11 (discussing the government's interests); Samuel Issacharoff, *On Political Corruption*, 124 Harv. L. Rev. 118, 118–21 (2010) (arguing that the *Citizens United* Court overly narrowed the concept of corruption); Wilson, *supra* note 85, at 740–45 (arguing for a broader definition of *corruption*).
87. *Citizens United*, 130 S. Ct. at 928 (Scalia, J., concurring) (quoting Zephyr Teachout, *The Anti-Corruption Principle*, 94 Cornell L. Rev. 341, 373 (2009)); *id.* at 898.
88. *E.g.*, Dennis v. United States, 341 U.S. 494 (1951) (holding that conviction of American communist leaders did not violate First Amendment); *see* Feldman, *supra* note 44, at 346–47, 415, 430–31 (discussing reasons for shrinking political support for civil liberties during and after World War II).
89. 421 U.S. 809, 812–13, 819–21, 826 (1975); Valentine v. Chrestensen, 316 U.S. 52, 54–55 (1942).
90. 425 U.S. 748, 763, 765 (1976); Central Hudson Gas & Electric Corp. v. Public Service Commission, 447 U.S. 557, 566 (1980); *see* Benjamin R.

Barber, Jihad vs. McWorld 14–15 (2001 ed.) (arguing that capitalism does not always promote democracy).

91. 424 U.S. 1, 19, 48–49 (1976). The Court, however, upheld a limitation on direct contributions to candidates. *See id.* at 143 (summarizing holding); Melvin I. Urofsky, Money and Free Speech: Campaign Finance Reform and the Courts 54–58 (2005) (explaining *Buckley*).
92. 435 U.S. 765, 776–77 (1978).
93. *Citizens United*, 130 S. Ct. at 906; *id.* at 948–49 (Stevens, J., dissenting); *see* Arizona Free Enterprise Club's Freedom Club Pac v. Bennett, 131 S. Ct. 2806 (2011) (following *Citizens United* to invalidate state-imposed campaign finance regulation). For examples of pre–*Citizens United* waffling, *see* Austin v. Michigan Chamber of Commerce, 494 U.S. 652 (1990) (upholding restriction on corporate political spending); FEC v. Massachusetts Citizens for Life, 479 U.S. 238 (1986) (invalidating restriction on nonprofit corporations); FEC v. National Right to Work Committee, 459 U.S. 197 (1982) (upholding restriction on nonprofit corporations); Urofsky, *supra* note 91, at 141–46 (describing Court's confusion); *see also* McConnell v. FEC, 540 U.S. 93 (2003) (reaffirming *Buckley* and upholding main sections of Bipartisan Campaign Reform Act of 2002).

CHAPTER 6

1. Murray Friedman, The Neoconservative Revolution 183 (2005) (quoting Kristol).
2. 545 U.S. 677, 683, 686, 690 (2005) (quoting Lynch v. Donnelly, 465 U.S. 668, 674 (1984)).
3. 545 U.S. 844, 859–60 (2005); *id.* at 887, 890, 893–900, 906 (Scalia, J., dissenting).
4. *Perceived Qualifications and Ideology of Supreme Court Nominees, 1937–2005* (data drawn from Jeffrey Segal & Albert Cover, *Ideological Values and the Votes of Supreme Court Justices*, 83 Am. Pol. Sci. Rev. 557–565 (1989); updated in Lee Epstein & Jeffrey A. Segal, Advice and Consent: The Politics of Judicial Appointments (2005)); Charles Lane, *Kennedy Seen as the Next Justice in the Court's Middle*, Washington Post, Jan. 31, 2006, at A4.
5. James Roger Sharp, American Politics in the Early Republic 8, 40–41 (1993); Melvin I. Urofsky & Paul Finkelman, 1 A March of Liberty 199–201 (2d ed. 2002); *Marbury*, 5 U.S. (1 Cranch) 137 (1803); Senate Journal, March 1, 1805, at 524–27; Erik W. Austin, Political Facts of the United States Since 1789, at 50 (1986) (Table 1.20, Partisan Composition of the United States Senate); Stephen M. Feldman, Free Expression

and Democracy in America: A History 70–100 (2008); William W. Van Alstyne, *A Critical Guide to* Marbury v. Madison, 1969 Duke L.J. 1.

6. Railroad Retirement Board v. Alton Railroad Co., 295 U.S. 330 (1935) (invalidating the Railroad Retirement Act); Nebbia v. New York, 291 U.S. 502 (1934) (upholding a state milk regulation); United States v. Butler, 297 U.S. 1 (1936) (invalidating parts of Agricultural Adjustment Act); Carter v. Carter Coal Co., 298 U.S. 238 (1936) (invalidating the Bituminous Coal Conservation Act); 81 Cong. Rec., Appendix at 469–71, 75th Cong., 1st Sess. (March 10, 1937); 81 Cong. Rec., 75th Cong., 1st Sess. 877–79 (Feb. 5, 1937); Feldman, *supra* note 5, at 350–59. *West Coast Hotel Co. v. Parrish*, 300 U.S. 379 (1937), and *NLRB v. Jones & Laughlin Steel Corp.*, 301 U.S. 1 (1937), marked the Court's 1937 turn.
7. David M. O'Brien, Storm Center 355–59 (8th ed. 2008); Robert A. Dahl, *Decision-Making in a Democracy: The Supreme Court as a National Policy-Maker*, 6 J. Pub. L. 279 (1957).
8. Barry Friedman, The Will of the People (2009) (arguing that Court follows prevailing politics); William E. Leuchtenburg, The Supreme Court Reborn (1995) (discussing Court-packing plan).
9. Pub. L. No. 109–62, 119 Stat. 2960 (2005); Pub. L. No. 106–386, 114 Stat. 1464 (2000). On the Court's dialogue with other institutions, see Stephen M. Feldman, *The Persistence of Power and the Struggle for Dialogic Standards in Postmodern Constitutional Jurisprudence*, 81 Geo. L.J. 2243 (1993); Stephen M. Feldman, *Republican Revival/Interpretive Turn*, 1992 Wis. L. Rev. 679; Barry Friedman, *Dialogue and Judicial Review*, 91 Mich. L. Rev. 577 (1993); Robert C. Post & Reva B. Siegel, *Democratic Constitutionalism*, *in* The Constitution in 2020, at 25 (Jack M. Balkin & Reva B. Siegel eds., 2009).
10. Patient Protection and Affordable Care Act, Pub. L. No. 111–48, 124 Stat. 119 (March 23, 2010); Endangered Species Act of 1973, Pub. L. No. 93–205, 87 Stat. 884; Americans with Disabilities Act, Pub. L. No. 101–336, 104 Stat. 327 (1990); Age Discrimination in Employment Act, Pub. L. No. 90–202, 81 Stat. 602 (1967); Cass R. Sunstein, Radicals in Robes 18–19 (2005); Bruce Ackerman, *The Art of Stealth*, London Review of Books, Feb. 17, 2005; Samuel R.Bagenstos, *Spending Clause Litigation in the Roberts Court*, 58 Duke L.J. 345 (2008).
11. Federal Communications Commission v. Fox Television Stations, Inc., 129 S. Ct. 1800, 1809, 1819 (2009); Walter Berns, The First Amendment and the Future of American Democracy 200–04 (1976).
12. *Citizens United*, 130 S. Ct. 876 (2010); *Morse*, 127 S. Ct. 2618 (2007); Arizona Free Enterprise Club's Freedom Club PAC v. Bennett, 131 S. Ct. 2806 (2011); McConnell v. Federal Election Commission, 540 U.S. 93 (2003); Buckley v. Valeo, 424 U.S. 1 (1976); Fox v. Washington, 236 U.S.

273 (1915); Patterson v. Colorado *ex rel.* Attorney General, 205 U.S. 454 (1907); Sunstein, *supra* note 10, at 18.

13. *CLS*, 130 S.Ct. 2971, 2979–81 (2010); *id.* at 3008–09, 3011, 3019 (Alito, J., dissenting); *id.* at 2999 (Kennedy, J., concurring); *Morse*, 127 S. Ct. 2618 (2007). The Court decided *Citizens United* on January 21, 2010, and *CLS* on June 28, 2010.
14. Lee v. Weisman, 505 U.S. 577, 587 (1992) (quoted in Santa Fe Independent School District v. Doe, 530 U.S. 290, 302 (2000)); *id.* at 640 (Scalia, J., dissenting) (quoted in *Newdow*, 542 U.S. 1, 52 (2004) (Thomas, J., concurring in the judgment)); *id.* at 593–94 (peer pressure); *Salazar*, 130 S.Ct. 1803, 1816–17, 1820 (2010); *id.* at 1822 (Alito, J., concurring in part and concurring in the judgment); Van Orden v. Perry, 545 U.S. 677, 893–900 (2005) (Scalia, J., dissenting); Elk Grove Unified School Dist. v. Newdow, 542 U.S. 1 (2004) (Kennedy joined liberal justices to form majority avoiding Establishment Clause issue); *id.* at 33–39 (O'Connor, J., concurring in the judgment) (applying endorsement test); Santa Fe Independent School District v. Doe, 530 U.S. 290, 311–12 (2000) (peer pressure); County of Allegheny v. ACLU, 492 U.S. 573, 659 (1989) (Kennedy, J., concurring and dissenting); Steven H. Shiffrin, The Religious Left and Church–State Relations 134 (2009) (arguing that Kennedy will move the Court rightward in Establishment Clause cases).
15. Stephen Breyer, Active Liberty: Interpreting Our Democratic Constitution (2006); Department of Justice Office of Legal Policy, *Guidelines on Constitutional Litigation* 5 (Feb. 19, 1988); Thomas B. Colby & Peter J. Smith, *Living Originalism*, 59 Duke L.J. 239 (2009) (originalists disagree about the meaning of originalism); *e.g.*, Rosenberger v. Rectors and Visitors of the University of Virginia, 515 U.S. 819 (1995) (majority and dissent disagree about original meaning); New York v. United States, 505 U.S. 144 (1992) (same).
16. Randy E. Barnett, Restoring the Lost Constitution 53–86 (2004); Randy Barnett, The Structure of Liberty 1–28 (1998); Richard A. Epstein, Takings 35–329 (1985); William J. Novak, The People's Welfare (1996) (detailing the many extensive nineteenth-century state and local regulations); Feldman, *supra* note 5, at 26–32 (on judicial determinations of the common good); Victoria F. Nourse, *A Tale of Two Lochners: The Untold History of Substantive Due Process and the Idea of Fundamental Rights*, 97 Cal. L. Rev. 751, 752–58, 799 (2009) (same).
17. James Kent, 2 Commentaries on American Law 276 (1827; Legal Classics Library Reprint); Commonwealth v. Rice, 9 Metcalf 253, 50 Mass. 253, 256–59 (1845); *see* Vandine's Case, 23 Mass. 187, 191–93 (1828) (upholding restriction on the removal of offal); Vanderbilt v. Adams, 7 Cow. 349,

351–52 (N.Y. 1827) (Justice John Woodworth explaining sovereign power over individual liberties).

18. Commonwealth v. Alger, 61 Mass. 53, 7 Cush. 53, 84–86 (1851); *see* Thorpe v. Rutland & Burlington Railroad Company, 27 Vt. 140, 156 n.a1 (1855). Given the pervasiveness of nineteenth-century regulations, those neocons who advocated for aggressive domestic governmental policies, so long as they were for the common good, remained most harmonious with the original republican democratic regime.
19. Thomas M. Cooley, A Treatise on the Constitutional Limitations Which Rest Upon the Legislative Power of the States of the American Union 160, 164–65, 168, 172, 174, 573–74 (Da Capo Press ed. 1972) (reprint of 1st ed. 1868); Lochner v. New York, 198 U.S. 45 (1905) (liberty of contract); Feldman, *supra* note 5, at 166–87 (discussing changes in concept of common good during post–Civil War period). Later editions of Cooley's *Constitutional Limitations* maintained the same substantive views. *E.g.*, Thomas M. Cooley & Walter Carrington, A Treatise on the Constitutional Limitations Which Rest Upon the Legislative Power of the States of the American Union (8th ed. 1927); Thomas M. Cooley, A Treatise on the Constitutional Limitations Which Rest Upon the Legislative Power of the States of the American Union (4th ed. 1878).
20. Cass R. Sunstein, One Case at a Time: Judicial Minimalism on the Supreme Court 9 (1999) [hereinafter Sunstein, One Case]; *Romer*, 517 U.S. 620, 623–25, 635–36 (1996) (quoting Colo. Const., Art. II, § 30b); Angela Onwuachi-Willig et al., *Cracking the Egg: Which Came First—Stigma or Affirmative Action?*, 96 Cal. L. Rev. 1299 (2008) (empirical study). Some progressives have argued that conservative justices simply ignore original meaning when it does not fit their political goals. For instance, the original meaning of the Fourteenth Amendment would seem to allow governments to institute race-based affirmative action programs. Robert Post & Reva Siegel, *Democratic Constitutionalism*, *in* The Constitution in 2020, at 25, 30 (Jack M. Balkin & Reva B. Siegel eds., 2009). Some progressives argue to invigorate the concept of citizenship. Bruce Ackerman, *The Citizenship Agenda*, *in* The Constitution in 2020, at 109 (Jack M. Balkin & Reva B. Siegel eds., 2009). For examples of other minimalist arguments, see Richard H. Fallon Jr., *Foreword: Implementing the Constitution*, 111 Harv. L. Rev. 56 (1997); Stephen M. Griffin, *Has the Hour of Democracy Come Round at Last? The New Critique of Judicial Review*, 17 Const. Comment. 683 (2000); Christopher J. Peters, *Assessing the New Judicial Minimalism*, 100 Colum. L. Rev. 1454 (2000); Robin West, *Progressive and Conservative Constitutionalism*, 88 Mich. L. Rev. 641, 650–51, 713–21 (1990).

21. *Romer*, 517 U.S. at 631–36; Sunstein, One Case, *supra* note 20, at ix, 137–57; Peters, *supra* note 20, at 1486–91. Because the Court has traditionally upheld almost any governmental action that is subject to rational basis review under equal protection, *Romer* can be added to that short list of cases where the Court has applied, in Gerald Gunther's terminology, rational basis "with bite." Gerald Gunther, Constitutional Law 604 (11th ed. 1985); Gerald Gunther, *Foreword: In Search of Evolving Doctrine on a Changing Court: A Model for a Newer Equal Protection*, 86 Harv. L. Rev. 1, 46–47 (1972); *e.g.*, City of Cleburne v. Cleburne Living Center, 473 U.S. 432 (1985).
22. Sunstein, One Case, *supra* note 20, at 54; Mark Tushnet, Taking the Constitution Away from the Courts 129–53 (1999); *see* Larry D. Kramer, *Foreword: We the Court*, 115 Harv. L. Rev. 4 (2001) (arguing for popular constitutionalism, where the people themselves would decide more constitutional questions).
23. Robin West, *The Missing Jurisprudence of the Legislated Constitution*, *in* The Constitution in 2020, at 79 (Jack M. Balkin & Reva B. Siegel eds., 2009); Richard Delgado, *Zero-Based Racial Politics*, 78 Geo. L.J. 1929 (1990); Erwin Chemerinsky, *When It Matters Most, It Is Still the Kennedy Court*, 11 Green Bag 2d 427, 427–28 (2008). I thank Richard Delgado for emphasizing to me the strategy of going to other institutions.
24. Elk Grove Unified School Dist. v. Newdow, 542 U.S. 1 (2004); *id.* at 26–33 (Rehnquist, C.J., concurring in the judgment); Lawrence v. Texas, 539 U.S. 558 (2003); Christian Legal Society Chapter of the University of California, Hastings College of the Law v. Martinez, 130 S.Ct. 2971 (2010); Sunstein, One Case, *supra* note 20, at 9 (categorizing Kennedy as a judicial minimalist); Mark A. Graber, *Rethinking Equal Protection in Dark Times*, 4 U. Pa. J. Const. L. 314, 325 (2002) (categorizing Kennedy as a country-club Republican).
25. Santa Fe Independent School District v. Doe, 530 U.S. 290, 311–12 (2000); Lee v. Weisman, 505 U.S. 577, 593–94 (1992); *id.* at 640 (Scalia, J., dissenting) (legal penalties only); *Newdow*, 542 U.S. 1, 52 (2004) (Thomas, J., concurring in the judgment) (same).

SELECTED BIBLIOGRAPHY OF BOOKS

NEOCONSERVATISM

Bell, Daniel. *The Cultural Contradictions of Capitalism*. New York: Basic Books, 1976.

Berkowitz, Peter, ed. *Varieties of Conservatism in America*. Stanford, Calif.: Hoover Institution Press, 2004.

Berns, Walter. *The First Amendment and the Future of American Democracy*. New York: Basic Books, 1976.

———. *Freedom, Virtue & the First Amendment*. Baton Rouge: Louisiana State University Press, 1957.

———. *Taking the Constitution Seriously*. New York: Simon and Schuster, 1987.

Bloom, Allan. *The Closing of the American Mind: How Higher Education Has Failed Democracy and Impoverished the Souls of Today's Students*. New York: Simon and Schuster, 1987.

Bork, Robert H. *Slouching Towards Gomorrah: Modern Liberalism and American Decline*. New York: Regan Books, 1996.

———. *The Tempting of America: The Political Seduction of the Law*. New York: Free Press, 1990.

Drury, Shadia B. *Leo Strauss and the American Right*. New York: St. Martin's Press, 1997.

Friedman, Murray. *The Neoconservative Revolution: Jewish Intellectuals and the Shaping of Public Policy*. Cambridge: Cambridge University Press, 2005.

Fukuyama, Francis. *America at the Crossroads: Democracy, Power, and the Neoconservative Legacy*. New Haven, Conn.: Yale University Press, 2006.

———. *The End of History and the Last Man*. New York: Free Press, 1992.

Heilbrunn, Jacob. *They Knew They Were Right: The Rise of the Neocons*. New York: Doubleday, 2008.

Himmelfarb, Gertrude. *Poverty and Compassion: The Moral Imagination of the Late Victorians*. New York: Knopf, 1991.

Kristol, Irving. *Neoconservatism: The Autobiography of an Idea*. New York: Free Press, 1995.

McAllister, Ted V. *Revolt Against Modernity: Leo Strauss, Eric Voegelin, and the Search for a Postliberal Order*. Lawrence: University Press of Kansas, 1996.

Murray, Douglas. *Neoconservatism: Why We Need It*. New York: Encounter Books, 2006.

Nash, George H. *The Conservative Intellectual Movement in America Since 1945*. Wilmington, Del.: ISI Books, 2006.

Pangle, Thomas L. *Leo Strauss: An Introduction to His Thought and Intellectual Legacy.* Baltimore: Johns Hopkins University Press, 2006.

Podhoretz, Norman. *The Norman Podhoretz Reader: A Selection of His Writings from the 1950s Through the 1990s.* New York: Free Press, 2004.

Stelzer, Irwin, ed. *Neocon Reader.* New York: Grove Press, 2004.

Strauss, Leo. *The City and Man.* Chicago: Rand McNally, 1964.

———. *Liberalism, Ancient and Modern.* New York: Basic Books, 1968.

———. *Natural Right and History.* Chicago: University of Chicago Press, 1953.

———. *What Is Political Philosophy? and Other Studies.* Glencoe, Ill.: Free Press, 1959.

Vaisse, Justin. *Neoconservatism: The Biography of a Movement.* Translated by Arthur Goldhammer. Cambridge, Mass.: Belknap Press of Harvard University Press, 2010.

OTHER POLITICAL AND CONSTITUTIONAL THEORY

Arendt, Hannah. *The Human Condition.* Chicago: University of Chicago Press, 1958.

———. *On Revolution.* New York: Viking Press, 1963.

———. *The Origins of Totalitarianism.* New York: Harcourt Brace Jovanovich, 1973.

Barnett, Randy E. *Restoring the Lost Constitution: The Presumption of Liberty.* Princeton, N.J.: Princeton University Press, 2004.

———. *The Structure of Liberty: Justice and the Rule of Law.* New York: Oxford University Press, 1998.

Bartels, Larry M. *Unequal Democracy.* Princeton, N.J.: Princeton University Press, 2008.

Bickel, Alexander M. *The Least Dangerous Branch: The Supreme Court at the Bar of Politics.* Indianapolis: Bobbs-Merrill, 1962.

———. *The Morality of Consent.* New Haven, Conn.: Yale University Press, 1975.

———. *The Supreme Court and the Idea of Progress.* New York: Harper & Row, 1970.

Binkley, Wilfred Ellsworth. *A Grammar of American Politics: The National Government.* New York: Knopf, 1949.

Bobbitt, Philip. *Constitutional Interpretation.* Cambridge, Mass.: Blackwell, 1991.

Bond, Jon R., and Richard Fleisher, eds. *Polarized Politics: Congress and the President in a Partisan Era.* Washington: CQ Press, 2000.

Boorstin, Daniel J. *The Genius of American Politics.* Chicago: University of Chicago Press, 1953.

Cigler, Allan J., and Burdett A. Loomis, eds. *Interest Group Politics.* Washington: CQ Press, 1983.

Dahl, Robert A. *Democracy and Its Critics.* New Haven, Conn.: Yale University Press, 1989.

———. *A Preface to Democratic Theory.* Chicago: University of Chicago Press, 1956.

———. *Who Governs? Democracy and Power in an American City.* New Haven, Conn.: Yale University Press, 1961.

Dewey, John. *Freedom and Culture.* New York: Putnam, 1939.

Dworkin, Ronald. *Freedom's Law: The Moral Reading of the American Constitution.* Cambridge, Mass.: Harvard University Press, 1996.

———. *Justice in Robes*. Cambridge, Mass.: Belknap Press of Harvard University Press, 2006.

———. *Law's Empire*. Cambridge, Mass.: Belknap Press of Harvard University Press, 1986.

———. *Taking Rights Seriously*. Cambridge, Mass.: Harvard University Press, 1977.

Ely, John Hart. *Democracy and Distrust: A Theory of Judicial Review*. Cambridge, Mass.: Harvard University Press, 1980.

Epstein, Richard A. *Principles for a Free Society: Reconciling Individual Liberty with the Common Good*. Reading, Mass.: Perseus Books, 1998.

———. *Takings: Private Property and the Power of Eminent Domain*. Cambridge, Mass.: Harvard University Press, 1985.

Fiorina, Morris P., Samuel J. Abrams, and Jeremy C. Pope. *Culture War? The Myth of a Polarized America*. New York: Pearson Longman, 2005.

Habermas, Jürgen. *Between Facts and Norms: Contributions to a Discourse Theory of Law and Democracy*. Translated by William Rehg. Cambridge, Mass.: MIT Press, 1996.

Hacker, Jacob, and Paul Pierson. *Winner-Take-All Politics*. New York: Simon and Schuster, 2010.

Hrebenar, Ronald J. *Interest Group Politics in America*. Armonk, N.Y.: M. E. Sharpe, 1997.

Keck, Thomas M. *The Most Activist Supreme Court in History: The Road to Modern Judicial Conservatism*. Chicago: University of Chicago Press, 2004.

Key, V. O. *Politics, Parties and Pressure Groups*. New York: Thomas Y. Crowell, 1942.

Olson, Mancur. *The Logic of Collective Action: Public Goods and the Theory of Groups*. Cambridge, Mass.: Harvard University Press, 1971.

———. *The Rise and Decline of Nations: Economic Growth, Stagflation, and Social Rigidities*. New Haven, Conn.: Yale University Press, 1982.

Schumpeter, Joseph A. *Capitalism, Socialism, and Democracy*. New York: Harper, 1942.

Segal, Jeffrey A., and Harold J. Spaeth. *The Supreme Court and the Attitudinal Model*. New York: Cambridge University Press, 1993.

Segal, Jeffrey A., Harold J. Spaeth, and Sara C. Benesh. *The Supreme Court in the American Legal System*. New York: Cambridge University Press, 2005.

Sinclair, Barbara. *Party Wars: Polarization and the Politics of National Policy Making*. Norman: University of Oklahoma Press, 2006.

Sunstein, Cass R. *One Case at a Time: Judicial Minimalism on the Supreme Court*. Cambridge, Mass.: Harvard University Press, 1999.

———. *Radicals in Robes: Why Extreme Right-Wing Courts Are Wrong for America*. New York: Basic Books, 2005.

Truman, David Bicknell. *The Governmental Process: Political Interests and Public Opinion*. New York: Knopf, 1951.

Tushnet, Mark. *Taking the Constitution Away from the Courts*. Princeton, N.J.: Princeton University Press, 1999.

Voegelin, Eric. *The New Science of Politics: An Introduction.* Chicago: University of Chicago Press, 1952.

———. *Order and History.* Baton Rouge: Louisiana State University Press, 1956.

Walker, Jack L. *Mobilizing Interest Groups in America: Patrons, Professions, and Social Movements.* Ann Arbor: University of Michigan Press, 1991.

Wolin, Sheldon S. *Democracy Incorporated.* Princeton, N.J.: Princeton University Press, 2008.

OTHER POLITICAL AND CONSTITUTIONAL HISTORY

Cohen, Lizabeth. *A Consumers' Republic: The Politics of Mass Consumption in Postwar America.* New York: Knopf, 2003.

———. *Making a New Deal: Industrial Workers in Chicago, 1919–1939.* Cambridge: Cambridge University Press, 1990.

Cross, Gary. *An All-Consuming Century: Why Commercialism Won in Modern America.* New York: Columbia University Press, 2000.

Dubofsky, Melvyn. *The State and Labor in Modern America.* Chapel Hill: University of North Carolina Press, 1994.

Elkins, Stanley, and Eric McKitrick. *The Age of Federalism.* New York: Oxford University Press, 1993.

Feldman, Stephen M. *American Legal Thought from Premodernism to Postmodernism: An Intellectual Voyage.* New York: Oxford University Press, 2000.

———. *Free Expression and Democracy in America: A History.* Chicago: University of Chicago Press, 2008.

Gillman, Howard. *The Constitution Besieged: The Rise and Demise of Lochner Era Police Powers Jurisprudence.* Durham, N.C.: Duke University Press, 1993.

Hartz, Louis. *The Liberal Tradition in America.* New York: Harcourt, Brace, 1955.

Herberg, Will. *Protestant, Catholic, Jew: An Essay in American Religious Sociology.* Garden City, N.Y.: Doubleday, 1955.

Higham, John. *Strangers in the Land: Patterns of American Nativism, 1860–1925.* New Brunswick, N.J.: Rutgers University Press, 2002.

King, Desmond. *Making Americans: Immigration, Race, and the Origins of the Diverse Democracy.* Cambridge, Mass.: Harvard University Press, 2000.

Leuchtenburg, William Edward. *Franklin D. Roosevelt and the New Deal, 1932–1940.* New York: Harper & Row, 1963.

———. *The Perils of Prosperity, 1914–32.* Chicago: University of Chicago Press, 1958.

Lowndes, Joseph E. *From the New Deal to the New Right: Race and the Southern Origins of Modern Conservatism.* New Haven, Conn.: Yale University Press, 2008.

Orren, Karen. *Belated Feudalism: Labor, the Law, and Liberal Development in the United States.* Cambridge: Cambridge University Press, 1991.

Pessen, Edward. *Jacksonian America: Society, Personality, and Politics.* Homewood, Ill.: Dorsey Press, 1978.

Purcell, Edward A. *The Crisis of Democratic Theory: Scientific Naturalism and the Problem of Value.* Lexington: University Press of Kentucky, 1973.

Rossiter, Clinton, ed. *The Federalist Papers*. New York: New American Library, 1961.

Teles, Steven M. *The Rise of the Conservative Legal Movement: The Battle for Control of the Law*. Princeton, N.J.: Princeton University Press, 2008.

Urofsky, Melvin I. *Money and Free Speech: Campaign Finance Reform and the Courts*. Lawrence: University Press of Kansas, 2005.

Watson, Harry L. *Liberty and Power: The Politics of Jacksonian America*. New York: Hill and Wang, 1990.

Wood, Gordon S. *The Creation of the American Republic, 1776–1787*. Chapel Hill: University of North Carolina Press, 1969.

SELECTED CASE CITATIONS

Adarand Constructors, Inc. v. Pena, 515 U.S. 200 (1995).
Adderley v. Florida, 385 U.S. 39 (1966).
Agostini v. Felton, 521 U.S. 203 (1997).
Aguilar v. Felton, 473 U.S. 402 (1985).
Alden v. Maine, 527 U.S. 706 (1999).
Arizona Free Enterprise Club's Freedom Club PAC v. Bennett, 131 S. Ct. 2806 (2011).
Austin v. Michigan Chamber of Commerce, 494 U.S. 652 (1990).
Bethel School Dist. No. 403 v. Fraser, 478 U.S. 675 (1986).
Bigelow v. Virginia, 421 U.S. 809 (1975).
Board of Trade v. Olsen, 262 U.S. 1 (1923).
Boumediene v. Bush, 553 U.S. 723 (2008).
Bowers v. Hardwick, 478 U.S. 186 (1986).
Brandenburg v. Ohio, 395 U.S. 444 (1969).
Bridges v. California, 314 U.S. 252 (1941).
Brown v. Board of Education, 347 U.S. 483 (1954).
Buckley v. Valeo, 424 U.S. 1 (1976).
Calder v. Bull, 3 U.S. (3 Dall.) 386 (1798).
Capitol Square Review & Advisory Board v. Pinette, 515 U.S. 753 (1995).
Carter v. Carter Coal Co., 298 U.S. 238 (1936).
Central Hudson Gas & Electric Corp. v. Public Service Commission, 447 U.S. 557 (1980).
Church of Lukumi Babalu Aye v. Hialeah, 508 U.S. 520 (1993).
Citizens United v. FEC, 130 S. Ct. 876 (2010).
City of Boerne v. Flores, 521 U.S. 527 (1997).
Cohen v. California, 403 U.S. 15 (1971).
County of Allegheny v. ACLU, 492 U.S. 573 (1989).
Dennis v. United States, 341 U.S. 494 (1951).
District of Columbia v. Heller, 554 U.S. 570 (2008).
Elk Grove Unified School Dist. v. Newdow, 542 U.S. 1 (2004).
Engel v. Vitale, 370 U.S. 421 (1962).
Everson v. Board of Education, 330 U.S. 1 (1947).

FCC v. Fox Television Stations, Inc., 556 U.S. 502 (2009).
FEC v. Massachusetts Citizens for Life, 479 U.S. 238 (1986).
FEC v. National Right to Work Committee, 459 U.S. 197 (1982).
First National Bank of Boston v. Bellotti, 435 U.S. 765 (1978).
Fiske v. Kansas, 274 U.S. 380 (1927).
Fullilove v. Klutznick, 448 U.S. 448 (1980).
Garcia v. San Antonio Metro. Transit Auth., 469 U.S. 528 (1985).
Gonzales v. Carhart, 550 U.S. 124 (2007).
Gonzales v. Raich, 545 U.S. 1 (2005).
Good News Club v. Milford Central School, 533 U.S. 98 (2001).
Gratz v. Bollinger, 539 U.S. 244 (2003).
Grutter v. Bollinger, 539 U.S. 306 (2003).
Hamdi v. Rumsfeld, 542 U.S. 507 (2004).
Hammer v. Dagenhart, 247 U.S. 251 (1918).
Hazelwood School Dist. v. Kuhlmeier, 484 U.S. 260 (1988).
Healy v. James, 408 U.S. 169 (1972).
Hill v. Wallace, 259 U.S. 44 (1922).
Kimel v. Fla. Bd. of Regents, 528 U.S. 62 (2000).
Korematsu v. United States, 323 U.S. 214 (1944).
Lamb's Chapel v. Center Moriches School Dist., 508 U.S. 384 (1993).
Lawrence v. Texas, 539 U.S. 558 (2003).
Lee v. Weisman, 505 U.S. 577 (1992).
Lemon v. Kurtzman, 403 U.S. 602 (1971).
Lochner v. New York, 198 U.S. 45 (1905).
Lynch v. Donnelly, 465 U.S. 668 (1984).
Marbury v. Madison, 5 U.S. (1 Cranch) 137 (1803).
Marsh v. Chambers, 463 U.S. 783 (1983).
McConnell v. FEC, 540 U.S. 93 (2003).
McCreary County v. ACLU, 545 U.S. 844 (2005).
Metro Broadcasting, Inc. v. FCC, 497 U.S. 547 (1990).
Mitchell v. Helms, 530 U.S. 793 (2000).
Morse v. Frederick, 551 U.S. 393 (2007).
National League of Cities v. Usery, 426 U.S. 833, 852 (1976).
Nebbia v. New York, 291 U.S. 502 (1934).
New York v. United States, 505 U.S. 144 (1992).
NLRB v. Jones & Laughlin Steel Corp., 301 U.S. 1 (1937).
Palmore v. Sidoti, 466 U.S. 429 (1984).
Papish v. University of Missouri, 410 U.S. 667 (1973).
Parents Involved v. Seattle School Dist., 551 U.S. 701 (2007).
Perry Education Assn. v. Perry Local Educators' Assn., 460 U.S. 37 (1983).
Planned Parenthood v. Casey, 505 U.S. 833 (1992).
Pleasant Grove City v. Summum, 555 U.S. 460 (2009).

Printz v. United States, 521 U.S. 898 (1997).
Railroad Retirement Board v. Alton Railroad Co., 295 U.S. 330 (1935).
Rasul v. Bush, 542 U.S. 466 (2004).
Reno v. Condon, 528 U.S. 141 (2000).
Richmond v. Croson Co., 488 U.S. 469 (1989).
Roe v. Wade, 410 U.S. 113 (1973).
Rosenberger v. University of Virginia, 515 U.S. 819 (1995).
Santa Fe Independent School Dist. v. Doe, 530 U.S. 290 (2000).
Schenck v. United States, 249 U.S. 47 (1919).
Schneider v. State, 308 U.S. 147 (1939).
School Dist. of Grand Rapids v. Ball, 473 U.S. 373 (1985).
Seminole Tribe v. Florida, 517 U.S. 44 (1996).
Stone v. Graham, 449 U.S. 39 (1980).
Stromberg v. California, 283 U.S. 359 (1931).
Tinker v. Des Moines School Dist., 393 U.S. 503 (1969).
United States v. Butler, 297 U.S. 1 (1936).
United States v. Carolene Products Co., 304 U.S. 144 (1938).
United States v. Darby, 312 U.S. 100 (1941).
United States v. E. C. Knight Co., 156 U.S. 1 (1895).
United States v. Lopez, 514 U.S. 549 (1995).
United States v. Morrison, 529 U.S. 598 (2000).
University of California Regents v. Bakke, 438 U.S. 265 (1978).
Valentine v. Chrestensen, 316 U.S. 52 (1942).
Van Orden v. Perry, 545 U.S. 677 (2005).
Virginia State Board of Pharmacy v. Virginia Citizens Consumer Council, 425 U.S. 748 (1976).
Wallace v. Jaffree, 472 U.S. 38 (1985).
Washington v. Davis, 426 U.S. 229 (1976).
West Coast Hotel Co. v. Parrish, 300 U.S. 379 (1937).
Wickard v. Filburn, 317 U.S. 111 (1942).
Widmar v. Vincent, 454 U.S. 276 (1981).
Zelman v. Simmons-Harris, 536 U.S. 639 (2002).

INDEX

ABOUT THE AUTHOR

Stephen M. Feldman is Jerry W. Housel/Carl F. Arnold Distinguished Professor of Law and Adjunct Professor of Political Science at the University of Wyoming. He has degrees from Hamilton College (B.A., Philosophy), the University of Oregon (J.D.), and Stanford University (J.S.M.). His most recent book is *Free Expression and Democracy in America: A History* (University of Chicago Press, 2008). Previously, besides writing numerous articles in the fields of Constitutional Law and Jurisprudence, he published *American Legal Thought from Premodernism to Postmodernism: An Intellectual Voyage* (Oxford University Press, 2000); *Please Don't Wish Me a Merry Christmas: A Critical History of the Separation of Church and State* (New York University Press, 1997); and *Law and Religion: A Critical Anthology* (New York University Press, 2000; editor).